Paths to Wealth through Common Stocks

INTRODUCING WILEY INVESTMENT CLASSICS

There are certain books that have redefined the way we see the worlds of finance and investing—books that deserve a place on every investor's shelf. *Wiley Investment Classics* will introduce you to these memorable books, which are just as relevant and vital today as when they were first published. Open a *Wiley Investment Classic* and rediscover the proven strategies, market philosophies, and definitive techniques that continue to stand the test of time.

Paths to Wealth
through Common Stocks

Philip A. Fisher

John Wiley & Sons, Inc.

Published by John Wiley & Sons, Inc., Hoboken, New Jersey.
Published simultaneously in Canada.

Originally Published in 1960 by Prentice-Hall, Inc.

Wiley Bicentennial Logo: Richard J. Pacifico

For general information on our other products and services or for technical support,
please contact our Customer Care Department within the United States at
(800) 762-2974, outside the United States at (317) 572-3993, or fax (317) 572-4002.

Wiley also publishes its books in a variety of electronic formats. Some content that
appears in print may not be available in electronic formats. For more information
about Wiley products, visit our Web site at www.wiley.com.

Library of Congress Cataloging-in-Publication Data:

Fisher, Philip A.
   Paths to wealth through common stocks/Philip A. Fisher, Kenneth L. Fisher.
      p. cm. – (Wiley investment classics)
   Includes index.
   ISBN 978-0-470-13949-3 (pbk.)
1. Stocks. 2. Investments.   I. Fisher, Kenneth L.   II. Title.
   HG4521.F59 2007
   332.63'22–dc22

2007014931

10 9 8 7 6 5 4 3 2 1

*This book is dedicated
to all investors, large and small,
who do not adhere to the philosophy:
"Everyone seems to believe it,
so it must be so."*

Contents

Foreword

PATHS TO WEALTH THROUGH COMMON STOCKS was my father's
second book, and was written very much as a follow-on to his 1958
classic, *Common Stocks and Uncommon Profits*. That first book became a basic text at the Stanford Graduate School of Business for
decades, and changed the way countless readers thought of investing—
including Warren Buffett, who said it pulled him away from his straight
Ben Graham approach and set him on his own approach ever after.
Although this book never had the sales, impact, or longevity of the
first book, it's important and useful for any serious market student for
two reasons.

First, this embellishes concepts in the first book—adding depth and
texture. It's a wide swath of what he later decided should have been
included in his first book. Anyone who was a fan of that first book
(and there were many) will find more here. Written less than two years
after *Common Stocks and Uncommon Profits*, this book was originally
published just before my father's time teaching the Investment course
at Stanford's Graduate School of Business. Here, he details even more
of his concepts of what separates a normal stock from a great one, a
normal business from a stellar one.

Second, this may be the best single slice on the state of the investment industry and what serious professionals fretted as they peered

into the 1960s. In some ways, it's a history book. Although it wasn't intended that way when he wrote it, that's what it has become. There are few professionals today old enough to have a serious memory of the 1960s. I don't. My memories of that period are through the hazy eyes of a boy whose father talked at the dinner table—and I'm 56. If you're 10 years older than I am and facing retirement, your eyes would have seen more, but at most you would have been a young beginner without much experience, canvassing the landscape as it blurred by you. The 1960s were a very important era in investing. They built a plateau above which equities would have difficulty climbing for two decades. Understanding how investors saw the opening of the decade, from the eyes of one of its top practitioners, is about as important a history book as you can find.

In 2007 my first new book in 13 years, *The Only Three Questions that Count*, was published and became a *New York Times* business best seller. It's based on the notion that much, maybe more than half, of what we commonly know as investing wisdom is demonstrably false mythology. You can know what others don't by learning to find and measure mythology and bet against it. So, I love the dedication to *Paths to Wealth through Common Stocks*:

> *This book is dedicated to all investors, large and small, who do not adhere to the philosophy: Everyone seems to believe it so it must be so.*

This says essentially the same thing in a simplified way. Don't forget, this was long before modern portfolio theory had been widely adopted (a scant nine years after Markowitz created the basis for modern portfolio theory).

He starts out by asking, "Is there any possible excuse for another book on investments?" Now, 47 years later, with more useless investment books than a normal mind can comprehend, it's always a good question. We rarely create more than a couple of really useful and enduring investment books in any year, and many years create none at all.

In Part 1, he starts with issue number one of the day: inflation. You'll find his analysis here both deficient and prescient all at the same time. It's deficient because he doesn't have in his arsenal the full array of monetarism that Milton Friedman would soon develop and popularize. After all, he was writing this three years before Friedman would publish his groundbreaking and world-changing book, A *Monetary History of the United States, 1867–1960*. (Moreover, it was years after that before Freidman's 860-page bomb had fully exploded and was absorbed by the world.)

Still, the discussion is prescient—he takes you through a stunningly correct analysis that Friedman would have loved: Why central bank rate hikes and cuts are not necessarily consistent with a monetary policy that controls inflation. He shows you how, in the right circumstances, the Fed raising rates can actually add to inflationary forces rather than dampen them. He argues the Fed shouldn't use rate hikes and cuts as the basis for fighting inflation. Friedman would have agreed completely. Still today we have a world both my father and Friedman disdained, where the prime mechanism central banks use to grapple with inflation is rate hikes and cuts.

Then, counter to Friedman, he paints an inflation picture that basically has the Fed largely subordinate to larger social trends in our society. I believe he is correct. If you view the Fed as a powerful victim in a huge system defined by our social values slowly shifting over time, it makes sense why in some environments the Fed has an easier time and in others a harder one. He predicted, quite correctly, that inflation was here to stay and even accelerate. The 1960s social trends towards more government, the increased spending of aging baby boomers, and shifting morals leading to the desire for higher prices rather than lower—all of this would create a wave of increased inflation. That of course, is what happened.

But he then points out there is opportunity. Although the average stock may or may not offset inflation, a great one will. By taking advantage of normal stock market volatility—timing done rarely, but done well—a single downturn can provide enough bounce to cover inflation for years. It is the closest he ever came to a justification for market timing.

Repeatedly my father justified science and technology as inflation's foes and the investor's friends. This book may be the first to herald the impact of science and technology on productivity, growth, and inflation. Make no mistake—my father was over-the-top on this point all his life. He saw the social pressures favoring inflation as never ending, whereas the efficiency and cost-dropping forces of science and technology were the antidote.

I will not recount his descriptions on this, but they are as valid today as ever. We live now in a world where inflation bears have been wrong because productivity in the last decade has skyrocketed beyond most seers' ability to fathom. What drove that? The same things my father foresaw in this book almost 50 years ago. He was adamant that new plants reduce costs and help fight inflation, while almost anything the government does—including raising short rates—tending to slow the development of new plants with new, cost-reducing technology is inflationary.

He saw unions and science as almost equally potent archenemies, where unions hurt and science helps. He simply couldn't fathom what actually happened, which is subsequently most unionism has withered (outside of government unions, which have grown immensely). Never would he have envisioned a world where government workers would need, want, or be allowed union protection from the government—any more than, as he points out, he could envision a world where the government's job was to ensure you a happy marriage.

His discussion of how taxes affect the stock market was ahead of his time—pre–supply-side economics. It's interesting to see his focus on foreign competition and foreign investing at a time when we presume no one thought about those things. Of course, they did—but you must read this as a history book to know that.

He has a single line that should be pressed into all aspiring rich people's memories. On page 49, he says, "In the first place it is nearly always the rich member of any family that the others envy and dislike." How true, but note how many of us aspire to become the disliked ones. Quite cute! Of course, he is using this in a different context, but it remains true: The way to have your siblings, nephews, and others envy and dislike you is to become much richer than they. Strange we should, so many, so aspire.

In Part 2, his description of Pioneer Metals Corporation is another perfect example of what we all know but never think about. One person, one idea, and the next thing you know, a boring, profitless company and useless stock is transformed in just a few years into an innovative world beater. My father said this theoretical example isn't any one company but a collage of many. Yet, in rereading Part 2 I was struck with how perfectly this example was illustrated a little more than a dozen years later at Nucor.

At Nucor Corporation (NUE), Ken Iverson flipped a near-bankrupt metals company into the world's low-cost producer of steel and, eventually, America's largest steel maker. I was part of that excitement in a small way, discovering Nucor in 1976 and leading an investor group into it—including my father, who held it until just before he died and had profited more than 100 to 1. Nucor's story and evolution over the decades almost perfectly parallels my father's fictional Pioneer Metals Corporation. If you're unfamiliar with Nucor, you are missing one of the great American stories and should read my friend Richard Preston's biography of the company, *American Steel*.

But there are more stories in this book. Just as fascinating is reading what my father wrote about people who transformed their realms. His description of Bill Hewlett and Dave Packard doing a parallel thing in creating Hewlett-Packard boggles the mind, considering the company's market value as my father wrote was a mere $150 million. Had someone simply bought Hewlett-Packard then and held on for a few decades, they would have been made. Texas Instruments is another such company he writes about—all someone would have had to do was buy this book then, buy these stocks, and they would have beaten almost everyone for decades, which by itself is a pretty great story.

In my mind, Part 3 is not my father's best work. There is little that is prescient in any regard, as near as I can tell. Since its original publication, so much has been written on how to pick a money manager that perhaps the chapter's most important concept is how truly primitive the process was in 1960.

But, then, Part 4 is stunning. Had CEOs of the day heeded his advice on mergers, the mess with 1960s conglomerates might have been avoided altogether. He drove nail after nail into the coffin of stupid mergers. He accurately defines and predicts the kinds of mergers that often work well and those that rarely do. Simply said, my father takes you through how acquirers who integrate forward or back or stay within their field of core competency often do well, while those that acquire for lateral diversity rarely ever succeed. Of course, the conglomerate craze of the 1960s was lateral diversity almost purely, and in retrospect gained nothing in efficiency for society. But his nine rules for mergers should be required reading for anyone contemplating either doing a merger or owning companies or stocks that do mergers.

This is particularly appropriate in 2007 as this edition is being released, because of the all-time record level of cash-based stock takeovers.

The section on voting rights in Part 4 shows how silly our current emphasis on corporate governance and shareholder voting is. He was 50 years ahead of his time on this. We took a wrong turn decades ago as a society on this matter (led by politicians, social scientists, and attorneys) and have never come back——much to our detriment.

He hits the nail on the head once again in a timely fashion for 2007 as he shows that politicians and politics aren't what we typically think they are, and that you have no rational basis for getting out of stocks, or even changing the type of stocks you have, because of a shift in power between our two political parties. His focus here is more on shifts in Congress than presidents, so it's particularly useful for 2007. However, he could as well be writing specifically about this year as about nearly half a century ago.

Part 5 is of interest partly for historical study and partly as a standard tool for business analysis. He focuses on then-contemporary industry analysis. On the surface, much of it won't relate to many readers seeking advice about buying stocks today. Most readers will be surprised at how much time he devotes to the chemical industry and will have difficulty seeing why. But in those days, it was a major growth industry and, as he says, was growing at about three times the growth rate of the national economy. But any material area today growing at three times the nation's growth rate gets lots of attention from everyone, so it isn't really surprising chemicals did then.

Chemicals then were a lot like technology is now—the big field that had grown at rapid rates for decades with huge, entrenched players as well as small upstarts trying to break in. He was clear that if you found the right established chemical firm, because of the safety of the growth, you could rely on it for a long time. He points out two in particular, Dow Chemical and DuPont. Today, they are America's two largest chemical companies, and if you bought either then and held them into the 1970s, 1980s, or even late 1990s, you would have beaten the market over that period. DuPont was then America's biggest chemical company and Dow was number five.

My father never mentions by name Union Carbide, Monsanto, and W.R. Grace, the other big independents of the day, but none of them remain in their original form as independent firms. All were broken up, split off, and sold to others, including pieces to Dow and DuPont. Other smaller but still big U.S. chemical firms of the day, such as Stauffer and Rohm and Hass, have all been gobbled up and taken private decades ago. So the fact that my father concentrated on Dow and DuPont is testimony to his being able to see the longer-term vision—who had depth and who didn't.

My father personally owned DuPont in the 1950s but sold it in the early 1960s after this book was completed. He held Dow until the late 1970s and finally sold it. By the time he sold Dow, it was number three in an industry that had consolidated greatly—now it's America's largest chemical firm. Today the chemical industry is commodity-like and has low growth rates. It largely is and long has been a straight cyclical play.

That might be true for technology in the not-too-distant future. My father didn't talk about technology in Part 5. He talked about the "electronics industry." Then it was the new and exciting area where little firms were slaying giants and becoming giants themselves at a gigantic pace. He discusses two in particular, Texas Instruments and Ampex. The former today is a long-time giant. The latter has disappeared, except in Silicon Valley history, as one of its early bright lights that flickered out.

He describes these areas as high growth with high risk, maybe a bit more like today's biotech than technology. To my thinking, the explosive technology leaders today aren't really leading because of technology (the way biotech firms do), but because of radical and innovative marketing and product design. Whether Amazon, Apple, Research in Motion (makers of the Blackberry), eBay, or Google, these firms aren't fundamental in technology and aren't growing based on their technological innovations. They are instead using technology to address consumer needs through innovative market research and product design and distribution.

Ironically, my father pointed out that success is best made by firms using multidisciplinary approaches linked to sales, marketing, and market research. The firms we have today that are truly based on advancing technology, like the leading semiconductor firms, are basically growing at much slower rates, more like my father's chemical companies. And that is how I would have you see electronics today, much like chemicals in the 1950s. And you should view biotech much like electronics then. Still, in Part 5 you'll see a multitude of tips on what to look for and how a firm should be run. My father's emphasis was regularly on management excellence. You can learn lots here about how explosive firms should manage themselves versus ones in more prosaic fields.

After devoting time to the pharmaceutical industry, he offers what may be his most prescient advice in Part 5 in his discussions of "Other Interesting Industries." In 1960, he viewed many emergent companies as being on the fringe of industries where there are more differences than similarities—and it is the differences that make the firms appealing. They may as well not be in any industry. He also sees companies creating their own fields inside the then-brand-new field of "services." Today, the services industry is bigger than manufacturing in America, but in 1960, services was largely new and tiny in the realm of investing.

In 1960, almost all investing was in what today we would see as manufacturing sectors. This book cameos A. C. Nielson and Manpower as very recent IPOs with huge potential. And, he focuses on a still fairly new Dunn & Bradstreet. Although seemingly old and boring names today—far from futuristically exciting—these were very hot stocks in the 1960s.

If someone had simply built a portfolio out of the stocks my father focused on in this book, he or she would have done well in the 1960s, far better than the market. They were, in the 1960s, testament to my father's approach, as laid out in *Common Stocks and Uncommon Profits* and embellished further here, in *Paths to Wealth through Common Stocks*. His fundamental view of finding stocks of outstanding firms with outstanding managements that would stay ahead of the competition for years to come by developing the next new thing—stocks that hadn't yet been fully appreciated or accepted by the institutional investing world, so they could later be bid up beyond their growth rate—that is still a valid approach these 47 years later.

Later, after he had completed this book, he devised a line he asked managers regularly. It's my favorite line he ever wrote: "What are you doing your competitors aren't doing yet?" The emphasis was on the *yet*, implying that by so doing they would be ahead of competitors, gaining an edge—or might simply force their competitors to follow. In my life I've applied that line so many times to good usage that I mightily suggest it to you. It's been a guiding light behind all my business endeavors.

What are you doing your competitors aren't doing yet? It's a pretty good thought to reuse regularly and is pretty well seeded throughout this book, if not said exactly that way.

However, as you read this book, you'll see the inherent risk in my father's approach—you can pick the wrong stocks by not seeing the management correctly. The approach laid out here is sound, but its biggest risk is, in my opinion, not just that you might presume a superior management where it doesn't exist, but also that you might see the management correctly when you buy it, but fail to notice that succession management is not as good. This is a very difficult thing to do. In my career, I've done it wrong many, many times. I use a lot of other risk controls today—ones that didn't exist then—to try to keep myself out of too much trouble when trouble arises. That isn't this book—yet I encourage you to embrace more modern risk-control techniques than were available in 1960.

The approach my father laid out is still one of the most basic and fundamental approaches to looking at stocks. That is why his first book has endured and continued selling so long, and why I'm pleased and proud to write the foreword for this re-introduction of his second book. Enjoy!

KEN FISHER
Founder and CEO, Fisher Investments
Author, *The Only Three Questions that Count*
and the Wiley Fisher Investment Series
Columnist, *Forbes* "Portfolio Strategy"

The Need for Additional
Investment Books

BOOKS ABOUT INVESTING in securities are getting to be like television commercials and crime comics. Most of us think there are far too many of them already. Therefore, before adding still more to the already bulging volume of material that can bewilder the investor with confusing and quite contradictory advice on how to handle common stocks, I gave considerable thought to whether the material presented herein would diminish or would merely add to that confusion. Two years ago, I added one book to this already overcrowded field. I did so because I believed (and still believe) it presented an investment philosophy that needed to be told. The astounding public response to that book vindicated this conclusion. But would adding a second book now do anything more than make the field still more overcrowded? Would it be like adding one more brand of soap when there might be twenty already on the market?

It was primarily because of my experiences resulting from having written *Common Stocks and Uncommon Profits* that I have come more and more to the conclusion there is a basic need for a book such as this. That book summarizes not only the method by which worthwhile profits have been and will continue to be made through common stock ownership, but the policies which I believe will make by far the greatest profits at the least risk. That book primarily attempts to do two things. First, it shows how the investor (or his adviser) can determine the occasional company with outstanding management that is likely to provide the vehicle for tremendous increases in market value over a long period of years. Second, it indicates when the shares in such unusual companies may best be bought and the much rarer situation when a stock that has been well selected in the first place should be sold.

Ever since my earlier book was published I have been hearing from investors all over the country. From these inquiries, repeated again and again, I have, I believe, been given an unusual insight into the type of additional information a tremendous number of stockholders and potential stockholders desire.

Their inquiries fall into two broad classifications. One of these is how to apply my philosophy of investment (or any philosophy of investment for that matter) to the specific conditions we will be facing in the period ahead. How significant, for example, is this matter of inflation, and what should we do about it? What about foreign competition and the prospects of investing abroad? Which will be the best industries for investment? The first and last sections of this book are largely devoted to answering such questions and to show how the investor can gain rather than be hurt by the powerful but quite divergent influences that in the years immediately ahead will cause some stocks to rise spectacularly, while others to disappoint the high hopes many now have for them.

In the second classification, a very large segment of investors seem to recognize something I accentuated heavily in my prior book: That highly profitable handling of common stock investments requires both a degree of knowledge and an amount of time that only a minority possess. Most investors, therefore, quite correctly want to go to an expert. From every adult age group and from people varying from the most modest means to some of extreme wealth, I am repeatedly asked this question: "How do I find an investment man in whom I can place real confidence?" I find a tremendous lack of basic understanding of the strengths and weaknesses of the various subdivisions of the investment business. Yet it is this background knowledge that will most help such people find the man they are seeking. To answer this type of inquiry, I have included the section: "You and Where the Investment Business Must Go." To this basic background knowledge, I have added the five steps which, in my opinion, an investor might take to select a suitable type of investment connection. Finally, I have indicated my views of what lies ahead—and why—and the road investment houses must eventually take to improve what they are now doing in this all-important function of offering sound investment advice.

To these I have added two smaller sections covering certain investment concepts concerning material which an abnormal amount of investor confusion still seems to exist. I believe one of these, in which I describe how the greatest increases in stock values come about, illustrates one of the most important matters in the entire field of common stocks so far as making important profits are concerned. Yet it is something concerning which nine investors out of ten seem completely unaware.

As in my other book, I have used an extremely informal style of presentation. I address you, the reader, in the first person, presenting many of these principles in almost exactly the same language and illustrating them with examples and analogies that I have used to make identical matters crystal clear to the few large investors whose funds it is my sole business to manage.

However, if I have tried to express myself in simple, everyday language, I have not tried to oversimplify the concepts I present. Such oversimplification results in making it seem quite easy to master the art of handling common stocks, but also results in the investor failing to get the benefits he anticipated, because the rules he was given were so simple they only fit some of the facts and not all of them. Before the publication of my first book, I was told I had thrown away all chance of making it a "popular" success, because by describing all the things that are needed to uncover outstanding investments other than by accident, I was describing something anybody and everybody obviously could not do at the drop of a hat. Yet the overwhelming public response to that book convinces me beyond a shadow of doubt that an important part of the investment public is tired of oversimplifications which, when put in practice, do not seem to work out as they should and welcomes a more complex treatment that describes investment matters as they actually are.

Again, as in my prior book, I have not hesitated to express what I believe to be the best financial course simply because some of the things I advocate run either partly or totally contrary to the generally accepted financial thinking of the moment. In the first edition of *Common Stocks and Uncommon Profits* I stated "There is a considerable degree of twisted thinking and general acceptance of half truths about a number of aspects of common stock investment. However, . . . in regard to dividends this confusion is little short of monumental." Now, only a little over two years after those words were written, there have been a number of rather spectacular stock market examples which confirm the points I made then on this subject. The false views that were so widely accepted only two years ago are already beginning to fade. Similarly, I am well aware that in a number of places in this book I have taken stands quite at variance with much of what I consider the easy and slipshod notions that are almost universally accepted by the financial community at the moment. My comments on the utter folly of the present "tight money" policy of the Federal Reserve Board as a means of fighting inflation, on investment trusts, and on the wisdom of making foreign investments, for example, are but a few instances of this. I can only point out that time and again, in matters of investment, the many beliefs that almost everyone accepted as a matter of course and without further thought have proved wrong, and those who thought the matter through to the right answer have been richly rewarded. Just two years of turbulent stock market history seem to lend strong confirmation to the soundness of the very points at which those who always blindly accept the popular view of the moment most raised their eyebrows when my other book first appeared. In comparable fashion, I leave passing judgment on the soundness of the views I am now presenting to the future and to you.

PHILIP A. FISHER
San Mateo, California
December 1959

PATHS TO WEALTH
THROUGH COMMON STOCKS

1

Adjusting to Key
Influences of the 1960's

F ROM TIME TO TIME, fundamental changes of great investment significance affect large groups of common stocks. Usually for some time after these new influences are felt, the great majority of the investment community have little appreciation of their true importance. Then as the real significance of what has happened dawns, a spectacular change occurs in the market price of the affected securities. Fortunes are sometimes made by those who appreciated the significance of what was happening early—before it was importantly reflected in changed quotations for individual stocks.

Let us examine two of the great adjustments to new conditions made by the financial community during the 1950's. Examining such readjustments of the past will better enable us to understand and anticipate some of those that will come during the 1960's.

One of these was the awareness of what a quarter century of progress in the art of corporate management had done to bring real investment stature to "blue chip" industrial equities. It is easy to forget that as recently as the late 1940's large segments of the investment community felt that those not in a position to face sizable risks should confine their security holdings to bonds, high-grade preferred and possibly a few public utility common stocks. Still remembered were the days when corporate management was largely a family affair. Those who controlled a corporation might be quite capable or just the opposite. However, following the practices of the times, authority was delegated only occasionally and almost never with the thought of building up continuity of management in the interest of the outside stockholder. When training a successor was thought of at all, it was usually from the standpoint of eventually handing authority to some favorite young relative who would continue managing in order to maintain the family interest. The corporate head was usually an autocrat, making decisions, good or bad, on the basis of personal conviction. The idea of assembling vast amounts of background material and a variety of outside specialized experts to provide a better factual basis for decision making was never considered. It hardly is surprising that the eventual realization of the enormous stride made by the more alert managements in the handling of their day-to-day affairs, in long-range planning, and in a sense of deep responsibility to the outside stockholder eventually caused a major upward revision in the price investors would pay for the shares of companies benefitting from these important new influences. What is surprising is that this trend toward making certain stocks intrinsically more valuable through radically improved management factors had been running on so long before stock prices began to reflect in a major way what had been going on for years.

Let us consider another and possibly equally important new development affecting certain classes of common stocks. This was the awareness by increasing numbers of companies of how properly guided "research" into one or another field of the natural sciences could open up a technique for ever greater growth in sales and profits through the creation and marketing of endless new but related products developed in this way. Again, important developments along these lines had started many years before. By the late 1940's, this trend had attained quite considerable stature. But it was not until the 1950's that the financial community gave widespread recognition to the enormous investment significance of companies that had genuinely learned to master this tremendously profitable management art. It was only as the 1950's progressed that these most promising companies began to sell at price earnings ratios actually reflecting this attribute.

I believe there are two important lessons that can be learned from studying the (then considered) "new" factors to which stock prices adjusted in the 1950's. One is a realization of the profit (or at times the avoidance of loss) which can accrue to those who take such new influences into consideration before everyone else also does. The second is that these so-called new influences only start to affect most stock prices after they have been running on for quite some time. Therefore, to anticipate some of the comparable influences that will make themselves felt in the 1960's, it is not necessary to anticipate future background forces. Rather, it simply requires examining some of the more recent background influences to which certain groups of stocks have either not sufficiently adjusted themselves or adjusted themselves in an unjustified manner.

A. STOCKS AND INFLATION

In the 1960's (as in the preceding three decades), the threat of further inflation will continue to be of major importance to all investors. However, as the 1960's progress, I believe it certain that the true relationship of common stock ownership to inflation will become more clearly understood. As a result, certain groups of stocks may sell at rather different price levels than they now do. Those who now understand these relationships may save themselves from considerable loss in the years ahead.

Because this whole matter has such great investment importance, I believe it may be worthwhile to explore inflation's fundamental nature before examining its relationship to various groups of common stocks. When its true cause is understood, the investor is unlikely to be confused in his basic thinking by various dogmatic comments of some of our political leaders.

The first thing to consider, of course, is just what we mean by inflation. While there are many complex definitions, I do not believe that for investment purposes it is either necessary or desirable to become involved in intricate definition. For practical purposes, it is sufficient to consider inflation as a condition whereby (with only minor and temporary reversals) the total amount of things and services that can be obtained for the same number of dollars (or other monetary units) grows less and less. Such a situation is in sharp contrast to the background condition that has prevailed over most of American history when the fairly long periods of years when the dollar would decrease in value were succeeded by roughly equivalent, lengthy cycles when the level of all prices would tend to fall and the value of the dollar to rise correspondingly.

The first and probably the most important thing for the investor to recognize about inflation is this: As long as the overwhelming majority of Americans maintain firmly held existing opinions concerning the duties and obligations of their government, more and more inflation is inevitable. Eliminating governmental waste and balancing budgets are highly desirable goals. If brought about without touching off a sharp downward spiral in general business, they can be extremely beneficial in slowing down the rate of further inflation and may even appear to have stopped it completely for a while. However, any talk by political leaders that in present-day America this by itself will put a permanent stop to further inflation is merely talk and nothing more.

Why is more inflation so sure to come? Because under the economic system we have established, the seeds of inflation sprout not in times of prosperity but in times of depression. About eighty per cent of our federal revenue is derived from corporate and individual income taxes. This basic source of federal funds is notoriously sensitive to the level of general business. It shrinks sharply on even moderate downturns in the general economy.

However, this is not all that happens when general business gets bad. We have enacted laws, including unemployment insurance and farm relief, which make mandatory a sharp increase of government payments in just these same periods of bad business when federal income is lowest. Furthermore, these laws already on the statute books are almost certainly but the smallest part of the special outpouring of government money that would occur whenever a truly severe depression might develop. Examine the actions of Congress in even the mild depression of 1958, and this becomes obvious. All sorts of proposals were immediately advanced for helping the economy at the expense of the national treasury. These ranged all the way from drastic reductions in taxes on individuals and corporations (so as to expand shrinking purchasing power) to setting up organizations to make special loans to distressed groups and to vastly expanded programs of public works. While most of these proposals failed to be enacted, the interesting thing is why they failed. Hardly a voice in either major party was raised in opposition to such a program "if it were really needed to end the slump." Rather, the Republicans took the stand that the slump gave promise of ending so soon anyway that it would be better to wait and only enact such inflation-producing measures if the expected upturn failed to materialize and "such measures became necessary."

While in 1958 events proved the slide so short-lived that few such measures were put into effect, can anyone with the least understanding of the practicalities of partisan politics doubt that in a more prolonged period of poor business our elected officials would almost unanimously choose tens of billions of annual deficits in preference to having the voters again undergo the hardships of a major depression? For that matter, can anyone say with even a semblance of surety that this deficit-producing course is not the right one in the national interest? It can be granted that huge deficits are bound to produce more inflation. We can also be well aware of the injustices and hardships that result from important rises in the general price level. However, are these injustices and hardships as great for those who feel their pinch as the suffering and hardships imposed on workers and proprietors alike by a great depression such as that of the early 1930's?

Whatever each of us as individuals may think of this matter, it has already been decided for us by the overwhelming weight of public conviction. One hundred and fifty years ago, public opinion would have no more held it was the business of our government to assure constantly prosperous economic conditions than, to mention the example I used when I wrote *Common Stocks and Uncommon Profits*, they would have thought it was the business of government to guarantee everyone a happy marriage. Fifty years ago, public opinion would have thought it necessary to do such relatively inexpensive things as to establish bread lines and soup kitchens so no one actually starved. At that time, public opinion would have done little more. In the then still strongly agricultural economy, this was hardly enough to have produced deficits of inflationary proportion. The federal income tax, of course, was still a thing of the future. Percentage-wise, the national government's incoming revenues did not fluctuate quite as violently with every change in the economic weathervane as they do today.

Where does all this leave us? The historically recent but now almost unanimous opinion of both our public officials and their constituents that it is the duty of government to maintain endless prosperity is not likely to change. Unfortunately, when hard times come, the only major cure known to government is to spend enough more than is taken in taxes to create sufficient new purchasing power to reverse the trend. This also produces more inflation. Occasional downturns in business seem as much a part of the price we must pay for all the other advantages of a system of free private enterprise as a lower standard of living for everybody, less goods produced, and a loss of personal freedom seem the price that must be paid by those living in countries where the government is the only employer. Therefore, as long as we maintain the benefits of our free economic system, unexpected downturns will occasionally appear. As long as we are democratically governed and public opinion reacts as it now does, these will be followed by more and more inflation.

However, at this point there is something else to be considered. Just as there are many people who erroneously hold that inflation can be halted short of dictatorship, so there are even more who have an equally false view. This is that there is something inherent in the inflationary process that inevitably makes it proceed at an ever faster and faster pace. Inflation is sometimes compared to a horse that may start at a slow walk but will eventually end in a furious and dangerous gallop. The often heard terms of "galloping" and "runaway" inflation have doubtless arisen from this analogy.

The arguments of those who believe in the inevitability of this speeding-up process of inflation run something like this: As prices start rising, far-sighted people realize the inflationary implications of what is happening. They start buying things they will need in the future before the price of these things rises still higher. This extra demand tends to make the prices of these things rise even faster than they otherwise would. These ever more rapid price increases alert still others to the inflationary implications of what is occurring. As they in turn anticipate future needs, further and further boosts are given to the momentum of this inflationary spiral. Consumers buying today what they normally would purchase in the future, businessmen piling up inventory materials far beyond normal practices, and speculators simply trying to make a quick profit from the situation all contribute their part to the whirlwind.

It is strange that in the face of all of the evidence to the contrary, so many people who evaluate the evils of our existing inflation quite realistically then go on to frighten themselves and totally mislead investors by proclaiming that our present leisurely type of inflation must inevitably break loose in a far more virulent galloping sort of inflation. Although these people have been forecasting this development for years and have so far been totally wrong, their convictions have gained considerable general acceptance. This acceptance has had important implications for the investor, which I will come to presently. But first, why does this view run contrary to what has actually happened? For some years, a sizable part of the business community has accepted the great probability of more and more inflation. Yet nowhere in the business world do we find any tendency in times of peace to build up inventories because of this. In contrast, we find constant effort to find more and more ways to cut down inventory totals. The reason for this is not hard to find. There are so many costs to carrying inventory that it does not pay to stock up just because eventually the general price level will rise further.

To understand this matter clearly, it might be well to examine these costs in detail. First, there is the interest that could be earned on funds tied up in excess inventory. If available funds are not on hand and excess inventory must be carried with borrowed money, this cost is even greater. Then there is the cost of warehousing or storing this inventory. To this must be added the cost of insuring it against fire, theft, or other damage. Next come local property taxes, which will be levied if the inventory is held at whatever time of year such assessments are made in the particular locality. Finally, in the case of certain commodities, there is the risk of physical spoilage with age. In other cases, there is danger of style or technical changes which would give them less value.

For these reasons, with all of the inflation and inflation awareness that has occurred in the United States since World War II, we find no tendency whatever to build up stocks of goods as an inflation hedge. Such advance buying as has occasionally occurred has nearly always been because of fear of physical scarcity (as in the early stages of the Korean War) or fear of a price rise in a particular commodity, but never because of concern about general inflation. At times, advance buying has not been stimulated even when immediate but moderate future price advances for a particular commodity have been announced. The increase was just too small in relation to the carrying charge.

None of this means that a speed-up to the type of truly galloping inflation witnessed in Germany and France shortly after World War I is an impossibility in the United States. It could happen here. However, to occur, the whole inflationary process first would have to be speeded up a great deal. There should be many advance signs of this well before it might happen. Furthermore, for reasons already discussed, such a speed-up, if it happens, will do so at a time of depression rather than prosperity. At such times, investment bargains in common shares usually abound. This has major significance to the investor for it means that when stock prices are high he need not rush surplus cash into the market for fear inflation will otherwise gobble up the value of his cash at any moment.

What is the actual pace at which inflation has been developing? No one can say with complete certainty exactly how fast inflation is growing (that is, just how much less the same amount of money will buy) each year. This is because no one can be positive that some margin of error may not exist in the various indices that have been devised to measure this matter. But the Consumer Price Index (CPI) of the U.S. Bureau of Labor Statistics has been compiled with so much care that it probably comes reasonably close to measuring accurately as complex a matter as this one. For the ten years from January 1, 1950 to December 31, 1959, it shows an average annual increase of a little over 2 per cent a year. Let us suppose this index should be inaccurate in measuring price changes by as much as 50 per cent, which seems quite unlikely. This would still leave us with an average annual increase of only a little over 3 per cent.

The full investment significance of this should be obvious, yet investors frequently fail to grasp it. It means that, from the long term standpoint, inflation is a major force to be reckoned with. Any investment which does not have within itself the means of increasing its value by at least from twenty to thirty per cent every ten years may be regarded as a poor one.

On the other hand, and here is where many investors go badly astray, just because cash, bonds, and many classes of stock contain no inherent inflationary protection, this emphatically does not mean that this type of asset should be pitched over and the right type of equity investment acquired at the first possible moment. In the average year, the shrinkage in the real value of cash might be in the 2 to 3 per cent range at most. This roughly represents about what (after taxes) cash is currently earning in interest income. This means that in as much as

8

four years there might be a real shrinkage of not over 8 to 12 per cent if the interest factor is ignored. Yet in any year, the most desirable types of common shares will fluctuate far more than 3 per cent in value, and over a four-year span, the fluctuations will be many, many times 8 to 12 per cent.

The wise investor should get the inflation matter in proper perspective. Long range, I believe this should be his goal: No investments that fail to give promise of at least enough gain to balance the inevitable further shrinkage of the dollar. But short range, he should also realize that selecting the right investment and buying it at the right time is tremendously more important than getting this inflation protection quickly. Conversely, when an investor has set aside a given sum of money for a given purpose for which he will want to use that money in a relatively few years (for example, to build a house or take his family on a trip abroad), I believe he should leave such sums in cash and not try to protect them against inflation. If he has bought the right type of inflation hedge, it may be down in price just when he wants his cash by far more than the relatively modest amount the purchasing value of his original savings would have shrunk in the meantime.

Why do so many investors in this inflation-conscious age get almost panicky about holding much cash? They rush in to buy with a total unwillingness to take the time necessary to find a genuinely outstanding investment opportunity. In some cases, this may just be the sign of an impatient or immature individual. Frequently, however, I believe there is something quite different behind their actions—the uncritical acceptance of the widespread fallacy that the tempo of inflation is so sure to increase, so that speed in disposing of cash or its equivalent becomes of paramount importance.

Because I have heard it so often, I am well aware of the objection to my basic conclusions that many thoughtful people will make at this point. They will say that my statement that major inflationary spurts will only occur as a result of the deficits caused by wars or business depressions (so that there is no tremendous rush to hedge against inflation at other times) is based entirely on the assumption that inflation is being caused by an expanding money base. Actually, they will claim steadily rising prices are being caused by something far different. This is the unfair advantage in our economy that our laws give to our labor unions. By enabling single organizations to have monopoly power to supply vitally needed workers or to withhold this supply from entire industries, these unions have been given a strength which the rest of the community cannot match. This has caused wages to rise so much that a business has no choice but to pass the increases on to the public in the form of higher prices. Here is a force that in good times even more than bad will be working for more and more inflation.

I agree with much of this argument, but I believe it to be only part of the entire picture. While it is a larger money supply and not higher wage rates that directly causes inflation, the two are still largely the same thing. This is because when wage increases are granted that are greater than increased productivity, management has no choice but to pass most or all of this on in the form of higher prices. This in turn is because, with the average of all business profits only a few cents of each dollar of sales and the total wage bill many times this amount, there is no place such a wage increase can be absorbed except in higher prices. Then, however, the government is also placed in a position in which sooner or later it has no choice. It can, through the Federal Reserve System, "ratify" a round of wage-price increases by increasing the money supply enough so the public can purchase the normal amount of goods at the increased price level resulting from this latest wave of wage increases. However, it can refuse to "ratify" and keep the money supply where it was before. If it refused to "ratify," there would then not be enough money to support the former normal volume of transactions at the higher price level. Bad times would then begin. Either the so-called "money managers" must reverse their own policy, or the depression deepens. Then with federal revenue shrinking and expenses rising, enough deficit occurs to increase the money supply through this means, and the wage price increase gets ratified anyway.

Fortunately, there is another major force which today is almost as powerful as the power of big labor unions and which tends to exert just the opposite effect on the general price structure. This is the amazing growth in recent years of scientific research and developmental engineering in industry. So profitable has been the teamwork of the business executive, the scientist, and the engineer, that what Professor Sumner Schlichter of Harvard University has so aptly called the "Industry of Discovery" has been growing at a truly amazing rate. It has tripled in the last six years and currently embraces annual expenditures somewhere in the neighborhood of nine billion dollars. This is almost a straight-line progression from expenditures only thirty years ago that totalled a relatively few million.

It is easy to visualize the influence on the price structure of the sizable group of engineering people who through new machinery and new methods are constantly finding ways of making things cheaper. Sometimes lost sight of—because their work does not lend itself so readily to statistical treatment—is the influence on the price structure of that other large group of researchers who are working to make things better. An example might make this clear. Suppose a tire costs the same price today as it did thirty-five years ago. Then, punctures were common every few thousand miles. Today they are quite rare. Then, the total mileage per tire, even at vastly slower driving speeds, was but a minor fraction of that which is standard today. Therefore, in total cost including maintenance, a sizable price reduction has occurred.

Here in the ever-growing "Industry of Discovery," we have a counter-vailing force that with its tendency to make things cheaper has gone a long way toward balancing much of the influence of rising wage rates to make them dearer. There is a considerable time lag between when expenditures are made in research and when the results appear in cheaper or better products. Since expenditures are steadily rising, there is every assurance that in the years ahead there will be an equally rising curve of benefits. Therefore, it seems rather sure that the price-reducing influence from this source will grow stronger not weaker. This is why I believe not that inflation will stop, but that with this powerful brake tending to hold down otherwise inflationary influences, excepting in times of large deficit producing depressions, the investor can take his time to find the occasional outstanding investment. He need not be so frightened of the speed of inflation's progress that he must rush into the first inflation hedge that comes along.

Once the investor realizes the certainty of more and more inflation, his natural tendency is to concentrate his thinking upon what to him is quite correctly the heart of the subject—where to place his funds in an inflationary world. However, I believe there is still one remaining background matter which it can be quite profitable for any investor to understand before getting to the specifics of just what type of hold-ing best fits into the kind of inflation most apt to be encountered in the 1960's.

What I am about to say will challenge the accuracy of an almost universally accepted belief. Just because so many accept something as true without further thought on the subject will cause some to feel that any questioning is out of place. To those, I would point out that history has shown that, in every age and in every field of human knowledge, many of the views which almost everyone accepted as true and never bothered to think about further were in time proven completely wrong. It took centuries of civilization before it was realized that the earth went round the sun and not the other way around. Only a generation ago, learned scientists would have ridiculed the idea that even the most solid of objects are almost entirely empty space, yet today we know this to be the case. Can you remember when pregnant women were told to eat enough for two, a practice we have since learned is highly undesirable? Because something is generally taken for granted and even though respected leaders in places of power tailor their policies accordingly, this does not of itself make it correct.

In modern times, nearly all bankers and many governments have held that the way to fight inflation is to raise interest rates. This would be an effective curb if, in our type of slow-moving inflation, people acted as they are supposed to do in the theoretical economist's traditional concept of inflation or as they actually do act in a faster moving inflation. Then businessmen, consumers, and speculators would all compete to stock up on things they do not need now but believe will cost more later. This would raise prices faster and faster until many became so overstocked and overbought that the boom would burst. Most such extra buying is done on credit or borrowed money. Therefore, raising the cost of such money by refusing to make more credit available would stop this type of dangerous procedure and would be a true inflation-curbing measure. However, since in actual practice none of these groups show any tendency to make unneeded or advanced purchases, raising interest rates to cure our type of inflation may be like using a drug that can quickly cure pneumonia on a patient whose ills result solely from overeating.

Because it can be quite helpful in the proper timing of investments, let us examine considerably more closely what raising interest rates actually does. First, let us see what our central banking authorities have been telling us. Remember, these are the people who have the power. Since they can control the supply of bank credit, they are in a position to exert tremendous influence on money rates.

Raise wages, they say, and that is inflationary. It increases the cost of doing business and therefore the cost of what the consumer must buy. Raise the price of raw materials, finished products, or services, and that is, of course, inflationary. It not only raises the cost of products directly affected, but by raising the cost for still other businesses who buy these products or services, it forces still other price increases. But raise the cost of money, say our central bankers, and this is deflationary! They say this even though, business must borrow money to carry on and grow, and though this raises the cost of doing business just as does any other type of price increase in the things which a business needs to operate. Does this make sense?

Strangely enough, under certain conditions it does. Unfortunately, these happen to be conditions which are quite different from those under which the American economy normally operates. But suppose our economy were operating close to capacity. Most major industries would then be turning out as much as could be squeezed out of their plants. Further suppose that the real rate at which, say steel, was being consumed were not as great as this demand. However, suppose the steel plants were being overworked trying to turn out enough steel not only to meet the real needs of the nation but also to build some additional steel plants to take care of the need that appeared to be there as long as the industry was being called upon to supply enough steel for *both* current demand and the proposed steel plants, too. In such an instance, choking back the amount of money business could borrow could do two quite worthwhile things. It could slow down how rapidly new steel plants would be built. This would force some of the extra steel demand into the future, thereby prolonging the boom. More important, it would force most companies to get along with the least amount of steel inventories that they could keep on hand and still carry on their business. In this way, it might well prevent the type of runaway rise in steel prices that would otherwise occur if all the customers of the steel industry were bidding against each other for just a little more steel than the mills could possibly turn out. Under circumstances like these—but only under circumstances like these—high interest rates and so-called "tight-money" can be of great help in curbing inflationary tendencies.

In the 1960's, however, the American economy is in a quite different position from the example just described. Except when faced by an industry-wide strike, most major industries are operating at rates varying between seventy and ninety per cent of capacity. Almost everywhere there is surplus unused capacity. There are, and may continue to be, several million people unemployed. Most importantly, a large part of new equipment and machinery projects under consideration by industry today, the type of projects which get approved in large numbers when interest rates are low but which are cut down drastically when they are high, are not for new capacity at all. Rather they are for modernization of old capacity. They are projects which will permit the turning out of products at a lower cost per unit, usually by the replacement of old machines and old methods with new machines and better methods.

Nothing could be more important in curbing the rate of inflation than this. Here is a two-pronged anti-inflationary weapon. On the one hand, through helping industry borrow at low rates to carry through many more of these modernization programs, industry is being helped to cut its costs. Because of the normal workings of our competitive system, such cost savings nearly always are passed on to the consumer, although at times this has only been in the form of enabling industry to absorb further wage increases without corresponding price increases. On the other hand, the volume of additional orders to industry which these additional modernization programs would produce would increase sufficiently the total volume of all business, to say nothing of the increase it would bring to total payrolls. It inevitably would bring dramatic improvement to a federal budget picture as dependent as is ours on the ups and downs of total corporation and individual income taxes.

It now should begin to become clear why creation of "tight money" does not accomplish what it is supposed to do in slowing down inflation. It actually sets in motion forces that in time are sure to speed up inflation. I already have tried to show how through constantly finding ways of making things cheaper or better, research and developmental engineering have been a powerful force slowing down this inflationary process. However, because nearly all of these cost-saving engineering developments require capital, their introduction into industry is directly affected by the money markets. When money is costly and hard to borrow, most corporations are under pressure to utilize only the most outstanding of the fruits of their research and engineering departments. Otherwise attractive programs tend to become postponed or abandoned as the means of financing them become unavailable or too costly. So the very interest rates that have been raised to prevent inflation curtail doing things that are designed to reduce production costs and bring about lower prices!

Nor is this the only or the most fundamental way that tight money brings on more and more inflation. I have also tried to show that the basic producer of inflation is business depression because of the huge increase in deficit financing that a period of severe business decline must bring. Whether it was as long ago as 1930 or as recently as 1957, whenever the Federal Reserve banks have encouraged a drastic tightening of money rates, the effect on general business has been the same. Industry curtails capital spending. Home building and other key industries in which financing costs play a big part in final prices to the consumer usually become equally affected. The decline in these "swing" industries begins to hurt other lines, and a general decline is on its way. Ever since the great depression of the 1930's, each of these business declines has resulted in still another hefty boost in the federal deficit and that much more inflation has become part of the economy.

If I have dwelled at what may have appeared to be an unreasonable length upon this matter of the effect of high interest rates, it is because I think it of far more significance to investors than most of them realize. While investors should never lose sight of the great probability of more and more inflation, in normal times, this inflation moves sufficiently slowly so that the investor should take his time waiting for an outstanding opportunity rather than grab anything that might be a hedge against rising prices. However, when money rates start climbing toward higher levels and the money managers appear to be encouraging the rise, the rules change somewhat. The investor should then move with even more caution than normally. Business may well be about to turn down. Even if it does not, the yield factor is likely to cause stocks to follow bonds toward lower levels. This does not mean that the investor should refrain from all buying during this period (for a genuinely outstanding opportunity should never be passed over because of the purely near-term influences) but that he should be more and more demanding of what he does buy.

After tight-money conditions have prevailed for some time, however, the picture changes radically. In tightening money rates to combat higher prices, the central banking authorities are like an individual who has a dangerous virus in his system and who decides to take no nourishment in an attempt to starve out the virus. He will die of starvation himself long before he eliminates the virus. Furthermore, the Federal Reserve, like most individuals, will usually give up the attempt and reverse policy as the starvation approach gets more and more painful. The investor has usually no sure way of knowing exactly when this change will take place. But the longer the starvation period has been going on and the more federal deficits are piling up while the capital goods and construction industry are suffering, the greater the possibility of a sharp reversal followed by another inflationary spurt. Therefore, the longer a deficit-producing period runs on, the more eager the individual should be to see that his securities are of a type suitable for long-range holding.

What type of holdings will provide protection from inflation? Here I think the crude and naive notions of the past decade are going to be in for a rude awakening as the 1960's unfold. It has been generally believed that almost any type of common stock which represents ownership of assets was, is, and will continue to be an inflation hedge. None of this is correct. So far as the past is concerned, this is easily demonstrated by citing the sizable number of stocks representing ownership of significant amounts of assets which over the past 15 years of steadily rising prices (and therefore shrinking purchasing power of the dollar) have shown no increase in their own price and in many instances have substantially declined. This in itself should refute the widely accepted and plausible sounding argument that since stocks represent the ownership of tangible things (as land, factories, inventories, etc.) and since in an inflation the value of things goes up in relation to dollars, owning these things through stock ownership will protect stockholders against further shrinkage in the value of the dollar.

Many investors carry this reasoning one step further. They claim that corporations which own vast amounts of natural raw materials in the ground, such as mining and petroleum companies, are ideal inflation hedges. As the dollar shrinks in value, ownership of such real assets will rise proportionately in value, so that shareholders in such companies have built-in protection. For reasons I will attempt to explain, some of these companies may prove quite worthwhile inflation hedges. However, this is due to a completely different set of factors, far removed from their happening to own sizable amounts of just any useful raw material. This is something which, in 1958 and 1959, many previously complacent owners of shares in oil-producing companies began to discover for themselves.

We can rid ourselves more easily of this common fallacy that "because stocks represent ownership of tangible things they automatically protect us against inflation" if we keep one basic concept in mind. Within the general price level, the things we buy are constantly changing their values in relation to each other. Even though this general price level may be steadily (but slowly) rising—within that great and rather glacier-like movement—some things are going up in price while others are going down. In these times of frequent inventions and the discovery of new processes that sometimes make possible major reductions in the cost of doing things, some of these downs can be rather spectacular. Similarly, shifts in public taste can cause noticeable increases or decreases in the price of the products or services affected.

To illustrate this point, I am going to cite an extreme case—one which may seem rather exaggerated. Nevertheless, I believe it to be one which stockholders might well keep in mind if they are to avoid the easy mistake of buying the wrong type of stock for an inflationary period. Furthermore, let us place our example in as extreme an inflation as the modern world has seen. Let us place it in Germany in the early 1920's. At that time, the German mark (worth about 25¢ prior to World War I) became so utterly worthless that a billion marks at one period had less trading value than ownership of a loaf of bread. Many Germans, recognizing what was coming, did their best to convert their deteriorating money into ownership of physical things. But suppose one of them acquired as his hedge against inflation a warehouse full of bustles. In the 1890's when the feminine population, for reasons far beyond my ability to comprehend, desired to disguise (or possibly accentuate?) a certain portion of their anatomy, this ownership would have been highly desirable. In that period, the merchandise would have retained much of its value. However, in the 1920's, outside of an occasional demand for theatrical costumes, bustles would have had no value whatsoever. It would not have made the slightest difference whether the price was high, low, or even if it was quoted in a currency which everyone thought soon to be worthless. No one would want

17

them, and no one would buy them. Bustles in the 1920's would not have been the least protection against inflation.

Now let us get to common stocks. Except when a company is about to be liquidated, the value of the assets behind each share of stock has very little to do with the price at which that stock normally sells in the market. Reason for this is essentially that unless assets are going to be passed out to stockholders, they are only desirable for either what they will earn or what the financial community as a whole thinks they will earn. If you doubt this and want confirmation of it, make a very simple test. The list of stocks traded on the New York Stock Exchange nearly always is presented in alphabetical order. Pick any spot at random on this list and study the next twenty stocks. Notice the complete lack of relationship between market price and asset value of whichever group you happen to choose. Some stocks will be selling at a huge discount from asset value. Others will be selling at many times their asset value. There is no relationship to be found at all. If this does not convince you, make another type of test. While they appear far less often than they did years ago, a broker will occasionally put out the type of bulletin that calls attention to stocks that are bargains because of their asset value. Get one of these that was published some years ago. With the ease of hindsight, compare the subsequent market action of these stocks with that of any of the recognized market indices. You will find that lots of assets by themselves have little relationship to what stocks are going to do in the market. These assets may or may not increase in value in an inflationary period. But this in itself is not enough to make the stocks go up proportionately. Asset value, by itself, has no power to produce rising stock prices.

What does cause stocks to rise in value are two things that are rather closely interrelated. One is an increase in a stock's earning power. The other, and usually the more important, is the consensus of investment opinion as to the future course of that earning power. The reason these are so closely related is the strong tendency of the financial community to conclude that because a particular company has been increasing per-share earnings at a brilliant rate year after year, this trend will continue for a long time in the future. Plus or minus the temporary influence of the business cycle, this line of reasoning is often quite correct, although occasionally it can be quite wrong. At any rate, it is steadily increasing per-share earnings upon which is superimposed a steadily rising ratio of market price to these earnings (as the financial community accords a particular stock more and more status) that produces much of the great increase in values commonly associated with growth stocks. This combination produces the greatest net gains for investors in times of sound money. It also provides the greatest protection against inflation in times of depreciating currency.

In other words, stocks that are going to have a big rise regardless of inflationary conditions are the only type of stocks that will safeguard the investors' assets against inflation. This is not because of any deep intrinsic relationship between common stocks and inflation protection. No such built-in relationship exists at all. It is solely because of the happy accident that the company involved is so conducting the affairs that it is making its shares intrinsically more valuable by a degree as great or greater than inflation is decreasing the value of the investor's money. This means that the investor's real assets will be maintained by as much as inflation would otherwise shrink them. If a true growth stock is bought before most of the financial community recognizes the full attractiveness of the company, it nearly always means in a slow-moving inflation such as ours that the stock will go up even more than money will shrink. Therefore, over and above his genuine inflationary hedge, an investor will have a sizable further real profit.

In other words, the rules for selecting the only type of stocks that will give real inflation protection are identical with those that I sketched in *Common Stocks and Uncommon Profits*. Find the company with a highly competent management that through research or some other means has found a way to increase its per-share earnings year after year (after allowing each year for the temporary ups and downs of the business cycle). Be sure that management is determined to continue this growth and safeguard it through the build-up of younger executives trained in the same general policies. Then, if you can buy these shares before most of the financial community fully appreciates the situation, get them and hang on to them, regardless of how high they go, for as long as these policies continue. Do all this, and you will have a real hedge against inflation and a great deal more. Buy this same company after its unusual qualities are pretty generally appreciated and you probably will still have your inflation hedge but not much more. In contrast, buy shares in a mediocre company, particularly when so many others are bidding up the price of any and all stocks, and you probably will not have any real protection from inflation at all.

Many people ask, "If most common stocks do not give full protection against inflation, do they not at least provide some protection?" After all, our type of inflation tends to make the periods of poor business shorter than they might otherwise be and may tend to stimulate activity when general business is good. Does not all this help create some additional earning power for nearly all stocks? Will not this earning power create enough additional real value to offset at least partially the declining worth of money?

I do not think enough dependable evidence is available to give a positive answer to this. However, I am inclined to suspect that as the 1950's progressed and the belief swept the investment community that common stocks are (just by being common stocks) a haven against inflation, far too much weight has been given these matters. This is because investors have been ignoring the other side of the same situation, that is, the way in which inflation hurts common stocks as well as helps them.

As prices rise, it takes more and more money to do the same physical amount of business. Assuming a company is already so efficient that it operates with the smallest amount of inventory needed to meet its customers' needs promptly, each round of price increases means it must set aside that much more money to maintain this same minimum level of raw materials, work in process, and finished goods on hand. Remember, excepting in accounting fiction, this is not a liquid resource. It represents a permanent additional investment that the company must keep on hand at all times, since it must maintain its minimum inventory at this level if it is to retain its existing position. Similarly, as prices rise, more and more money must be tied up in accounts receivable to finance not more but the same amount of business. Finally and most important of all is the financial drain resulting from plant and equipment. Remember, some of these machinery and building items have shorter periods before they wear out and become useless while others may have a longer life. However, all of them wear out in time. The depreciation rate a company is allowed to charge depends on the taxing authorities' estimate of how long it takes to wear out each item. However, this rate under our archaic and rather unfair depreciation laws only allows a company to recover the amount each of these assets originally cost, not what it will cost to replace it when a new one must be put in its place. Therefore, in an inflationary period, there is a constant financial drain and erosion on the plant and equipment of all companies. This amounts to the rather sizable sum that represents the difference between the price at which these items are being depreciated on the books and the real cost of replacing them.

From the standpoint of the common stockholder, there is only one protection against all this inflationary produced financial attrition. This is a management of such ability that it can produce a steadily increasing stream of profits. Such increasing profits usually come from increasing the size of existing activities or starting new activities in related lines. To be great enough to nourish a business in inflationary times, this growth must be truly large; for in addition to supplying the additional capital needed by the older parts of the business, there is the problem of supplying the capital for the newer lines as well. To do this requires management of great capability and great judgment in selecting the right spot for expansion. Companies with such managements are usually exactly the same ones that in non-inflationary times would make the most worthwhile investments. This is why the common stock of just any company with a mediocre management is not likely to prove much protection against inflation.

As the 1960's start, I believe, understanding this one point can be of tremendous importance in avoiding losses that might otherwise occur when greater financial sophistication concerning inflation develops in the years immediately ahead. In the 1940's and the early part of the 1950's, all the signs pointing to the inevitability of more and more inflation were just as clear as they were later on in the past decade. However, for some reason, until a very few years ago, a great many investors did not read these signs. Then in 1956 to 1957 and even more so in 1958 and 1959, millions of investors heretofore not overly concerned about the matter began developing a great mass phobia about inflation. With no change in fundamentals whatsoever and inflation no more (and no less) dangerous than it had been for many years before, they acted as though their funds would be wiped out if they did not get protection by acquiring common stocks (almost any kind of common stock) immediately. The result was a great uprush in the quotations for and the price-earnings ratios of all sorts of common stocks. Some are of a sort that should genuinely protect against further inflation. Others, because of situations affecting the course of their own future earning power, may prove either inadequate protection or no protection whatsoever.

Most of the many wealthy individuals who flocked into the market to make their first common stock purchases in the period of 1956 through 1959 might be considered genuine long-term investors and not speculators. They became sincerely concerned about inflation. This made them lose their fondness for tax-free municipal bonds and the greater net income after taxes which these tax-free securities offer to wealthy investors. They bought their common shares, sometimes almost regardless of price. They put them away in their strong boxes with the comfortable feeling that they were now protected against the further inflation that was sure to come and that, no matter how much they paid per share, in time inflation would make the price a lot higher.

I believe this has created a situation which in the early 1960's the shrewd investor will watch with close attention. I say this because I think it reasonable to conclude that many of these wealthier new-comers to the stock market may have great ability in other directions but are people with relatively low investment I.Q.'s. Otherwise with all of the inflationary signs just as apparent at least ten years earlier, they would neither have concentrated upon the inflationary dangerous tax-frees for so long nor so quickly and uncritically have embraced the doctrine that any stock—regardless of price—would protect them against inflation.

What I believe may very well occur is this: Many of these recent inflationary-induced converts to common stocks may well act about as you might expect someone to behave who had previously spent his whole life underground and who knew almost nothing of celestial mechanics. You show such a person the moon at exactly eight o'clock in the evening. You tell him that as the night goes on the moon will appear to travel clear across the heavens. He looks at it with intense interest. But he cannot see it move. So he keeps watching. At 8:01 it seems to be in just the same place. At 8:02 he can still see no change. 8:03 still brings nothing he can see for himself, and by 8:04, he gives up in disgust as still things seem the same. He decided he can spend his time to better and to greater advantage doing something else. Yet by two o'clock in the morning if he came back and looked, there would be the type of spectacular change for which he got tired of looking at 8:04.

I think this is just what is rather apt to happen to many of the relatively recent converts to the ranks of those who hold common stocks primarily because of inflation. Many months, perhaps several more years, will go by. At the speed inflation has been advancing it may be pretty hard to see that in the time since they bought their common shares inflation has been a mighty force. Their psychological 8:04 P.M. will come. They will be influenced by the prevailing feeling of the moment that "inflation really isn't so important" just as when they bought they were influenced by the mass fear of not protecting themselves at once. If this happens, and it could happen just when the real need of protection against inflation is greatest, before the 1960's are too far advanced, a mass movement away from common stocks might prove a major influence for a short period of time.

To the alert investor, such a possibility opens up two avenues of possible immediate action. Now, when many routine stocks are selling at what, judged by most past standards, seems extremely high prices, he might re-examine his holdings with the thought of eliminating any investments that are not of truly outstanding character. On the other hand, as I reiterated again and again in my *Common Stocks and Uncommon Profits*, any possibility that the really unusual stock may be temporarily overpriced should not be the least inducement toward causing an investor to sell that type of security. There are just too many chances that (1) the expected price reaction will not occur, (2) if it does the investor will wait for still lower prices and will not get back until the stock has again climbed to even higher levels, or (3) by the time the reaction does come the stock will have continued to climb so much that at its coming bottom it will still be above present prices.

Mass disenchantment with the idea of "any stock as an inflation hedge" might also, at such time as it may come, open up future avenues of action for the alert investor. The always hard to find genuine growth company will, for the moment at least, go down in the general selling. If such a selling wave should come, it might present that rare buying opportunity in the type of stock that represents true inflation protection. In typical, normal major-market setbacks, all kinds of stocks go down sharply during the decline, but only the truly good ones make the kind of sharp recovery that leads on to new all-time highs.

In summary, I think there is every probability that by the end of the 1960's there will be general investor confirmation of the current view that more and more inflation is inevitable and that one of the most important considerations in making any kind of investment is protection against this tremendous force. However, I think by that time the investor will have a degree of sophistication undreamed of today regarding the mechanics of so protecting his holdings. Not just any stocks but solely stocks that would do unusually well in any non-inflationary period will be recognized as the only true common-stock inflation protection. It will be realized that there is no direct relationship causing common stocks to rise as the purchasing power of money goes down. Meanwhile, it will also be recognized that, excepting in times of depression when common stocks are likely to be cheap anyway, there is seldom any reason for rushing into such buying for inflation protection. Selecting exactly the right stock to buy is so important and the shrinkage in the real value of cash occurs so gradually that there is every reason to take several years, if necessary, until just the right purchase comes along. However, the process of obtaining this degree of general investor sophistication on this subject may not be easy or painless. Earlier in the 1960's, there may well be a period of considerable frustration and disenchantment with "any common stock as an inflation hedge." The alert investor might well consider whether any of his present holdings are not intrinsically attractive but are selling at abnormal prices chiefly because of an erroneously imputed value given them as a possible inflation hedge. Later on, he may also have an opportunity to make some unusually attractive purchases if a period of mass disenchantment should occur.

B. Institutional Buying

Institutional buying in the stock market comes largely from five major sources. These are (1) pension and profit-sharing funds, (2) trustees for the benefit of private individuals, represented mainly by the trust departments of large banks, (3) investment trusts, (4) insurance companies, and (5) educational and charitable organizations, including the sizable transactions of our wealthier universities.

The importance of the impact of these institutional buyers on the stock will not be unique to the 1960's any more than the inflationary influence we have already discussed are brand new. Just as in the case of inflation, what will be different will be increased investor awareness of the real significance of this relatively new influence—a better understanding of how to take advantage of it and, even more important, how to avoid being hurt by it.

In order to understand these matters, a little financial history might be helpful. A relatively low level of common stock prices prevailed over most of the 1930's. Two influences are usually considered to be the principal reasons for this. One was the correspondingly low level of general business. The other was the uneasy feeling of a very large number of investors about what the Roosevelt administration might try to do to them next. However, in addition to these, there was a third and much less understood major force tending to push stock prices down. This was a financial mechanism that our tax laws had built into the market.

In the 1930's, our state as well as our federal income taxes, while not as high as today, had reached levels that by previous peace-time standards were tremendous. This meant that when most wealthy stockholders died, sizable blocks of shares had to be liquidated to pay the necessary taxes. This dissavings (or forcing on the market of large amounts of shares that otherwise would have remained off the market in strong boxes) was occurring just when high income taxes were cutting heavily into the ability to save by the wealthier classes. It was this wealthy group from which most stock buying had always come. In other words, all during this decade there was a built-in downward bias to stock prices. The fresh savings of those interested in buying stocks was not enough to meet the combined new stock issues of the period together with the sizable and constant supply of shares from the liquidation of estates.

Then after World War II, a largely new force appeared that, in time, was completely to reverse this imbalance. This was the institutional buyer. Of course, all institutional buying did not have its origins in this period. Private and bank trustees, insurance companies, and educational and charitable institutions had owned a considerable volume of common shares for many years. Also, there were a number of investment trusts in existence, although not nearly as many as were soon to flourish. Rather, what was to occur were several new influences, all in logical sequence and all to exert the same type of increased pull on certain parts of the stock market.

First was to come the sharp upgrading of the general public's opinion about the respectability of common stocks for conservative investment. This was to result in importantly increasing the per cent of their total assets that professional trustees and educational and charitable organizations invested in common stocks. It was to increase moderately the proportion for insurance companies. It was to pave the way for the spectacular growth of the common-stock slanted open-end investment trusts and for the most important development of all—the tremendous growth of the common-stock-slanted pension and profit-sharing funds.

One of the financially most significant aspects of the steady growth of these pension and profit-sharing funds is that they tended to tap an entirely new and important source of savings for common-stock purchases. Funds that would normally flow into the pockets of factory workers and lower-income office workers, neither of which groups had been conspicuous for the size of their common stock holdings, were now flowing toward the stock market. Similarly, a steadily growing number of salesmen for investment trusts are finding it profitable to sell to these same groups who had never thought of putting their savings in common stocks. In this way, still more demand for common stocks has come from groups whose savings have previously gone into other types of assets.

In short, as the 1950's developed, institutional buying became a force that far outbalanced with an upward bias the prewar tendency of high estate taxes and high income taxes to provide the stock market with a downward slant. Furthermore, as has been pointed out many times, the buying of most of these institutional groups had an even greater impact on stock prices than would have occurred from even a comparably large volume of fresh buying from individuals. This is because (while one stock holding might be switched into another) most of these fresh purchases of stocks would remain as common-stock investments for a long period of years, if not forever. It would not be subject to sale sooner or later as so often happens with many individual holdings. The available supply of stock was being reduced. Only a major change in basic thinking as to the intrinsic desirability of common stocks in contrast to other types of investments would be likely to cause most of this stock to come back on the market. Such a switch in fundamental concepts usually comes about quite slowly and (as when stocks acquired their present high regard), years later, changed background conditions started to warrant a change in general thought.

No one knows for sure exactly how to measure quantitatively just how much fresh buying arose from these institutional sources as the 1950's progressed. Nevertheless, a few random figures will show something of the size of the forces involved. Toward the close of 1959, Byron K. Elliott, President of the John Hancock Mutual Life Insurance Company, in a speech in San Francisco predicted that by the end of 1960 private pension fund reserves would show a twenty-fold' increase over 1940 and would total $48 billion. In July of the same year, Victor L. Andrews, Assistant Professor of Finance in the Massachusetts Institute of Technology School of Industrial Management, reported in the *Monthly Labor Review* published by the U.S. Labor Department that the amount of common stocks held by pension-plan trust funds had risen from 12 per cent of total assets in 1951 to 27 per cent of such assets in 1958. In the same month, the *Wall Street Journal* reported that estimates made by the American Bankers Association, based on a nationwide survey that used scientific sampling and was "far more dependable than estimates that had been made in the past", showed that $30,664,500,000 or 61.7 per cent of the total assets held by U.S. banks in personal trust accounts was invested in common stocks. In November 1959, the Boston Fund (a mutual fund) reported a survey showing that on June 30, 1959, 68 colleges and universities owned $3,912,919,958 of common stocks which accounted for 56.6 per cent of their assets as against 51.7 per cent being represented by this class of investment one year earlier. Even life insurance companies, which traditionally have negligible appetites for common stocks, seem to be beginning to join the trend. Recently, James F. Oates Jr., President of the giant Equitable Life, reported that, while until recently his company had relatively few common stocks in its $9.6 billion portfolio, it plans to buy them at a rate of about $40 million yearly for the next ten years. Some idea of how big a potential impact on the stock market might arise from a life insurance company trend toward more common stock holdings can be seen from a recent *Wall Street Journal* survey showing that

Equitable had less than two-fifths of 1 per cent of total assets in common stocks; Metropolitan, the largest life insurance company, had less than one-fifth of 1 per cent; Prudential had 2.3 per cent; New York Life had 3.1 per cent; and John Hancock Mutual had 5 per cent.

Similarly, the National Association of Investment Companies estimated that investors bought $2.3 billion of mutual fund shares in 1959 as against $1.6 in 1958. As this organization also reported redemptions at $780 million in 1959 as against $511 million a year earlier, it would appear that new cash available for investment from this source was about $1.8 billion in 1959 and $1.1 billion in 1958. It therefore seems probable that investment trusts are each year taking in excess of $1 billion of common stocks out of the market and adding them to their portfolios.

Possibly all of these trends may be summarized by a recent study made by the New York Stock Exchange. This study showed that, at year end 1959, institutions as a group owned $51 billion of all stocks listed on the exchange, which was by value 16.6 per cent of the total. Ten years earlier they were reported to own $9.5 billion or 12.4 per cent of total value.

However, all this is history. Understanding what has happened will only make money for us, as it helps us to form a more accurate judgment of what will happen. Turning now to the 1960's, the first question that confronts us is this: Will institutional buying be an even greater force during these next ten years or will it diminish in importance?

The first thing to consider here is that by no means have all the huge impact of institutional purchases on the stock market come from the investment of fresh funds. An important part came from switching into common stocks a proportion of funds previously invested in other media. Today common stocks are so highly regarded that from a historical standpoint a quite high proportion of total assets are already so invested. Will this proportion grow even higher in the 1960's? If so, the impact on the market would be great, even without any further growth in these various types of stock-buying institutions themselves.

I believe the answer to this is that there will be somewhat of a further switch in overall institutional holdings into common stocks, although the switch will not be of as great a proportion as occurred in the 1950's. However, it need not be as big a percentage to have very great implications for stock prices. Remember that the institutional purchases of the 1950's (I refer to overall stock acquisitions, not the switch from one stock to another) have already taken the purchase of the 1950's off the market. Therefore the purchases of the 1960's are in addition to this in their impact.

There are several reasons which I believe forecast a further switch toward common-stock investment. However, it will be of more modest proportions than in the recent past. Favoring common-stock increases is the important fact that among states and other political subdivisions a trend has just barely started toward investing in equities part of the tremendous assets some of these units hold as pension funds. Unless this quite new development gets nipped in the bud by the sudden emergence of a bear market before this recent trend gathers enough momentum to survive such a one-time setback, it may grow to quite important proportions.

Meanwhile, particularly among trustees in the older age bracket, there is still a tendency in some quarters to hold bonds at some fixed proportion of a particular trust. This is not because of any specific logical reason why bonds fit into the needs of that trust but because they formed their financial habits at a time when bonds were considered the natural backbone of any trust. They simply cannot visualize any properly run trust fund without bonds. As these older men are replaced by younger trustees reared in an atmosphere where bonds have been less highly regarded, the proportion of bonds held in such trust accounts will shrink still more. Common stocks in many instances will replace them.

Partially, but far from entirely offsetting all this, there are certain other influences. It is probable but not certain (political influences can play a major part here) that the relative yield of bonds as compared to stocks will be much more favorable to bonds than it was in most of the 1950's. If this happens, there are always many (including a few who may have good reason for so doing) who prefer a larger current income and a risk of decline in the real value of principal to a smaller income and a long-term increase in the value of principal. This well could cause some movement back toward bonds. This would be noticeable particularly in periods when either (a) bond prices are so low that bonds might be expected to have enough of a recovery to more than balance in the near term any further inflationary inroads into their value or (b) stock prices are so high that instead of the usual rewards of further growth, the near-term outlook might be for significant declines.

Furthermore, there is another and, I believe, even more important influence that will tend to cut down on the proportion of existing funds that institutions as a group will place in stocks in the 1960's. *If properly handled*, in an economy where technology is opening up as many opportunities for investment as it is now doing, common stocks are magnificently suited to be one of the mainstays of much institutional investment. However, there are many such investment managers, both trustee and otherwise, who I suspect are quite inept at handling stock investment. The great bull markets that prevailed in much of the 1950's largely helped conceal the incompetence (so far as common-stock management is concerned) of such people. This largely one-way trend of the stock markets is abnormal and cannot be expected to go on forever. Sometime in the 1960's, a more long-lived bear market than that of 1957 to 1958 is apt to uncover this type of past management weakness. Institutions and the beneficiaries of trusts who perhaps should then become disillusioned with the individual managers will find it easier on their pride to become disillusioned with common stocks instead. This too will probably cause an important further offset to the 1960's institutional trend toward more common stocks, but I doubt more than a year or two's time will be strong enough to reverse it.

All of these influences affect the percentage of funds that will flow to common stocks from assets already managed by institutions. Now we come to a matter that can have an equally important influence on the markets. Will the total funds of the institutions grow or shrink? Will important *freshly raised funds* flow into the stock market in the 1960's as they did in the 1950's? If so, all common-stock investors must reckon with this force! I believe the clearest answer to this question can be obtained by appraising the individual outlook for each of the quite divergent groups of institutional holders.

However, before doing so, I believe we should take into account a basic change that with little fanfare is steadily improving the performance of many of the larger types of institutional buyers. This is not a change in form. On an organization chart, most such groups are conducting their affairs just as they did a decade ago. Some have made little or no change in actual practice. Nevertheless, many of the more important have made noticeable changes with corresponding improvement in their performance record. If their activities have grown significantly in the face of less-adept handling of common stocks in the past, the probabilities are that their growth is that much more assured as their efficiency increases.

As large banking, charitable, insurance, or investment trust organizations first tackled the intricate job of buying and selling sizable holdings in common stocks, they did so to quite a degree by setting up "investment committees." These groups would consist in some instances solely of major full-time officers of the organization. In others, some members would be officers of the organization, others would be prominent businessmen, frequently members of the board of directors. One or more full-time investment specialists would then be hired to make recommendations to this investment committee. However, it was (and in form in nearly all cases still is) the investment committee which had the final authority and made the actual decisions.

In many instances, these full-time investment specialists, often called "security analysts," were anything but outstanding experts. Mediocre, as is apt to be the work of an institutional investment committee, it was probably quite necessary in the early days when institutions had their first big experience with common stock purchasing, that there be such committees to pass upon the recommendations of unproven full-time advisers.

However, here and there, security analysts of real ability started to be heard in investment committee meetings. Frequently at first, this was a morale shattering experience for a thoroughly competent investment man. Being cashier or treasurer of the organization, president of the local public utility, or having inherited three million dollars might cause a man to be appointed to an investment committee. It would not necessarily qualify such a member to be any more efficient at judging what stock should be bought or sold than it would qualify him to pass judgment on whether the Vice President's appendix should be removed by surgery or whether a lawsuit should be compromised rather than brought to trial. However, while these investment committee members might be the first to defer such medical or legal decisions to qualified experts in those fields, the fact that they all

31

handled money and had been appointed on an investment committee usually resulted in erasing any possible suspicion as to the wisdom of their exerting their full legal right to pass judgment on each recommendation of their full-time alleged experts.

Everything was stacked against a capable investment employee in dealing with a skeptical investment committee. Usually most (if not all) of the committee considerably outranked him, not only in the organization but also in the general business and social hierarchy of the community. This made fighting for his ideas that much more difficult. Furthermore, the investment expert was usually for a course of action. Therefore, any committeeman who opposed him would in general prevail, since with a division of opinion no action is apt to be taken. All of this tended to limit results down to the denominator of the least-able member of an investment committee. Time and again, I have heard an outstanding investment man who was still fairly new in an organization say, "I know that is a stock we should buy. But there is no use recommending it. It will never get by my committee."

However, in instance after instance as the 1950's progressed, many of the most able of the full-time investment men began enjoying a quite different status within their organizations. As events proved the majority of their recommendations to have been far better than the committee's own choice, in substance if not in form, certain investment committees began leaving the real choice in these investment men's hands. If this worked well and the trust department of a bank, the insurance company, or the university did noticeably better than others in its field, the tendency would be to leave the decision making more and more to the qualified experts, not to a large investment committee. I do not know if the samples I have seen represent a large enough per cent of the total to enable me to say that there may not be important exceptions, but it has been my experience that the more power given to the investment specialist and the smaller the influence of the individuals on investment committees, the better the quality of the work accomplished. This is partly because in principle it makes sense to leave decisions in the hands of those best qualified to make them. It is partly because only where thoroughly competent investment men are found have they been able gradually to dominate rather than be dominated by the prominent names often found on such committees. At any rate, competition will cause this trend to develop even more as the 1960's continue. As it does, the work of many of the larger institutional stock buyers will still further improve in quality. As this goes on, more and more people will turn to such organizations for their services, and the impact of these organizations on certain sections of the stock market will become greater and greater.

Turning now to examine one by one the coming trend of the major subdivisions of institutional buyers, it is noteworthy that, by far, the most rapid growth among any one subdivision of this group during the past ten years was in the pension and profit-sharing fund classification. I see nothing in the next ten years indicating that these organizations will do anything but continue to increase their total stock holdings by enormous amounts. It is true so many such funds have been organized already that the number of additional ones may not be so great. However, the established funding plans of the already existing pension funds and the additional contributions that may be expected in the years ahead for the profit-sharing trusts all indicate a steady, persistent demand for more and more common shares.

I believe the forward plans of these pension and profit-sharing funds are so well established that only one thing could prevent them from exerting a strong, bullish influence on the market in the years ahead. This is if incompetence or dishonesty in the financial management of these funds should cause the whole idea of them to lose its present appeal. The affairs of so many of the smaller funds of this type are shrouded in secrecy, so it is impossible to pass judgment on them. However, some of the largest appear run with sufficient skill so as to make it seem rather unlikely the entire system will become discredited.

As to the trust funds for individuals, I think it equally certain that there will be further growth for them too in the 1960's. This should largely parallel the probable growth of the trust business (and investment management business) of the large metropolitan banks and independent trust companies. My frank opinion, with which many would disagree, is that prior to World War II an unpleasantly large amount of such business was managed in a way somewhat less than brilliant. However, starting with the post-war period, a number of banks extending all the way across the nation from Boston and New York to San Diego began making giant strides toward much higher levels of investment management. Competition forced others to adopt similar changed ways. The results have been that trust departments as a whole have prospered. If this growth has gone on in the 1950's when standards were improving, I see little reason why it should stop in the 1960's when the overall level of efficiency gives promise of being higher. Therefore, this important group, too, should add fresh demand for common stocks.

Similarly, I see no great reason why total additional stock purchase by insurance companies should not occur at about the same moderate growth rate that has prevailed in the recent past. As to educational and charitable organizations, the advent of the first Sputnik focussed public opinion on the need for the former. The endless strains of modern living keep everyone aware of the need for the latter. If times remain prosperous, more fresh gifts and major capital donations are likely to flow toward such organizations than if adversity comes, but in any event, whatever changed totals occur should be in an upward direction.

This leaves only investment trusts among the major classes of institutional buyers. As to this group, I believe an estimate of the future trend is impossible. Almost anything might happen in the 1960's. The better-run investment trusts do perform a useful service in that they offer those needing some diversification and with too few assets to obtain it elsewhere, a means whereby they can attain a diversified investment. Furthermore, because of this diversification, many investment trusts include in their portfolios a significant amount of "non-institutional" type holdings, that is, stocks of companies which would not meet the full qualifications of most other classes of institutional buyers. Under today's conditions, they also provide a useful service to a certain number of larger investors who for one reason or another seem unable to find qualified professional investment sources to advise them. The great diversification of most of these trusts gives promise that the assets placed in them will not shrink much except in bear markets and then not much faster and quite probably slightly less fast than the market may decline as a whole. All this is distinctly to the good.

On the other hand, this great diversification also means that in rising markets most of these funds will probably also rise about as the market does. Many will disagree with me about this, but I believe it so hard to find genuinely outstanding investments that no individual or organization is likely to end up with a huge list of them. There-fore, I believe investment trusts by their basic nature are to a degree tied in with mediocrity and the concept of average performance. The able investment-trust management is usually striving for and achieving something above average performance. However, it is still a long way from the type of outstanding performance it would seem to me most investors should desire to attain.

For these reasons, I think that whether investment trusts increase or decrease in importance in the 1960's may depend a lot on whether the security business as a whole develops during the 1960's any better facilities than it has done so far in giving the small- and medium-sized common-stock buyer the service he may be trying to get today. I will discuss this matter of possible future trends in the security business in another section of this book. However, if radical developments do not take place within the structure of the investment business itself (and certain unpleasant things do not happen in the stock market) the investment trust business will continue to appeal to many and should grow.

There is, I believe, one other threat to the investment trust field. Since the great growth of open-end trusts got under way, cynics have been pointing out that all would be fine in a bull market. However, the right of stockholders to redeem their shares at or close to liquidating value at all times might cause self-generating trouble in a bear market. Heavy calls for redemption of these shares would force the sale of so much of the investment trusts' general holdings to raise the funds to pay for this redemption so as (in an already falling market) to drive down the liquidating or redemption value to a point where still more holders might become frightened and want cash. This in turn would force more liquidation of assets which would further depress share prices and might cause still more holders to want cash.

In theory at least, this self-generating downward spiral could go a long way. In practice, however, no significant trouble has occurred at all in the bear markets of the 1950's. However, on the whole, the 1950's had what may prove to be an abnormally bullish tinge. If bigger or more prolonged bear markets should develop in the 1960's, will the open-end trusts lose shareholders and therefore shrink in size?

I do not know. However, I do not believe it safe to toss the matter off by claiming that because this did not happen in the last ten years it will not in the future. I believe the average investment-trust holder may now be having an extremely optimistic expectation of what his trust shares will do for him in the time ahead. I think it is unreasonable to believe that this expectation can be matched by the performance of most trust managements, because the great diversification in the portfolios of so many of them is almost sure to mean results somewhere near the average, rather than results that are spectacularly good or spectacularly bad. With so many stocks involved, the mediocre performance of some is almost sure to dilute the highly creditable performance of others. If most investment trusts produce results that are really rather favorable if allowance is made for this "built-in stabilizer" but still are not as good as many of their stockholders think they should be, a period of disillusionment and share liquidation may well be accentuated.

If this happens, the situation will be aggravated by a practice many of these trusts have encouraged but which I believe to be quite deceptive to the unsophisticated stockholder. This is the matter of capital gains dividends. All investors know that capital gains (which in tax language means a profit on an investment held for six months or longer) are taxed at only half the rate of current income and never at a rate greater than 25 per cent of the profit. Investment trusts that make such gains are allowed to "pass them through" to shareholders. They can declare dividends from these profits. These dividends understandably have great appeal to investors, since they are taxed at a so much lower rate than other investment income.

What is wrong with this system? Nothing if non-tax considerations made the sale a wise one and if the stockholder would only consider as genuine profit the amount by which the shares sold had gone up *more* than the market as a whole. Unfortunately, this is not what often happens. Stockholders have come to like these tax-saving dividends. They always want more of them. The fund's salesmen know how effective a selling argument are these capital gains dividends. They, too, want more. The whole market has risen. So the fund sells something that has gone up just about as much as the market. After paying out the capital gains, it reinvests the balance in something else that has also risen by this amount. However, the fund has already paid out its profit to stockholders in the form of the capital gains dividend. Therefore, all it can reinvest is the proceeds less the dividend. Since the stock being bought has also about risen with the market, it must buy considerably less of this stock than it formerly owned of the stock it sold. Therefore, excepting when an extremely clean-cut case can be made for the stock that is being bought having much better prospects than the stock that was sold, these capital gains dividends come very close (in a true investment sense, although not in accounting theory) to resembling dividends paid out of principal.

Because so many people do not understand this, let us take a theoretical example. Ten thousand shares of Northern Steel were bought by an investment trust at 20, for $200,000. It goes to 30 and is sold for $300,000. Under conventional accounting, this is a capital gains profit of $100,000. Since the stock was held for over six months, this $100,000 is passed on to stockholders in the form of an appealing capital gains dividend. The remaining $200,000 is then reinvested in Southern Steel which was at 40 when Northern Steel was bought at 20 but which, in line with a generally stronger steel stock market, is now at 60. So, instead of buying the 5,000 shares which would give the trust the same relative position in the industry (half as many shares of a stock selling at double the price), only 3,333 can be bought. In a real sense, the fund has lost one-third of its position in the industry because that third has been passed out as a so-called "profit."

Of course, if Southern Steel does increase in value 50 per cent more than Northern Steel, this loss will be made up and the capital gains dividend will be compensated for by a real—rather than just an accounting—profit. Furthermore, in the day-to-day transactions of investment trusts out of which these capital gains dividends arise, it is not quite this simple to see what is happening. Instead of an investment trust selling one steel stock and buying another in the hope of making a greater profit, it may, for example, sell an oil and a motor stock and buy copper, container, and merchandising shares. However, the point remains that because of the amount it has passed on as capital gains dividends it cannot reinvest as much as it has sold. The only real test that will show whether these capital gains dividends do not impair the amount of the stockholder's accrued principal at the time the dividend was declared would be to discover a few years later if the smaller amount reinvested in other securities had appreciated in value enough more than the subsequent change in value of the securities that had been sold to make up the capital gains dividend. Some day, enlightened legislation enacted for the stockholders' own protection may demand that investment trusts either prove that funds have been reinvested sufficiently wisely to have made up for these capital gains dividends within a given period of years or the investment trust will lose its right to declare such dividends until they do. However, until this happens, when bear markets occur and the securities sold and the smaller amounts repurchased both react to about the same degree, the way in which these capital gains dividends can erode capital may be a lot more clear to many investors than it seems to be today.

It is at this point that in the hands of an unscrupulous management these capital gains dividends could become a real investment hazard. Stockholders and salesmen are used to them and want them. But there has been a general market decline. Only one or two stocks in the portfolio still show a big profit. A basic rule of good investment practice is to let your profits run and take your losses. Put another way, the only reason these few stocks are up, when the rest of the market has gone down, is because they are unusually attractive. Will the investment trust yield to stockholder and salesmen pressure and sell the very stocks out of its holding that give promise of bringing the greatest future gains? Will it sell the very last stocks with which it should part? If it does, future performance may be rather bleak.

Because problems of these sorts might overtake the investment trusts during the 1960's, they are the one segment of the institutional stock market that might (but not necessarily will) break away from the general upward trend. However, regardless of whether the buying power of investment trusts grows or shrinks, further demand from every other segment of institutional common stock buyers is going to have terrific impact on common stockholders all during the 1960's. The reason this force is one no investor can afford to ignore is that there are two background causes, one economic and the other legal, that almost guarantee that this steady demand, this constant taking of shares out of the market, will be concentrated on a rather restricted number of stocks. It cannot and will not be spread over the market as a whole.

Let us first look at the economic reason for this. A dollar of earnings from a low-cost producer in an industry has always been so much safer than from a marginal producer that the low-cost producer has always been the choice of the conservative investor. Similarly, if production costs are about equal, the company that could year in and year out do a large volume of business in a given industry has investment appeal over another that could never attain more than a small volume. When, as often happens, size and low-cost operations go together, the investment appeal is that much greater.

However, in the last thirty years, a number of basic business trends have combined to give large or fairly large low-cost companies a greater and greater degree of investment attractiveness in relation to others. There is the increase of scientific research as one of the great influences causing companies to rise or fall. The large company can afford a combined effort of a size that permits flexibility of approach in a way the small company may find difficult. The rise of big government and large labor unions has created need for a whole host of specialists on the business staff. The large company does enough business to warrant various tax specialists, industrial (or labor relations) experts, sales representatives in Washington, and experts on foreign trade in various regions of the world, to say nothing of innumerable other specialists. The manager of a small company may have to be a jack-of-all-trades. In today's complex world, this is sometimes quite expensive. The large company often has a distinct advantage in the basic matter of management itself. It has more maneuverability in achieving both management in depth and continuity of management policies. In a company that is generally well run, all of this has real investment value and is well worth the payment of a considerable premium in the price-earnings ratio. Finally, a large company is usually in a somewhat better position to be in touch with alert managements in fields far removed from its own, to become aware of what others are doing to make business operations more efficient, and to take advantage of this quickly. All this has dollar value, too.

For all of these reasons, even if no huge institutional stock market had developed, at least a part of what is sometimes called "blue chipitis" would have appeared. A relatively small number of magnificently run large companies would gradually have sold at more and more of a premium over most other companies—the rising premium of course, being expressed in financial terms as a gradually increasing price for such shares in relation to their earnings over that commanded by companies that did not have these investment advantages. The greater safety and the strong probability that continuity of good management would assure growth trends at least somewhat above average would have assured this much.

However, an ever-growing institutional demand did come with the 1950's. The nature of the ultimate beneficiary of the overwhelming majority of such institutional funds calls for placing nearly all of them in the intrinsically strongest class of security. While there may be strong reason for putting into something as risky as common stocks large amounts of the funds of the university, the widow, or the corporate-pension trust, it just makes business and economic sense to select only the finest class of such equities for this type of investor.

However, these basically sensible economic reasons are not the only ones focussing this huge institutional demand upon just one segment of the stock market. The men who have the responsibility for most institutional buying are trustees with all of the legal responsibilities of a trustee. The rules of trustee liability as they have been built up, as a result of many court decisions, are fairly clear. They are not comparably conducive toward providing the wisest management of common stocks in an age where conditions are changing with ever increasing rapidity. These background rules should be understood by all investors, whether they are trustees or not, because these rules have and will continue to have a most important influence on the prices of all kinds of common stocks.

A trustee is seldom specially rewarded for handling investments out-standingly well. His fee is fixed in advance and is never increased because his performance has been unusually good. In contrast, he can be penalized heavily if he loses money. However, he will not necessarily incur this penalty just because he does his job badly. He will only incur significant risk of personally having to make good a loss in the trust if in losing money for his beneficiaries he violates certain rules! Now, remember that a beneficiary suing a trustee for a recovery of losses has all the benefits of hindsight. After the events have happened, he can take action claiming the trustee should have known better at the time. In contrast, the trustee can only use foresight. Under such cir-cumstances it is hardly surprising that any trustee will pay the closest attention to the legal rules which will protect him from incurring heavy personal liability, even though as a result of his actions the trust has heavy losses.

What is the legal rule that will protect a trustee against suit for honestly incurred losses? In legal language, it is that a trustee can not be held personally responsible if he does as any prudent man would have done at the time. This is beautiful language, but what does it mean? How can you prove what a prudent man would or would not have done? In practical language, as most attorneys would explain it, this means that if the trustee buys or holds the same securities that most other trustees are holding and holds them in about the same proportions, he is running little risk of personal liability. Since again you cannot prove what all other trustees are holding, this puts great weight on what the largest, most prominent, and presumably best-informed trustees (the trust departments of New York banks, for example) are holding. As one cynic put it, "It is all right to lose heavily, as long as you do it in good company!"

Under rules like these, it is rather surprising that results for beneficiaries have not gone from bad to worse. Even the courts that have set this pattern must know that constant change is taking place in the business world. A stock that may have been eminently suited for trustee purchase five years ago may have had a change of management, so that it should not even be considered for this type of holding today. Stock of another company that five years ago, in spite of its superb management, was still too small and new for trustee acquisition, today and for years to come might be just the security a conscientious trustee should buy. Yet under the rules, a trustee might be penalized not for holding the former but for buying the latter, should hindsight prove his judgment wrong.

It is to the great credit of courageous individual trustees and the pioneering trust departments of a small number of metropolitan banks that in spite of the legal background against which they must work, trust management has progressed as much as it has.

What essentially has happened, is happening, and will continue to happen is this: A relatively small number of particularly strong companies (mainly the ones intrinsically most suited to trustee purchases) get what is called "institutional acceptance." Most of them have attributes that would warrant a quite high price-earnings ratio anyway. However, because these stocks are the ones into which trustee buying is concentrated, they have a certain scarcity value and the price-earnings ratio becomes even higher. Other non-trusteed institutional funds, such as insurance companies and most investment trusts,* for at least part of their holdings feel that since these are the strongest companies they, too, should have them. With all of these buyers taking stock out of the market, the "spread" in price between such companies and those without institutional acceptance remains extremely wide.

As the 1960's progress, sophisticated non-institutional investors as well as the more able institutional stock buyers will become far more alert as to how they will benefit from these background conditions than they are today. They will recognize that the composition of the small group of stocks attaining greatest institutional acceptance changes quite slowly, but it does change. It is like the membership list of a very exclusive and very expensive club. Each year there are very few changes. However, a few people who have recently risen to great wealth and power are taken in. A few die or resign because the cost of keeping up their membership is too much for them. But these are the exceptions. The great majority of the membership remains the same.

No method of making important profits in common stocks is ever easy. However, this background condition permits what will probably prove one of the least difficult ways of making major gains available in the 1960's. Careful study can be made of stocks just on the edge of institutional acceptance. By this, I mean medium-sized corporations that are having or are about to have a steady upward trend in earnings. They may already be included in the approved purchase list of a small segment of institutional buyers, or they may not as yet be so approved by any. However, they must have a management of outstanding ability, those attributes of growth, relatively wide profit margin for their industry, and adequate size to appeal eventually to institutional investors. If they are growing into a position where intrinsically they will be highly suitable for purchase by professional trustees, sooner or later the pressure of all the funds such trustees must invest and the relatively high price of much of what shares they can invest in will cause such companies to "be included in the club," that is, to win widespread institutional acceptance and enjoy the sharply higher price-earnings ratio that this acceptance brings.

---

* Investment trusts are usually corporations controlled by boards of directors, in which cases they are technically not trusts at all.

The fortunate owners who have bought such a stock before it gains this sort of financial status makes a double profit. In the first place, the stock would not be gaining this status if its earnings were not growing faster than those of industry in general. Therefore, the shareholder first gains the benefit of this rising earnings trend. But the shareholder also gains something else. Let us suppose such a company, still considered by most of the financial community as run-of-the-mill or mediocre, was earning $2 per share in a year of neither great depression or great boom and was selling at 12 times earnings or 24. Five years later, in another year of neither great boom nor depression, earnings had shown a year by year rise and were now at $4 a share. This of itself would double the value of the shares which at the same price-earnings ratio of 12 times earnings would cause the stock to sell at 48. However, in the meantime, the financial community had started to accept this as truly an institutional stock—something undreamed of five years before. Instead of selling at 12 times earnings, such a company would easily command a price of 24 times earnings or 96. In other words, because the alert buyer had correctly anticipated this institutional acceptance and the changed market price this would bring, he had converted a doubling of his earning power into not a doubling but a quadrupling of the value of his holding.

This investor's wealth has quadrupled in five years. It has come about partly because of an increase in the price-earnings ratio at which his shares are now selling and partly because of an increase in the earning power of these shares. Is this investor entitled to feel that the increase in his net worth is as sound and rests on as firm a foundation as though all of it had come about through a quadrupling of the earning power of his stocks alone?

In a sense, we already have the answer to this question from our lengthy discussion of whether overall institutional demand for common stocks will grow or shrink in the time ahead. If the indications are as clear as I believe them to be that in the years ahead there will be at least as much concentrated demand focussed on a relatively small number of stocks as there is now, the investor need have no worry as to the best of the institutional stocks continuing to sell at a very much higher price in relation to earnings than does the great body of stocks as a whole. Therefore, if he is sure that the significant increase that these changed price-earnings ratios have made in the value of

43

his holdings is due to his stock now having a justified institutional acceptance it did not previously enjoy, he can be rather certain that this state of things will continue and that his gain is just as "real" (i.e., permanent) as though it had come solely from improvement in earning power.

There is one thing in this connection about which the investor should be on guard, however. Every so often, for one reason or another, a particular industry becomes the momentary darling of the market place. Sometimes the reasoning behind this great enthusiasm by the investing public is quite sound. At others, the favorable factors may all be true, but prices can get well out of line with reality because little or no weight is momentarily given to the unfavorable factors. Chemicals, aluminums, life insurance companies, uranium companies, and drugs are all groups that have enjoyed this type of great, momentary investment acclaim in one period or another since the close of World War II. The electronics were such a public favorite as the 1950's were drawing to a close.

When the reasoning behind such general enthusiasm has been sound, the eventual ebbing of surface public excitement about this particular class of stock has usually resulted in not too severe a drop from the peak for the stocks of the best-run companies in the industry. More important, within a few years and usually with much less public fanfare, these outstanding stocks have gone on to new highs. However, even when this background excitement about an industry's investment prospects are basically sound, the stocks of secondary and less well-run companies in that industry can be carried up to price-earnings ratios which do not represent sound values. When excitement about a whole industry may be greatly overdone (as could have been the case with the uraniums and life insurance companies in the mid 1950's), this danger can be even more pronounced.

In other words, the investor who wants to take great advantage of the more permanent type of higher price-earnings ratio that will accrue from a heretofore non-institutional stock obtaining institutional acceptance should always do this: Whenever a stock he owns has attained a major upward revision of its price-earnings ratio in relation to those of stocks as a whole, he should examine the matter most carefully. He should determine whether this change is actually due to institutions starting to hold his stock or to some completely different set of factors.

In either case, he should determine for his particular company (not for the industry as a whole) whether its management, its prospects, its inherent risks, and all the other factors on which its true investment status will depend justify the increased price in relation to each dollar of earnings. If they do, he need not be afraid that the increase in his net worth coming from this source is any more fictitious, temporary, or unsound than if it came from increased earning power of his shares.

This brings us to the other side of the coin—the second thing for which alert investors will have to watch if they would gain rather than lose from the great impact institutional buyers will have on the price of many stocks in the 1960's. Long accepted stocks take as long to disappear from the approved institutional groups as new ones are slow to be added. However, eventually these changes do take place. Just as rising companies eventually get included, so, usually years after the weakness should have been clearly apparent, other companies, with managements that have become stodgy and lost their drive or in industries no longer able to hold their own, get dropped from institutional favor.

The thing to remember here is that the prices of institutionally accepted stocks resemble what would happen if it were the custom of our country for all of the unusually fine and able people (but only those recognized as being unusually fine and able) to go around on very high stilts. Getting up on these stilts would be the only way to associate with these leaders. Furthermore, as long as these people kept their fine qualities, there would not be the slightest danger they would fall off their high stilts. However, if any one of them was to lose his fine and unusual traits (not immediately but after considerable time) his stilts would have become rotten and suddenly he would come crashing down off them with a spectacular tumble.

In just this way, the price of the intrinsically finest investments are up on stilts because of institutional demand. There is nothing particularly dangerous about this. They will stay at this high price-earnings ratio and will continue to go up in price about in proportion to how their earnings expand so long as they retain their unusual qualities. If they lose the characteristics that put them on stilts, then they become extremely dangerous. They will decline not alone in proportion to the decrease in their profits but a great deal more. As institutions

45

eventually sell them, they lose their premium value. However, this price decline usually will not occur until long after an institutional stock has begun to lose much of its former attractiveness. This lag is partly because of the normal tendency of investors to recognize belatedly the changed characteristics of a stock that has attained a reputation for being particularly attractive. To this must be added the sluggish response that results from the legal pressure on trustees to follow in the accepted paths, particularly the paths being followed by trustees bigger and more prominent than they are. For these reasons and with all the advance warning that should be available, the holders of the highest price-earnings ratio stocks need have no fear of the high price-earnings ratios themselves, as long as they have strong reason to believe their holdings will continue in the intrinsic nature warranting them.

But why should the individual investor of the 1960's continue holding these institutionally favored stocks at all? Once they are at or near the peak of institutional acceptance, they will only grow in value about as fast as their earnings. Therefore, would not the investor be wiser to sell them? Then he can reinvest his profits in some other stock on the verge of institutional acceptance. If he is right in his judgment, he will then continue to have his assets grow at the unusually fast rate that results from multiplying the increase in per-share earnings by the improved price-earnings ratio that institutional acceptance brings. Obviously, stocks growing in value just from increased earnings alone can seldom grow in value at this fast a rate.

While all of these things are true, I believe the investor who follows such a practice exclusively fails to understand the true nature of institutional stocks. The very fact that a stock has gained institutional acceptance and is now selling at this new and sharply advanced earnings ratio is usually because *it has such assured prospects of further profit growth at such risk.* As an investor becomes successful and amasses a significant amount of wealth, one of his benefits, I believe, should be to have at least part of this wealth in the finest and safest type of investment. Further growth with security, particularly for those who have already amassed a fair sized profit, can be as desirable as the prospects of still faster growth in market value at much greater risk. Since, to use my analogy, stocks, once they get investment status for being outstanding, tend to come down off their stilts so tardily that the alert investor should have ample warning, there seems but little reason for any large investor who watches his holdings reasonably carefully not to enjoy the benefit of this highest class of equity assets for a worthwhile part of his assets. This will avoid the heavy toll of the capital-gains tax on the work of the more successful investor. After all, the history of American business has shown that many of the most prominent of these high price-earnings ratio institutional stocks keep their managements fresh and vigorous to a point where they never do come down off their stilts but keep on growing decade after decade.

C. Foreign Competition

Until mid-year 1957, most Americans were complacent to the point of smugness about their country's economic supremacy. The European compact car had already made sharp inroads into the U.S. home market. In most markets abroad, U.S. automobiles, machine tools, and numerous other domestic products were beginning to disappear before the onslaught of European and occasionally Japanese goods produced by much lower-cost labor. The long-range implications of this, however, had not yet been recognized by the average U.S citizen.

Then came a dramatic reversal of public sentiment. The deepening business slump, a sizable outflow of gold from Fort Knox, and a steadily rising sales total of heretofore exotic low-priced foreign cars all contributed to the changed outlook. Prior to this time, plenty of people had been aware that hourly wage rates abroad, depending upon the country involved, were from one-quarter to one-ninth those paid here. But, so the reasoning went, those countries did not have the technical skills. U.S. "know how" could make up the difference. Overlooked was the fundamental fact that basic intelligence abroad was comparable to that found here. Frequently aided by export of U.S. "know how" and U.S. machinery, which was often financed by our own government, alert foreigners were becoming as efficient as we were.

As the 1950's drew to a close, the true magnitude of the problem became more and more apparent. There is no easy solution in sight. During much of the 1960's, the alert U.S. investor is going to be confronted with the dilemma: "How can I manage my affairs so as not to be dragged down either by investments in companies directly hurt by low-cost imports or by investments in companies with important customers that will be weakened in this way?"

Already, three separate routes to hoped-for investor safety are discernible. The first of these is the obvious one of investing in these foreign companies themselves. This has gained great popularity. However, in time, many of those who have been rushing to buy shares of leading companies in the "European Common Market" and elsewhere may be in for some rather unpleasant surprises. The heart of any type of successful common-stock investment is knowing what you are doing. Companies headquartered much farther from home than the average U.S. corporation are usually correspondingly more difficult to investigate than similar types of companies here. This problem is compounded not only by language barriers in the case of all but British companies, but by so many of the customers and other normal suppliers of investment information also being abroad. Even more important, foreign companies have grown up in a quite different investment atmosphere. They are traditionally far less free with basic information than are U.S. companies. At times, even their accounting systems may be considerably different. Finally, the shares of many such companies sell in markets much less liquid than our own. Therefore, small amounts of buying or selling may have a far greater effect on prices than the changes with which the investor is familiar here.

All of these things do not mean that it is impossible to make a magnificent investment in a foreign company. It does mean that for most Americans it is a much more difficult thing to do than making a correspondingly good domestic investment. It also means that much of the uncritical and undiluted enthusiasm with which the U.S. financial community was greeting most kinds of foreign investment as the 1960's arrived may fade noticeably as the decade goes on. This may occur even if special problems of foreign exchange taxes or political confiscation do not arise to further threaten investment safety.

The second route sought by investors also does not lend itself to easy analysis. This is to buy into U.S. companies with major (and often increasing) investments abroad. Such foreign plants with their low labor costs and American management methods usually offer a far better return on the investment than do the domestic operations of the same companies. At times, these plants will enable a domestic company to survive against foreign imports by making all or part of its products sold in the U.S. market at a price comparable to that at which purely foreign competitors are shipping into this country.

Why may these foreign based plants not be as attractive as they seem? We do not have to travel far from our shores to find the answer. Let us take one of the countries in which U.S. corporate investments seemed particularly strongly entrenched. Cuba is a striking example. Here is a country which owes its very freedom to U.S. action, which for the first forty-eight years of its forty-nine-year history was the friend of the United States. Its basic economic well-being has been due to preferential treatment for sugar, its largest industry, in the U.S. market. Yet all this did not prevent a revolutionary and supposedly popular government from taking action after action that gives promise of eventually resulting in the investments of U.S. corporations in Cuba having about the same value as those which were located in Shanghai after the Communists took over. Incidentally, it is well to remember that the Chinese Reds were never so impolite as to confiscate or even threaten to confiscate American investments in their country. At first they merely "regulated" these companies so they could not earn a profit, assuring them all the while that foreign investments would be respected. Then more and more "unpaid" back taxes and employee claims were found. Before too long, particularly if the former managers wanted to keep out of jail, it just seemed better to turn over the properties in settlement of these claims.

It might be argued that Cuba is an extreme case, although in the same part of the world, the Central American experience of the United Fruit Company can hardly be called encouraging to long-term investors. But is Cuba so extreme or is it symbolic of what can and probably will happen in many parts of the world? Why, psychologically, is the Cuban development so liable to be repeated time and time again?

In the first place, it is nearly always the rich member of any family that the others envy and dislike. To most of the ordinary people all over the world, the U.S.A. is a land of incredible riches. Our movies and the ever-present American tourist have carried this impression to people in every part of the globe. I would guess that 90 per cent of our tourists act in a manner that does our nation credit. However, anyone who has been abroad has seen the bad manners, freely-expressed criticism of the ways of the area, and generally loud-mouthed boorishness with which other compatriots comport themselves. Unfortunately, one ill-mannered American of this type can do more damage to international goodwill than fifty other Americans who act as visitors to a country should. Our tourists have left us with a sizable residue of ill-will in most parts of the world.

Add to this the almost universal tendency of all people to dislike the foreigner with his different ways of doing things, and what do we find? The foreign investor, particularly if he is an impersonal U.S. corporation, is a natural target to be used by the native politician desiring to increase his influence. Why should what has happened in supposedly friendly Cuba not happen again and again elsewhere?

If it is going to happen, why has it not happened more often already? The reasons for this are not hard to find. In the first place, as the 1950's were drawing to a close, stimulated by the much lower labor costs abroad, the amount of U.S. investment in branch plants in foreign lands was reaching almost tidal wave proportions. This was both creating abnormal prosperity in the affected countries and a certain amount of competition between various countries to get as much as possible of this golden flood. As long as more and more prosperity was flowing in with new construction contracts and other benefits to be gained, it is only natural that the foreigner be made most welcome. It is when money stops pouring in and operating profits start to flow back toward home that sentiment is more likely to change. Perhaps this is not so different from the comments wryly made by competent observers in Europe at the time the United States was negotiating with Franco for bases in Spain. Almost everywhere else in Western Europe, into which United States funds had been poured, anti-American feeling was rising and in some places had reached sizable proportions. But in Spain, to which nothing had been given but where there was hope of getting something soon, United States popularity was never higher.

The other reason Cuban-type developments are more likely to happen in the future than in the past is that such movements get much of their momentum in times of depression, not of prosperity. It is in hard times that either by ballot or bullet, those in power traditionally are turned out and others take over. If Cuba had not been so poverty-ridden, Castro might well have failed in his attempt. Those in power in many foreign lands today are eagerly bidding for more U.S. branch plant investments and are therefore favorable to the U.S. investor. Does not this suggest what the stand will be of many of the opposition politicians who may topple such regimes when and if a depression may strike?

For these reasons, investing in companies with a major stake abroad may not always appear as desirable as current earning figures indicate. Companies with many foreign plants may do magnificently for a few years. However, if such foreign earnings are capitalized in the price of these shares as highly as domestic earnings, a year may come when a lot of the profits along with some even more important assets may disappear rather suddenly. Of course, the experience in different lands may vary. In some, no serious troubles may come at all.

If, therefore, these branch plants abroad provide no easy answer to the investor seeking protection against foreign competition during the 1960's, is there any other route to safety? I believe there is. Attaining and maintaining technical leadership in one or another field of a rapidly advancing technology is the one sure way a U.S. corporation can make itself independent of the threat of low-cost foreign competition. Investors with shares in such companies need not fear the general threat of low-cost foreign labor to the U.S. economy and may actually benefit from it without having to run the great risks of foreign investment.

Why is this? Since research costs are also cheaper abroad, why would not a foreign competitor soon take the technological lead? The answer definitely is not because there are more or better scientific brains here than there are abroad. Rather, it is because some of these technologies are so complex and there are so many of them developing in such different directions that some U.S. companies are building up commanding leads in certain highly technical areas while other foreign companies are developing similar outstanding leadership in completely different areas. The thing to do is to find the management with technical teams capable of staying in front. In other words, some companies seem to develop enough skill in their particular field (or important parts of it) so that the competition is forever trying to arrive tomorrow where they are today. By tomorrow, when the competition attains this objective, they will have again moved one step ahead. If a company can do this, it need not fear foreign competition any more than domestic.

Furthermore, such a company may benefit from the strength that foreign industrial nations will undoubtedly have during the 1960's. If the company's product line is technically superior, foreigners will want to buy it just as they would have in the period prior to the recent great rise of foreign industry. But until recently these potential foreign buyers would have been limited by currency problems as to how much U.S. goods their governments would let them buy. In the 1960's this should be much less of a problem. Therefore, the technically superior company may have export markets open to it of a size undreamed of in prior decades.

Finally if the company has outstandingly superior products that foreigners can not come close to matching and if it should also have some branch plants abroad, it may have protection against anti-foreign taxation or confiscation such as less fortunate companies will not have. Hitler's extreme persecution of the Jews is too well known to need much discussion. However, extreme as was his treatment of the great majority, a handful of Jews were left completely unmolested because they had unusual technical skills which Hitler badly needed. Similarly a company which alone has the know-how to produce a key product that a foreign nation needs is in a position to bargain with an otherwise hostile foreign government in a way most corporations are not. In case the Hitler example seems exaggerated, the experience of the major oil companies in parts of the Near East might be recalled. It is not contractual agreements or love of those companies, but realization that they alone have the marketing facilities to transport and sell petroleum, that may be considered the reason these companies have not been treated a good deal worse than they have. Knowing how to make a vital product could be even more important should a wave of nationalism sweep a foreign land.

What does all this mean? From the investor's standpoint, the rules for protection against the great foreign competition of the 1960's are no different from those for finding outstanding investments regardless of foreign competition. If he seeks and finds the company that because of outstanding business management and technical superiority would have proven an investment bonanza in the days before foreign competition was such a general threat, he need not fear low foreign labor costs in the 1960's. It is the run-of-the-mill company making products the foreigner can easily copy which can be in danger.

All this is looking at this problem of foreign competition in the narrow sense—the means whereby individual investors can gain rather than lose. However, how about the broader picture? Will our entire nation suffer from being unable to compete with a flood of imports produced by lower-paid foreign workers?

I do not think the answer will be clear until it is known what kind of man or men will occupy the Presidency in the years ahead and what kind of leadership he or they will provide on this vital matter. Evidence is beginning to accumulate that American business management can meet this problem of wage discrepancies and equalize costs if from this point on domestic wages advance no more rapidly than foreign (which are also climbing) and provided the further burden of featherbedding is not added on to the cost load U.S. products must carry.

This problem of featherbedding, that is, of continuing work rules which call for job classifications that are not genuinely needed, is not an easy one. Business management can proclaim that featherbedding is outrageous (which it is), but workers are apt to fight stubbornly for these rules until such time as those affected have some assurance that as they are displaced by more efficient equipment other comparable paying jobs in the same community will be found for them. With the countless new industries that developmental engineering is creating at the same time that it is making it possible for older industries to turn out more products with fewer workers, this guaranteeing of comparable (or possibly even better) jobs to displaced workers should not be too difficult if major attention were given it. Should good fortune bring to the government in the 1960's an administration or administrations that will face up squarely to the problem of featherbedding, I believe most American industries can be brought around to the point where they can hold their own in domestic markets and still maintain current wage differentials. If this does not happen and U.S. wage costs rise still further in relation to those of the rest of the world, sizable unemployment and generally hard times will occur. However, I see no basis for predicting as yet which will happen. Too much of the outcome may depend on whether an as yet unknown President lets the nation drift into a totally unnecessary business crisis or whether he can exert the personal influence and magnetism needed for all groups to see what must be done if, without sacrificing our high current standards of living, American-made goods are to be permitted to hold their own against the current vigorous competition from much cheaper foreign labor. Leaders of business and of labor should work together on these matters. To date no sign of this has arisen. Should we reach a point where leadership can only come from government, it will all depend on who heads the government and how he acts. These are matters on which, as this is written, it is still too early to pass intelligent judgment.

D. Increased Population

Strictly speaking, this matter of the influence of the great population surge of the 1960's should not be included at all in comments on the major investment influences of the period ahead. This is because I do not believe it is in any sense going to be a major investment force, comparable in its influence to those we have already discussed. However, so much publicity has been given this matter and so closely has it been tied in to the concept of the "golden sixties" that I believe it worthy of examination, if only to judge it in its proper perspective.

In general, those who expound the pleasant-sounding but somewhat superficial line of reasoning that the population figures assure a great advance in business levels in the years just ahead rely on an extremely simple argument. They point out that the great increase in births started at the time of World War II. With but minor interruptions, this has continued ever since. So far, however, this population surge has caused the increase to be largely among infants, young school children, and more recently the younger teen-agers. These groups have relatively simple requirements compared with those they will be seeking in the period immediately ahead. As the population increase spills over into the older teen-age group, the demand will grow for automobiles and all that goes with them, more expensive clothes, additional travel facilities, and all the other economic desires of young adulthood. This, in turn, will be followed by a great increase in new family formations and the even greater economic demand this brings in the way of need for more homes, appliances, furnishings, etc. With the birth rate still holding up so that there is no slackening in demand from the infant and children's groups, the need for all of these things will create boom-time conditions and ever-increasing prosperity.

The cynics have a standard reply to this. They claim population of itself does not create prosperity. If it did, India, Egypt, and China would be among the most prosperous countries on earth instead of the most poverty-stricken. This young population will, by the very limitations of its age, largely be spending money, not working at high enough paid jobs to produce much wealth. Therefore, all that will happen will be that the already overloaded family budget will have to be reshuffled still further. The average family has just so much income to cover its needs. The extra spending of the teen-ager and the young adult will be about balanced by lesser sums the parents will spend on their own needs. The total volume of business done will be about the same. All that will happen is that there will be a further shift in how the money is spent and, with more mouths to feed, the per capita income and the standard of living will go down.

Which of these two estimates will prove correct? In the American economy as it exists today, probably neither. As so many parents have learned, the greater normal needs of children as they grow older do create problems in the family budget that to a considerable degree get solved by shifting how family income is spent and by the parents spending less on themselves. To this degree, the pessimists are correct and a great increase in demand for goods unaccompanied by an increase in the wherewithal to pay for these things certainly will not produce a major spurt in total national prosperity.

However, this is not quite all the picture. Unlike Egypt, China, and probably much of India, our economy does provide considerable leeway enabling individuals and more particularly families to increase their wealth (as well as the community's) if the urge to do so is great enough. Wives who might not otherwise work get useful jobs and become a second source of family revenue. Under the spur of greater family need, husbands work harder, make more effort to get ahead financially, and move into more important and more productive jobs. As the teen-agers grow older, they too, add to the work force. Therefore to some degree, at least, there is an increase in the total amount of wealth produced to meet the increased demands of the family unit with older children. To some degree, the total volume of available business does genuinely increase.

In short, insofar as the overall level of business is concerned, the influence of the growing population will fall somewhere short of the much talked of guaranteed boom for the golden sixties, but not as far short as claimed by those who visualize the only effect being a sharp decline in the standard of living. However, from the standpoint of the holder of common stocks, what increase in the total of all business is produced by these population changes and is much less significant than it might appear at first glance. This is because the investor does not hold common stock in the economy as a whole but in individual companies. While the potential market for these companies' products will expand with the growing work force, so will the competition. In many lines of business there will simply be that many more units dividing up the market.

Meanwhile, in many families the need to make changes in the family budget will partially apply. In some it will necessitate a major rearrangement. This means there will be many shifts in overall demand between one type of product and another. Some will gain, others will be fighting a declining trend.

Why not attempt to forecast which companies will gain most and make investment plans accordingly? Except in extremely rare instances, I do not believe this a wise course to pursue. The reason is the extreme complexity of trying to judge how, under the pressure of increased demands on the budget, family decisions will shift from one product to another. It is not, for example, simply a matter of whether the family will forego repainting the house to buy an extra car. They may switch to lower-priced model cars or to buying only used cars when previously they had always bought new ones. They may start serving more spaghetti and less meat. They may do any number of other things as they shift and reshift their expenditures. They may even find the necessary savings almost handed to them by a technological advance resulting in producing one of the products they desire at much lower cost than before. With the number of family units in this country and the number of choices they can exercise, about the most that can be done is to observe what is happening and then make a reasonable judgment as to whether this trend will continue. Only in rare instances is it likely to be of sufficient significance by itself to cause making many investment decisions. In short, this matter of population change has been overstressed.

Since this population influence has been one of the main props upon which has been based this whole concept of the "golden sixties" with its almost guaranteed built-in prosperity, is the whole idea little more than a mirage? It may not be. The steadily expanding pace of technology and invention could well create a flow of new industries and refurbishing of old industries that will provide an expanding and prosperous background such as the world has seldom seen. Whether it does or not will largely depend on whether unwise or restrictive policies in regard to taxation, credit, labor policy, and similar largely government-regulated matters are handled with such folly as to dam up the benefits of this flow. These are things which can only be judged as the decade progresses. In the meantime, it is well to keep in mind that the huge rise that had occurred in the price of so many stocks as the 1950's drew to a close has probably to a considerable degree already discounted much of this prospect. In other words, the spectacular gains among common stocks in the 1960's will almost surely be even more selective than in the 1950's. Such a general and widely publicized matter as the expanding population curve will, except in the rarest of instances, have little relationship to such gains.

The Economists Go Out—The Psychologists Come in

I have already commented on the strange tendency of the supposedly forward-looking financial community so often to fail to recognize a changed set of circumstances until the new influence has been in existence for many years. I believe this is why the man who attempted to forecast the course of general business was regarded as so important a factor in the making of investment decisions during all of the 1940's and much of the 1950's. Even today, a surprising number of both investors and professional investment men still believe that the heart of a wise investment policy is to obtain the best business forecast you can. If the outlook is one of expanding business, then buy. If the outlook is for a decline, sell.

Many years ago there was probably considerably more merit to such a policy than there could possibly be today. The banking structure was weaker. There was no assurance it would be shored up by the government in times of real trouble—a process bound to produce a massive dose of inflation. There was no tax system of a type that can hardly fail to produce strong inflationary spending whenever business (and therefore federal tax revenues) are at abnormally low levels. No public opinion had crystallized to assure that whenever business levels dipped sharply, the government would take strong countermeasures to stem the tide. Finally, the industrial base was much more narrow. The large number of industries in today's complex economy that bear little relationship to each other in their basic characteristics probably assures that even without the actions of government, the modern business recession would be somewhat less severe than its former counterpart. Some industries would be enjoying unusual background conditions enabling them to expand, while the majority might be in a declining phase. This tends somewhat to stabilize the economy as a whole.

All this means that a depression is of less significance to the investor than it was many years ago. It does not mean knowing what business is going to do would not be quite useful information to have. But having such information is not vital for obtaining magnificent results from common stock investments. Simple arithmetic should show this. When a stock market decline coincides with a fairly sizable economic slump as happened in 1937 to 1938 or 1957 to 1958, most stocks sell off from 35 to 50 per cent. The better ones then recover when the slump ends and usually go on to new high levels. Even in the greatest slump of all time, only a small percentage of all companies failed, that is, went down 100 per cent. Most of these were companies which had had fantastic amounts of debts and senior securities placed ahead of their common. After one of the wildest speculative booms ever known, much of it financed by borrowed money, the average stock slumped 80 or 90 per cent. In contrast, when stocks rise over a period of years, even the most casual study of stock market history shows many figures of a very much greater order of magnitude. Compared to the temporary declines, usually of 35 to 50 per cent, that frequently accompany depressions, the outstanding stocks (those of the unusually well-run companies that have maneuvered themselves into growth fields) go up several hundred per cent, stay at these levels, and then go still higher. Many can be found for which a decade's progress can be measured in multiples of 1000 per cent rather than 100 per cent.

All this is fortunate for, as I endeavored to point out in *Common Stocks and Uncommon Profits*, there are definite rules by which the unusual managements that produce these equally unusual and highly profitable stocks can be selected with at least a workable degree of precision. On the other hand, I think the record shows that economics in its present state of development has not reached the point where depression forecasts can be used as a reliable investment tool. In today's highly complex economy, there are too many factors that can affect these forecasts. The intricate interrelation between this evergrowing number of different influences is not yet sufficiently understood. This, I believe, is why so many economists tend to disagree with each other and why so many are sometimes so spectacularly wrong.

From the standpoint of obtaining results, I have noticed that investors who place heavy emphasis on economic forecasts in the making of investment decisions usually fall into one of two main groups. Those who are inclined to be cautious by nature can nearly always find an impressive sounding forecast that for quite plausible and persuasive reasons makes it appear that important economic difficulties lie ahead for the business community. Therefore, they seldom take advantage of opportunities when they present themselves and, on balance, these missed opportunities mean the economic forecasts have done them considerable harm. The other group are the perpetual optimists who can always find a favorable forecast to satisfy them. Since they always decide to go ahead with whatever action they are considering, it is hard to see how all the time they spend on business forecasting does much good.

More and more investors are coming to recognize the wisdom of making their decisions about common stocks largely on the basis of such outright business factors as appraisal of the quality of the management and the growth potential of the individual company's product line. These things both can be measured with a fair degree of preciseness and have a far greater influence on how good a long-range investment will be. Until such time as methods for forecasting the business cycle become vastly more scientific than they are today, I believe the role of the economist in the investment community will continue to shrink. I think economists themselves, many of whom are men of great intelligence, recognize increasingly that their specialty is not yet ready for the role of business forecasting, in which so many people both within and outside this specialty rushed to place it. Thus, press reports of the first annual convention of the National Association of Business Economists, held in the fall of 1959, told how there was a growing but not unanimous sentiment among

these advisers to private business that they should drop their forecasting activities. There was noticeable sentiment for serving their
employers by such functions as keeping management informed of
the "perspective of the social, political and business environment in
which their business functions" and providing a perhaps broader viewpoint on anti-trust work than the legal department might have. As
one speaker was reported to have said, "I am out of the forecasting
business" having lost confidence in "numbers placed off somewhere
in the future." While this group were economists for private industry
(i.e., largely manufacturers, merchandisers, and transportation companies), I believe the same thing is at least as applicable to stock market
economists.

I believe it can be assumed that for these reasons forecasts of the
trend of general business will play a steadily decreasing role as the
1960's go on. Is there, then, any other area outside of such already
recognized influences as business management, variations in interest
rates, and changes in such legislative fields as taxation to which investors will be paying increasing heed? I believe there is. For lack of
a better term, I will call it the psychological factors affecting security
prices.

To understand this, let us look at a few investment fundamentals.
Why does a stock sell at a certain price at a certain time? It is not
because of what it is doing, has done, or will do. It is because of
what the majority of those investors who are actually or potentially
interested in this stock *think* it will do. When we talk of what opinion
people have about a stock at a particular time rather than about the
intrinsic nature of the stock itself, we are talking of a psychological
factor.

It is, of course, true that this psychological factor is nothing more
than a short-term characteristic. A majority of the financial community
may get carried away by overappreciation of the attractiveness of a
certain stock or an entire industry. For a year or several years they
may, as a result, continue to pay a premium for this stock (or most of
the shares in this industry) well beyond what that stock is intrinsically
worth. Sooner or later, however, when the stock or the industry fails
to measure up to the glowing anticipations, a period of disillusionment
sets in. The price-earnings ratio of the shares will then decline by
enough to bring the stock closer to intrinsic value. Frequently, the

reaction goes too far the other way and the shares for a while sell below what, for lack of a better term, I will call "intrinsic" value.

This means that the price of any particular security can be pictured as something resembling a captive balloon attached, not to the ground, but to a wide line traveling through space. That line represents "intrinsic" value. As time goes on, if a company's earning power and true prospects improve, the line climbs higher and higher. If these or other basic ingredients of intrinsic value get worse, the line declines correspondingly. At any one time, the psychological influences (i.e., how the financial community is appraising these more fundamental matters of intrinsic value) will cause the price of the particular stock to be anywhere from well above this line to well below it. However, while momentary mass enthusiasm or unwarranted pessimism will cause the stock price to be far above or well below intrinsic value, it, like our captive balloon, can never get completely away from the line of true value and will always be pulled back toward that line sooner or later.

This whole matter of common stock evaluation is made more difficult by no one being able to pinpoint intrinsic value to an exact price. This is why I have, in our captive balloon illustration, described "intrinsic" value as a broad line and placed the word intrinsic in quotation marks. Enough can be known about a group of companies, some in the same field and others with comparable growth rates but in quite different industries, to make general approximations of intrinsic value. Thus, it is possible to say that from such a comparison and after taking into account such relevant factors as quality of management, growth rate, vulnerability to depression, etc., etc., the stock of the XYZ company currently has an intrinsic value of somewhere between $25 and $30 per share. I doubt if it can be pinpointed more closely. In the case of extremely rapidly growing companies, which legitimately are worth quite high price-earnings ratios, I doubt if it can be approximated anywhere near this closely. Too big a factor is not the current growth rate but how long into the more distant future this abnormal growth rate will continue.

The further off you get into the future, the greater your chances of misjudging what will happen. Therefore, the greater the allowance needed for a possible margin of error the more difficult it becomes to determine true value. In any event, there are so many factors involved that it is never wise to attempt to judge intrinsic value to the last eighth of a point or even point. If a stock has an attractive enough future (so that its true value line will be rising) and you can buy it within a range of not over 25 per cent or 30 per cent of what you estimate might be intrinsic value, that should be more than good enough to afford magnificent profit opportunities. The danger lies in being so carried away by overenthusiasm that you might buy at prices several times real worth.

In short, whether a stock is selling at a low price-earnings ratio or a high one has of itself nothing whatever to do with whether that stock is intrinsically cheap or overpriced. The vast differences in the quality and prospects of one company when compared with another fully warrant such wide variations. What does matter is whether the facts warrant this high or low price-earnings ratio. Has mass opinion so overaccentuated the appealing factors of an intrinsically good stock that while the investment would normally be a good one, it is anything but appealing at the current price? Or is just the opposite occurring, as also quite frequently happens? Is such a large part of the investment community so frightened at the high price-earnings ratio at which this inherently attractive company is selling that even at these levels it still has not been bid up to the levels that its future genuinely warrants? In other words, is the financial community's current psychological outlook on any particular stock causing it to be significantly above or below a point within striking distance of its real value?

It is important to understand the true role of this type of study in the proper handling of investments, if only so as not to overrate its importance. Current financial community psychology should have nothing whatever to do with what stocks should eventually be bought for investment. This should be determined solely on the basis of fundamental facts affecting the companies themselves. Under existing conditions, select good enough growth companies and in enough time you will be handsomely rewarded. This has been shown again and again throughout the entire business history of the twentieth century. Fundamentals, that is, ignoring the psychology of the moment, will bring you a good profit if you have enough patience. However, it may require a rather considerable amount of patience (as well as skill in mastering the fundamentals), and it will come rather short of providing the degree of profit that can come from allowing for current investors' psychological foibles in timing your purchases of otherwise properly selected common stocks. In other words, the psychologist far more than the economist may be of help in deciding when to buy. He can only be of help in the more important matter of what to buy in the secondary sense that if, on the basis of fundamental matters, two or more stocks appear highly desirable from the standpoint of long-range growth. He may help determine which is currently the most or the least attractive at current prices. He can do nothing on the basic matter of whether any of these stocks are worthy of investments in the first place.

Calling this a psychological approach means that we are considering how the investment community is evaluating particular stocks in relation both to their intrinsic worth and to how they may be evaluated similarly in the future. Thus, for example, even if the majority of investors had overvalued the shares of rocket-fuel manufacturers prior to Soviet Russia's surprise launching of the first Sputnik, the psychologist would have been on rather safe grounds in concluding that this event was proving such a shock to the American people that the overvaluation would go a great deal further.

An even simpler and far more important psychological conclusion was crystal clear in the spring of 1958. "Wall Street" was nearly unanimous in its view that the sharp declines that had occurred in corporate earning power as a result of the business depression that had begun a few months before was inadequately reflected in the stock market break that had reached its low point on November 15, 1957. I remember one representative after another of the larger stock brokerage firms saying he expected much lower prices and under prevailing conditions would buy nothing. Seldom have I seen the investment community so unanimous. Few seemed to consider that just as you would not cut the value of a good farm in half just because bad weather conditions caused a crop failure in a single year, so stocks should sell on the basis of what they might be expected to earn in the next several years, far more than as a multiple of what they were earning in a period that had all the economic earmarks of being of fairly short duration. Equally few seemed to give weight to the amount of cash available for investment that would be focussed on the stock market because of the then existing psychological appeal of common stocks for their reputed protection against inflation. Here was a psychological background that was almost ideal for acquiring any stock that was intrinsically a good long-range investment. If the depression had continued, the almost unanimous bearishness made it probable that much of the selling had already been done and that good stocks would decline only moderately further. If as actually happened, the business tide turned, the vast sums that had been moved from stocks into cash "to buy back at lower levels" would stampede into the stock market with the resulting rise that shortly was to prove so spectacular. This proved to be almost a perfect example of how constant alertness, as to whether current mass psychology may be out of step with fundamentals and as to how long such a trend may continue, can help enormously in determining when to buy into an outstanding company. It can frequently show us when to wait for a better opportunity and when to look around for a comparable opportunity in some other industry that is momentarily less popular.

However, there is a quite different way in which psychological-type studies of human behavior in regard to the handling of common stocks may prove even more helpful to investors. It is in this area that I believe sizable developments will come in the period ahead. For years, it has been known that few fields of human activity are inherently as deceptive as the managing of equity investments. What seems like so obviously the right thing to do is time and again exactly the wrong thing. Experienced stock brokers report that not just a few but the great majority of their clients make exactly the same mistakes over, and over, and over again.

I do not believe these things are happenstance or coincidence. In many ways, the art of common-stock investment has changed radically over the past fifty years. However, human nature en masse in relation to its attempt to make profits through buying capital assets does not change at all. What figures are available show that a chart of prices for tulip bulbs during the great speculative mania that occurred in that exotic commodity in Holland many centuries ago would parallel with amazing closeness a comparable chart of the rise and fall of leading stock prices in our own hectic period just before and after 1929. Even more illuminating is a study of what happened when nationwide optimism about the profit possibilities of the British East India Company caused a great wave of eagerness for common stocks to engulf the British Isles in the eighteenth century. The parallel between the difference in action of leading and secondary stocks then and in recent markets is astonishingly close. So are the resemblances in size and duration of the various dips or rallies that ran against the general price trend both on the way up and the way down. While these parallels are colorful, they merely confirm what most shrewd observers have recognized after they have had enough experience with the investment public: Human beings en masse always react about the same way to the same investment stimuli.

Now how can psychological studies take advantage of this constant factor to open up means of greater profit to the informed investor? Let me furnish an example of just one area where nothing is known today but where adequate study might give answers of great dollar value. I will make this example something that occurs not occasionally but time and again in our fast-moving technological age.

The research department of a publicly owned company develops a new process that up reaching full commercial fruition will probably produce about a 50 per cent increase in that company's total profits. The management submits the matter to a meeting of the Board of Directors to obtain authorization of the needed capital expenditures. This is granted. Work starts on the new plants with a scheduled calling for start-up operations in eighteen months. It actually takes twenty-four months. Six months after this start-up, the new process becomes profitable for the first time and three years later the full goal of a 50 per cent increase in total corporate profits is attained.

Obviously, such a development will produce a significant increase in the market price of the affected shares. But when will this happen? I am under the impression (so far as I know no one has ever made enough study of matters of this sort to enable anyone to be sure) that a key date is the presenting of this matter to the board of directors. These men can usually recognize a real investment opportunity. They may have the wealth themselves to cause enough buying significantly to change the stock's price. They are even more likely to have friends or associates in this position. At any rate I suspect, for I still have no data to support my general impressions, that from this point on the stock will follow a U-shaped course. It will go up to a surprising degree in the ensuing weeks as Wall Street excitement about the new process mounts. Months later, as profits from the new process are still far in the future, some of the eager recent buyers lose their enthusiasm and the shares sag. How far they sag may depend upon the time span that must elapse until the new process hits black ink figures. Then when the anticipated profits finally are attained, another rise occurs which, if no other new favorable developments have occurred in the meantime, strangely enough may or may not be as high a peak as on the original excitement.

All this is only my guess, which may be quite inaccurate, as to how the typical good stock behaves in relation to a situation that occurs time and time again. The remarkable thing is that with all the man-power employed by the financial community in the attempt to build up business by finding profit opportunities for present or prospective clients, thorough studies of this sort of thing (corrected, of course, for the influence of any major change in the general market level that may have occurred while these events were going on) have not been made. The reason they have not been made is that most of the financial com-munity has paid so little attention to the psychological aspect, that is, how people were thinking about an event, and have concentrated upon the event itself. Also, such work requires close knowledge of internal affairs of any company being studied. When the board of directors recognizes the significance of a new product can only be learned from someone who is close enough to one or more directors to get the facts at the source. It can not be learned by an investigator who merely reads an annual report.

The example I have cited of the type of psychological study that will vastly improve informed investor performance in the time ahead leads to a still more fundamental psychological stock market problem. Particularly in periods of general market enthusiasm, stocks discount these favorable developments quite some time ahead. Some of these good things are almost sure to happen but will not occur for several years. How far ahead is it safe to discount such developments without a major danger of stockholders becoming tired of waiting and prior to the favorable development having its impact on earnings, selling their shares, and causing sharply lower stock prices? Does this time element vary significantly between periods of general optimism and general in-vestment pessimism? If so, is there any approximate relationship that can be measured? In this day and age of such complex technology that greater and greater lead time is required between the completion of en-gineering on a product and its profitable production, these are matters affecting the shares of more and more outstanding companies. Since human beings en mass respond to the same investment stimuli of hope, confidence, fear, and impatience in exactly the same way, not alone year by year but century by century; these are all matters which proper financial psychological study should be able to solve. I believe that as the 1960's continue, increasing attention will be given such studies.

Is there any method by which some of these inherently psychological problems can be solved other than by accurately appraising how particular news items were being regarded at a particular time in a sufficient number of instances to permit the drawing of general conclusions? There seems to be. In 1950, an experiment was conducted by O. K. Burrell, Professor of Finance of the School of Business Administration of the University of Oregon. While this was subsequently reported in the *Commercial and Financial Chronicle*, I do not believe the financial community gave it the attention it deserved. It pioneered a technique which might be carried much further to learn how the average investor reacts to a particular kind of influence. By uncovering common investment errors, such a method can be invaluable in enabling investors to guard against actions which can prove quite costly.

Professor Burrell told each of a class of forty students they had $20,000 of theoretical purchasing power, which they must invest at once in any of six stocks designated "A" through "F." The only information they had about these equally imaginary stocks was the price arbitrarily set by Professor Burrell, the last year's earnings, dividend rate, and ex-dividend rates. The students had complete freedom of choice as to how they divided their funds between these six stocks, with no diversification being required.

The prices of each of the six stocks were then arbitrarily changed at regular intervals to simulate price changes that occur in the marketplace. Students were told to switch their holdings in whatever way they felt was most likely to increase their profit. Careful records were kept of total position in each stock after each price change and of the gains or losses of each student for the entire period. Because one of the matters Professor Burrell was trying to test was whether the average stock buyer would lose money in a period when some stocks were going up while others were declining, the students were required to keep fully invested at all times. Then at the end of the simulated three-year period, although some stocks had advanced and others declined, these gains and losses exactly balanced.

Some of the things this experiment showed were of considerable interest. In the first place, it indicated the strong tendency of all stock buyers to associate in their minds the price they pay for a stock with its real value. To this, Professor Burrell attributes the tendency of his entire class to average down, that is, to feel that if they paid 40 for a stock, it must be even more attractive now because it is selling at, say, 28. In addition to letting their losses run, he noted the tendency on the part of the students who were least successful (so far as this game was concerned) to take quick profits and for the more successful to let their profits ride somewhat longer. Another interesting observation which may confound those who are always advocating "splitting" high-priced shares on the grounds that it broadens the market, was the very slight preference for a lower-priced stock to a higher-priced one, deliberately designed to test this point by selling at the same price-earnings ratio and on the same yield basis.

However, possibly far more important than what this experiment may have shown is the opportunity it pioneered to develop a method that can test public reaction to a particular investment influence, isolated from all the other influences that in the real market are constantly pulling on investors' fears and hopes. For example, six actual stocks could have been chosen with their identity concealed so as to avoid the advantages of hindsight. These could have been six which over the same three-year period varied considerably from each other in their market action. Instead of students, experienced investors might have participated. As in real life, the participants might not be required to keep fully invested at all times, but would have a fixed original amount that they could invest or keep in cash as they pleased. The only motivation for buying or selling would be changes in quotation, as there would be no other data available to aid in decision making. Today, we know that price changes in themselves cause a good deal of buying and selling, but we do not know much more than this. Such an experiment, if carefully conducted, might greatly add to our knowledge of how (and probably why) investors act as they do. If (as would probably happen) a consistent pattern developed between the minority of participants who are highly successful and the majority who are not so successful, even more useful data would emerge on how the investor should or should not conduct himself.

It does not take great imagination to see how Professor Burrell's experimental method could be tailored to throw light on the significance (or lack of it) of many other investment matters besides stock split-up and investor response to price changes. Because the relationship of all of these essentially psychological matters to proper investment action has been so scantily explored, I am in no position to make dogmatic statements about all of the ways that such methods might enable an investor to improve his performance. All that can be said is that in place of some of the attention that the 1940's and 1950's put upon forecasting the business cycle, the 1960's may well devote to this completely different forms of endeavor. The pace of competition will probably cause this. For while no studies of this kind will have much bearing on the most basic problem of investors, which is selecting the particular stock to be bought or sold, it can have considerable bearing on the next most important problem of when to buy or sell it.

2

How the Greatest Increases in
Stock Values Come About

Most of the larger stock brokerage firms keep files of the principal "security analyses" put out by themselves and many of their competitors. While purporting to be "analyses" of the investment nature of certain stocks, many of them are essentially recommendations to buy the particular shares under discussion. These reports will vary tremendously from one another in length and scope. However, regardless of size, they tend to stress the reasons why a particular security is likely to prove profitable to its owner. There are relatively few such reports that are bearish or neutral in viewpoint.

Go to your broker and examine a fair sized sample of such material. Notice the diversity of reasons presented as to why one or another stock should rise in value. A far from complete list might include these reasons:

(1) There is an abnormal amount of assets behind each share of stock.
(2) The dividend yield is abnormally high.
(3) An increase in cash dividends is coming.
(4) A stock dividend or stock split is coming.
(5) The stock is abnormally cheap in relation to its earnings.

(6) The earnings have been steadily increasing year by year.

(7) The earnings are about to increase.

(8) The sales are about to increase.

(9) An appealing new product is about to be marketed.

(10) The company is spending an unusual amount on research.

(11) Occasionally (but oh, so very occasionally) because important changes are taking place in the management resulting from the appearance on the scene of one or more individuals of unusual business ability.

It is unfortunate that in many aspects of our crowded lives we are so busy doing this or that that we never take time to consider whether getting this or that done is the best way, or even a good way, of bringing about the thing for which we were doing this or that in the first place. Instead of spending quite so much time reading about the huge asset value and high-dividend return offered by the shares of the Hooligan and Van Astor Brickyards, it might be much more profitable first to give thought to some pretty basic matters. Are the different reasons why people urge us to buy one stock or another of equal importance? Are some of them of any particular importance at all? What does cause the really large spectacular rise in the occasional stock that results in wealth for its fortunate owners? Most important of all, do these breathtaking increases in value (several thousand per cent or more in five to ten years) occur because of generally little understood influences seldom even hinted at in most discussions of securities?

The hard competitive pace of the 1960's will unquestionably cause real progress in general understanding of these matters. Fortunately, enough advances already have been made so that much of the deadwood can easily be cleared away. Even now we can begin to see how financial theories will crystallize.

I have already mentioned in another section of this book how easy it is to see that the value of the assets behind a share of stock has little to do with its market value—unless a company is about to be liquidated and the proceeds of the assets turned over to stockholders. While generally recognized today, this, incidentally, is a relatively recent advance in investment understanding. Prior to World War I, most investment people in making their appraisals would have believed that assets were as important as earnings. Gradually, they have learned from the actions of the market place itself. Recommendations to buy based on asset considerations appear less and less often with the passing of time.

Alert Corporate Management

Before brushing off this matter of asset value completely, however, the investor would do well to remember there is one negative way in which it does have some significance. Just having a lot of valuable assets behind it—again in the absence of prospects for liquidating the company or selling it to others—will never send a stock up. But in one set of circumstances, lack of assets can send a stock down. Alert corporate management is looking for places where it can earn an abnormally high rate of return on additional investment. If such a management sees another company earning such a return on a relatively small amount of assets, it may be tempted to see if it cannot enter the business and share in the lush profits. Usually there are good reasons why this is not possible. Such reasons may include production know-how of the high-earning and low-asset producer, patent protection, customer loyalty to an established brand name, or any one of a dozen other factors. However, if it should be relatively easy for newcomers to enter the business that enjoys an unusually high rate of return on a small amount of assets, enough others may be expected to enter the field so that competition soon reduces the former rate of profit. Therefore, whenever an investor finds one of these low-asset value, high-earning power situations, he should regard it just as would the manager of an outside business considering entrance into the field. If he finds an absence of good business reasons preventing others from entering the field, he had better consider the low-asset value a warning signal and keep away. However, most of the time he will find strong reasons why the established units in the field have a big advantage over those who might want to enter it. If this were not so, these others would probably have already started to compete long before. In such event, he can completely ignore asset or book value as having anything to do with the future price trend of the shares.

It is even more recently that investors are beginning to recognize that dividends have much less influence on the course of stock prices than heretofore has been believed. As I pointed out in much greater detail in *Common Stocks and Uncommon Profits* income taxes take a huge toll from the dividend receipts of many stockholders. There are also the problems and risks of reinvestment of surplus dividend income in contrast to the relative ease and safety of having an outstanding management reinvest this same surplus in the type of expansion which they have already made so profitable for their stockholders. For these reasons, there are some who prefer non-dividend-paying stocks and others who prefer quite low dividend-paying stocks as well as those who like the high dividend payers and welcome every dividend increase. This means that increasing the regular dividend rate can and does have some moderate effect on a stock's value since it appeals to one class of stockholder. However, it also means the influence of such increases is very much less than was formerly believed and that such increases have nothing whatever to do with the great gains of many hundreds of per cent in market value that are the benchmarks of outstandingly successful investment. The tremendous stock market success of such rapidly growing companies as Texas Instruments and Ampex which neither pay dividends nor offer prospects of paying any for a long time in the future finally is driving home to many that, while dividend gains can produce one relatively small spurt in value, dividend payments have nothing whatever to do with major capital gain. The many years of stellar market performance of such traditional followers of a low dividend payout as International Business Machines, Dow Chemical, Minnesota Mining & Manufacturing and Eastman Kodak, to select random samples from widely diverse industries, has helped drive home the same point.

If real (cash) dividends are much less important in creating increases in market value than had formerly been believed, increasing amounts of highly impressive data are beginning to appear showing that stock dividends and stock splits (excepting to the degree that they increase the cash dividend) have an influence that is virtually nonexistent. A number of excellent studies* have been made showing that once a stock split has been made, it has no effect whatsoever on the future price curve of the shares. While in the period just prior to announcement of a split such stocks appear to have done somewhat better than the market,

---

* See "Split Stocks Before and After" by A. Wilfred May, *Commercial & Fin. Chronicle,* Jan. 31, 1957; or "Stock Split Results Can Vary Too," *Business Week,* February 18, 1956.

there seems to be considerable question whether such betterment (which seldom is of major proportions) is due to the split or whether the splitting action usually is not taken by the Board of Directors at a time when the company is doing particularly well and therefore its shares probably would have gone up anyway. In any event insofar as big changes in value are concerned, the total impact of stock splits and dividends is minor. It can be argued that some investors like to buy shares selling at less than, say, $50 per share so they can obtain more shares for their money and that this will create more demand for low-priced shares. However, it can also be argued that most investors who would let as superficial a matter as that influence them in selecting one stock in preference to another probably have too little investment sense to appreciate what makes a good investment and to remain long term shareholders anyway. Therefore, splitting stock may increase turnover and the amount of weakly held shares without any long-term influence on value. It is hard to argue with the brilliant market action of some of the higher priced issues.

The tie-in between growth in sales, introduction of new products, etc., and a hoped for resulting growth in profits is pretty obvious. Therefore, this brings us to profits as the next factor to consider in judging what makes major changes in stock values. The correlation between growth in per-share earnings and major increases in market price of common shares is so close and can be so easily demonstrated that I see no point in taking up a lot of space discussing something everyone knows and in which every investor can have confidence. It is a rare case when per-share earnings are advancing and give promise of continuing to advance and the security in question is not doing better than the market as a whole. However, is there any other factor—one not so generally understood—that plays a part along with changed earning levels in causing a particular stock to go up (or down) more than the general market?

I believe there is. I believe the investor who understands this influence can put himself in a position so that over the years—if he can appraise correctly what he sees—he may benefit enormously. However, since the concept will be new to many, it may be a trifle more difficult to grasp. Because I believe it so important and because I want to be sure it is fully understood, I plan to attempt to start explaining it in a somewhat indirect and round about manner.

A NEW CONCEPT

Dr. Smith is a brilliant surgeon. He is recognized as the most skill-ful in his community. His large fees are readily paid. His business expenses are chiefly rent for his office and salary for one office girl. After deducting everything but his personal income taxes he is making $60,000 a year.

Now at the age of 61, he sees a magnificent investment opportunity if he could raise some capital quickly. However, between his tastes which are expensive, and his two former and one present wives who are even more expensive, he has never saved any money. He hits on what seems to him like a brilliant idea. The doctor's closest friend inherited a large sheet metal plant from his father. He has sold stock in it for quite a sum of money. Why not start a medical corporation? He has $60,000 a year's earning power to support it. He would keep 20 per cent of this and sell shares entitling their owners to 80 per cent of this $60,000, or $48,000. How much would people pay for corporate shares having a pretax earning power of $48,000 per annum?

He called on an investment banker. He learned they would pay so little that it could not possibly be worth his while to make such a move. I suspect you already know most of the reasons for this. However, as I have already explained, I think it worthwhile to build up step-by-step the investment concept I am about to introduce, and therefore, I want to explain these reasons anyway. Our doctor might get sick or hurt in an accident, so that his earning power, which is dependent solely on his unusual abilities, could stop at any moment. Each year as his age increases the probability of its stopping increases as well. Eventually it must stop. He has trained no one to take his place. If he had, there is not the least assurance the assistant would remain working for the corporation. The chances are, in a profession such as this, he would do better working for himself. Meanwhile, since the doctor is already working about as hard as one man can, there is little way the earning power might increase. In contrast, there is every chance it might decrease since once the doctor is only making from his medical practice about 15 per cent of what he had previously done (20 per cent of $60,000 less corporate income tax), and since he now presumably would be getting rich from his other investment, there would be little inducement for his working as hard as had formerly been the case.

A one-man personal business like this, if it could be sold at all, would bring at most only two or three times his earnings. There are just too many risks and too few prospects in the business. Now let us turn to the friend of Dr. Smith: The one who had sold a 45 per cent interest in the sheet metal plant. Actually Jones, the sheet metal plant owner, had not sold these shares for such a fancy price at all. The reported high price resulted solely from Jones' being such a congenital liar. Since it had been a private transaction with no records being available to the public, Jones greatly had exaggerated the price he claimed to have received. Robinson had paid just under four times earnings for his shares.

Why should he pay any more? A fundamentally less attractive business could hardly have been found. It required very inexpensive equipment and little specialized know-how to operate this type of sheet metal works. Anybody easily could get into the business, and many people had. There were so many small shops competing for the relatively simple type of jobs that were the only kind Jones' plant could handle that to get the low bid always meant accepting a profit-margin so small as to be almost non-existent. The only way to survive at all was to pay just as low wages as a hostile union would tolerate, give nothing to the employees that was not forced, and turn out just as inexpensive or slipshod work as could be gotten away with under each contract. If Jones had any goodwill or loyalty from anyone with whom he dealt, Robinson could find no trace of it.

Robinson's friends warned him against making this purchase. He had only a minority interest. The business was controlled by a man without moral scruples. If by some miracle a real profit could sooner or later be earned, there was nothing to prevent Jones from grabbing most of it through increasing his own salary or his own expense account.

Young Robinson knew all this. But he also knew something else. Jones was a sick man, and two years later after Robinson had learned the business thoroughly Jones died. Robinson bought the remaining 55 per cent of stock from Jones' estate for five times per-share earnings. Since this was control stock, the estate tried to get a higher price, but Jones' business had such a poor reputation there were no other bidders.

Robinson now made a move that he had been considering for some time. He knew that only some of the most complex steel alloys and certain exotic new metals could stand up under intense heat. But he knew that in aircraft and missiles, in chemical plants and oil refineries, as well as in atomic reactors, there would be greater and greater demand for such products in the future. He also knew that these materials were all so difficult to handle neither he nor anyone in his whole section of the country could fabricate them profitably. He offered Brown, a brilliant young metallurgist at one of the universities, an option on buying some unissued stock in his company (the name of which he had changed to Pioneer Metals Corporation) if he would join it.

Robinson and Brown took on two small fabricating jobs in these newer metals and alloys. They lost money on both. They did learn, however, just which parts of their existing facilities could be used for these new materials and how to design the special equipment they needed but did not yet have. It almost exhausted the assets and borrowing power of the business to acquire these things. However, somehow they got them.

In the year that followed, they made very little money. But they acquired more and more knowledge of just how to handle these difficult metals, a field so full of problems that everyone around them seemed happy to leave it alone. However, as their knowledge grew so did the volume of incoming business and modest profits began to appear.

Then came the episode that was to mark the turning point in their business. They took on a job for one of the largest manufacturers in the area. Although the metals involved were too tricky for this experienced fabricator to want to handle himself, Robinson gave a verbal promise of delivery in eight weeks. Relying on this, the large manufacturer in turn had contracted to furnish a major piece of equipment to his largest customer in time for the seasonal peak of that customer's business. Failure to deliver on time would be very costly. Robinson felt almost physically ill when four weeks from the day of promised delivery his men made a mistake in judgment and all the work done to date was hopelessly ruined.

Robinson was not bound by contract to deliver on time. However, he felt his word was pledged. Although his financial resources were already severely extended, he authorized overtime and double time without stint. He even hired extra helpers to get the full eight-week job done in the four weeks that still remained. He insisted his company was to blame for the difficulty and asked no extra reimbursement from the buyer. When he made delivery exactly when promised, he estimated his liquid assets against his outstanding bills and ruefully calculated his business career had ended.

Instead of being finished, he was on the verge of his first real taste of prosperity. The president of the large company to which he had delivered as promised invited him to lunch. He was told that his small company was exactly the type of dependable supplier the large company had long been seeking. He was also told that if he would take no extra payment to cover his losses on this job, the large manufacturing company would insist, in its own interest, that it loan Pioneer whatever was needed to keep Robinson in business. Equally important, word of just what had happened spread through the business community and to many other potential customers in a way such things so often do. Company after company, in not one industry but many, decided it wanted a supplier upon which it could really depend. Business began to pour in. Furthermore, this was not the rough competitive bidding business of the old Jones Sheet Metal days, with its frighteningly small margin of profit. The Pioneer Metal Corporation had knowledge and reliability which was unique and for which prosperous companies felt it to be to their interest to pay. Profit margins were healthy. Although much additional equipment was purchased, loans were in time all paid off.

Meanwhile, compared with the old Jones Sheet Metal days, the relationship of Pioneer with its employees showed as much contrast as did Pioneer's relationship with customers. Even in the tough times when he could not afford it, Robinson tried within the limits of his financial ability to treat his men as individuals and give them every possible break. The men quickly sensed this and productivity improved. Then, as prosperous days arrived, another episode occurred, equally dramatic but far more tragic than that which won him the respect of his customers. He sent one of his men in a company automobile on a company errand. On an open road an oncoming car went out of control. There was a head-on crash. Through no fault of Pioneer, an employee was killed.

Robinson could think of nothing he less wanted to do, but he felt he should call on the widow immediately. She had three preschool children. He had no legal financial liability. Nevertheless, he told her the company felt a responsibility for the children and that trust funds would at once be started to see that they, at company expense, would get not only a high school but also a college education.

Word of what happened spread through the shops with the speed such things usually do. It spread from family to family. Both among Pioneer personnel and others, the feeling grew that this was the right sort of place in which to work—where you are treated right all the time and they stand behind you in an emergency. From that day on, the quit rate at Pioneer stayed far below the average for the area. As the business expanded, it was no longer necessary to hire just anyone available. With a policy of constantly seeking to find men capable of promotion and a growth rate so rapid that many opportunities for promotion existed, this was one company with so many applicants for every available position that there was no problem in finding the right one. Only the most promising talent would be added to the payroll.

This may have been the most rewarding of any of Robinson's management moves. First one, then another, then three more of the employees showed outstanding management talent—men who understood Robinson's goals and policies, who could think like he did, and carry on for him if necessary. Instead of one-man management, a real management team was emerging. Like the key research people, these management men were tied into the picture by attractive options on unissued stock of the company.

At this point, many a business man would have rested on his laurels, but Robinson was of a different stripe. He encouraged his men to look for another growing field where the company's special skills might open up possibilities too difficult for most competitors to tackle. It was found that certain kinds of bearings—not any kind but ones with special advantages obtainable in no other way—might be made of some of the exotic metals with which the company was already familiar. It was also found that some of the designers of special equipment already on Pioneer's staff had the knowledge and imagination to design the needed production machinery. The new line was a success almost from the beginning. Now it began to appear that if the company could find the money to finance several similar plants around the country, there would be every prospect of their becoming the national leaders in the new but rapidly growing field of this kind of specialized bearing.

However, it was important that this be done quickly before someone else caught up with Pioneer's technique and became established first as a main supplier.

Borrowing more than part of this money would have put too great a debt load on the business for safety. Robinson decided to sell stock to the public for the balance of the needed funds.

In the ten years since he bought out Jones, he had increased the per-share earnings ten times. But now we come to something even more important, in fact, so important that it is my only excuse for having taken up so much of your time in a largely (but not entirely) fictitious example. I say not entirely fictitious because some of the things I have described for Pioneer actually happened just as I described them, but not all to the same company.

Robinson talked to some investment bankers about the price that would be reasonable if Pioneer sold some additional stock. He found that from the investor's standpoint things had changed dramatically from the old Jones Sheet Metal days primarily because of three things. These were:

(1) Instead of one rather weak manager with no one ready to replace him, the company had a team of several outstanding business people, any one of whom could head the company and continue existing policies. Moreover, the same methods of handling people that had enabled these men to rise from the ranks and make themselves fit for leadership gave every assurance that others would also emerge to take their places as these men grew older.

(2) In place of profit margins so narrow that the slightest mishap could mean disaster, the great technical lead the company had acquired (based on many small bits of experience, not on a single big secret) and the tendency of customers to prefer a supplier on whom they knew they could depend, made any reasonable price acceptable so that profit margins were good.

(3) The lines in which the company were already entrenched gave promise of considerable growth while the same technical teams that had uncovered entirely new opportunities in the past gave promise of discovering still others in the future.

For these reasons, Robinson was told Pioneer could sell the required amount of stock at eighteen times current per-share earnings—four times the price to earnings ratio at which Robinson had bought his shares ten and twelve years before.

This change in the price-earnings ratio is the vital point so often overlooked, because it is here that the biggest segment of stock-market profits can be made. Let us see, by simple arithmetic, how important the factor is. Let us suppose that Robinson originally had acquired his 100 per cent stock ownership of the Jones Sheet Metal Works at a total cost of $30,000. When he planned his first public financing, he had increased these per-share earnings ten-fold so if the price-earnings ratio had remained the same his holdings would have increased in value by $300,000. However, because the price-earnings ratio had quadrupled the price others would pay for his shares (now that a superb management team was geared into the picture) was four times this amount or $1,200,000. In other words, $900,000 of the amazing profit available to him (in addition to his modest but fully taxable salary for the period) as a result of 12 years of brilliant work came because of the change in the price-earnings ratio at which his holdings could be sold on the market. Only $300,000 would have come from the magnificent increase in earnings if no changed price-earnings ratio had occurred.

Sometimes a fairly sizable but purely temporary increase in this price-earnings ratio will come from a stock market fad. This happens when investors en masse get an exaggerated idea of the prospects of one glamorous industry or another and for a time bid up the shares to unrealistic levels. Also, at times investors will get overenthusiastic (or underenthusiastic) for stocks as a whole. For a year or two, the whole market will sell at temporary dangerously high (or appealingly low) price earnings ratios. However, the biggest changes in these price-earnings ratios—the ones that continue on through the years and the ones that increase independently of what the rest of the market is doing—arise from one cause and one cause only. They happen because fundamental changes have been going on within the company. These changes make the particular shares a great deal safer and more appealing to investors than had been the case before. I hope that all the detail in which I indulged in my Pioneer Metal example will help make obvious why management matters of the sort I described are not theoretical affairs of only abstract interest. Instead, they intrinsically increase or decrease in a major way the real value of current earnings to any investor.

This being the case, would an investor be smart to buy Pioneer Metal stock after it had already gone up 4,000 per cent from Robinson's original purchase price? Assuming Pioneer lived up to its promise of still further growth in earnings, does not this very point of the importance of price-earnings ratios make it unwise for the farsighted investor to buy any stock after this big a rise in the price-earnings ratio—even if a nice, further growth in earnings appears probable? To understand the answer to this question, let us (without going into quite so much detail as before) see what happened in the next ten years of Pioneer's history—the second decade of Robinson's management.

The specialized bearing venture went well, and in time, the company became the acknowledged leader in this field, too. But in so doing something even more important had happened. The management team had learned the technique of finding new fields on the frontiers of technology in which big commercial growth lay ahead and in which the company had special advantages enabling it to excel. Several such additional ventures were begun. Not all prospered. The majority, however, did. As the initial investment in each was small, the successful ones into which big capital was poured, as each project became profitable on its way, far exceeded the small cost of the few failures. To finance these worthwhile new ventures, additional stock had to be issued several times. However, this only was done when the additional profits would be great enough so that after the financing, per-share earnings on the increased number of shares outstanding would be enhanced, not diluted. The result was that 10 years after its first public financing, Pioneer's per-share earning had increased by another 300 per cent. Its total earnings had of course increased even more, but the larger figure was, from an earning standpoint, meaningless to stockholders because what affects them earningswise is the amount their individual share of the earning power has increased.

The Role of Institutional Buying

However, meanwhile, something else had also been happening. As the company had grown in size and diversity, the great financial institutions of the country had become interested in Pioneer's development. By now, it had so proved itself that investment trusts, pension funds, and even that most difficult to satisfy and yet that most desirable class of stockholder, the trust departments of banks, were ready to entrust some of their funds in these shares. For one thing, there were now enough shares outstanding, with the resulting broad market for the stock, that these institutions felt there was a liquid market where they could buy or sell the size blocks of shares in which they normally deal. This condition had not existed when Pioneer shares were first offered to the public. For another, Pioneer's ability to keep branching out into additional growth lines too complex for ordinary competition to enter made the stock peculiarly well suited to the needs of many of these organizations.

Elsewhere in this book, I discuss the influence of the institutional buyer upon the market. I point out why the relatively small number of stocks into which this class of buying must be concentrated tends to make the comparatively few stocks so selected sell (usually legitimately) at higher price-earnings ratios than stocks not so chosen. Now that Pioneer fully qualified in this group, it was selling at 36 times earnings.

So to the decade's tripling of Pioneer stock due to earnings must be added a doubling of that increase due to a further advance in the price earnings ratio. In short, a gain of 600 per cent in ten years was enjoyed by those who bought Pioneer's first public offering. Few investors would turn up their collective noses at this type of return provided it can be made with a relatively small degree of risk—a matter to which I will return presently. On the other hand, this return was paltry compared to the gains of Robinson (or of his backers) if others had purchased some of Jones' shares to help Robinson obtain control. These people would have run up an' original investment of $30,000, made from 20 to 22 years before to the $1,200,000 figure of ten years ago and to six times this amount now, or $7,200,000—a 12,000 per cent appreciation for the entire period.

Are the figures in this admittedly fictitious example exaggerated? No, actually they are small compared to what dozens and dozens of outstanding managements have done in every industrialized section of the nation. Thirty miles south of my office in San Francisco, the early 1930's saw two brilliant engineer-businessmen found a business in a tiny shop. They were William R. Hewlett and David Packard, co-owners of Hewlett-Packard Company, electronic laboratory equipment manufacturers. Without having sold any company stock to the public (they have in very recent years sold a minority of their own stock for personal diversification and to have a more liquid asset for estate tax purposes) the current market value of this company's shares is considerably in excess of $150 million. The greatest part of this is still owned by these two men. This was accomplished in about the same time span as our "fictitious" Pioneer Metals. About six miles north of the Hewlett-Packard plant are the main activities of the Ampex Corporation. In the late 1940's, four individuals took over the management of this, then, tiny company. Their total investment, including loans and advances to the company, was in the neighborhood of $400,000. If these four businessmen had kept all the shares they received as a result of the transaction, these shares would, as I write this, have a market value in excess of $40 million! Their present holdings, as revealed by the last Ampex proxy statement, do represent around 80 per cent of this or about $32,000,000. Nor can the other 20 per cent, which was sold as the stock rose, be considered inconsequential. It must have produced several additional millions of cash as these owners diversified somewhat.

These two examples are by no means unique even for the small area near San Francisco. One of that city's ablest financiers risked $10,000 in the very early days of the International Rectifier Company. Now, 15 years later, his holdings in this Southern California manufacturer are worth over $3,000,000. This same man told me recently that not much more than this original investment, placed in still another young company in the San Francisco Bay area less than five years ago, today has a market value in excess of $1,500,000. To the north, in the Portland area, an even greater source of personal fortunes will probably be revealed shortly if, as is expected to happen, there is a public marketing of the stock of Tectronics.

Elsewhere in this book, I discuss such companies as A. C. Nielsen Company of Chicago and Texas Instruments, Inc. of Dallas. A glance at the latest proxy statements of such companies is rather revealing. Although the Nielsen company was only founded in the 1920's and only started to become prosperous about 12 years later when present policies were established, the holdings of its able founder are today worth in the neighborhood of $12,500,000. The Texas Instruments story is even more spectacular. This company was founded just a few years later than Nielsen. None of its three principal stockholders nor another of its major executives who arrived on the scenes somewhat later were men of wealth. Yet the present holdings of one of these four men are currently valued at almost $80,000,000; two more have holdings in the general neighborhood of $60,000,000 and the worth of the holdings of the relatively newcomer still totals a modest $25,000,000!

I could easily make long lists of other companies which in relatively recent times have produced fortunes vastly greater than my Pioneer Metals example. I am a little reluctant to do this as in many instances I am insufficiently familiar with the corporate background to be completely sure that the huge rise can be significantly attributed to fundamental improvement in the intrinsic worth of each dollar of per-share earnings, together with the earnings increase that this management betterment helped bring about. However, just to mention a few more Pacific Coast companies, one is the fabulously successful Litton Industries, another is the slightly older Friden Calculating Machine Company, which could have been bought lock, stock and barrel for a few hundred thousand dollars in the mid-1930's (this was well after the 1932 to 1933 period when everything was on the bargain counter) and which today sells for $85 million in the open market. Statham Instruments and Electro Instruments are two other West Coast companies (in rather different types of business in spite of their somewhat similar names) that quite recently have produced this kind of fortune for their able managers and major stockholders.

If instead of just taking younger companies you go back to those founded 50 or 60 years ago, the number of such instances swells by the hundreds. The sensational number of millionaires made by the General Motors Corporation or by the very much smaller and once desperately struggling young Dow Chemical Company is now a matter of business history. The thing so many people do not realize is the amazing number of such companies that have grown up decade by decade since the industrialization of our country began.

Another thing of interest is the number of these companies that did not start off in particularly attractive lines when they commenced operations. As with our Jones Sheet Metal Works, many of them obtained their great impetus toward success by finding attractive associated lines into which they might go but in which they would have some advantage because of their original business (as when Texas Instruments went into transistors). Others, like the spectacularly successful chemical companies, soon found that the heart of being successful in their field lay in having continuously to make the right decision (or at least having a high batting average regarding such decisions) as to which subdivisions of their field to enter and which to leave alone.

If you are fully convinced that the results quoted in my Pioneer example are an understatement, not an overstatement, of what is continuously occurring in the real business world, let us return to a rather basic consideration. Let us go back to a fundamental question I raised but have not yet answered. Why, to continue with our Pioneer example, should any wise investor buy the stock at 18 times earnings and content himself with a mere 600 per cent in ten years (good as that may be) when he might look around and find a situation such as Pioneer was ten years earlier that would have paid him 4,000 per cent?

The answer, of course, lies in the degree of risk involved. The standard by which any investment should be judged is not just how much can be made from it if all goes well. Rather, it is how much can be made *in relation to the amount of risk involved.* In our Pioneer example, it was touch and go whether the business would even survive during its earlier stages when the low price-earnings ratio might have been available. Good luck as well as good judgment can well have entered the picture. Suppose Robinson had become seriously ill during those crucial early days when he had on his payroll no other keen business mind to carry on? Suppose a brilliant technical discovery by a research group thousands of miles away had demonstrated some other economically new metals or alloys to be vastly superior to those in the fabricating of which Pioneer was just beginning to establish a reputation? Suppose the president of the large manufacturer, who was so pleased with Pioneer's performance that he advanced the needed loans to avert financial collapse, had been in Europe on vacation and his assistant, while also admiring Pioneer's policies, had not felt he "should stick his neck out" by volunteering company funds for this purpose? Any of these entirely possible events, or many others, could have caused an entirely different ending to the story of Robinson's investment.

In contrast, when the stock offering was made at 18 times earnings, there was much less prospect of anything preventing important further growth. Even discovery of better competitive metals and alloys would not have been too serious. By this time the company had the technical talent capable of mastering a switch to the new materials and, equally important, the financial strength to weather the costly period of learning. Furthermore, even by this time, Pioneer, with its new bearing venture, had enough diversification so that parts of the business would have remained highly profitable during the expensive transition period. In short, 600 per cent at quite little risk might have been a considerably more attractive investment than 4,000 per cent with the tremendous dangers involved.

But how about the third ten-year period? The stock is now selling at 36 times earnings. It has almost all if not all the investment status of the very highest class of investment. Under these conditions, its price-earnings ratio is not, in a normal year, going any higher. Under these circumstances would it not be rather silly to buy Pioneer stock at all? The only increase in its value from here can come from improved earnings. There is no way this increase in earning power can have as great an effect on market price as when it could be multiplied by a legitimately earned increase in the price-earnings ratio.

A Reward Usually Overlooked

I have already discussed the investment characteristics of these institutional stocks in a prior section of this book. There is no point in repeating those comments here. However, this should also be pointed out: Outstanding corporate management brings the stockholder two rewards, not one. The enormously valuable reward of irregularly but continuously increasing the price-earnings ratio until the stock in question reaches the "institutional ceiling" (which our Pioneer example has now attained) is one about which investors seem largely unaware. Therefore, because of its tremendous dollars significance, I have devoted this entire section of this book to it.

However, outstanding corporate management also brings investors a second and comparably important reward. This is that beyond temporary gains or setbacks due to the current phase of the business cycle, the stockholders' proportionate share of earnings will continue to grow decade by decade at a well-above-average rate. If our Pioneer stock is *legitimately entitled* to sell at 36 times earnings, this means that management is so good and company position is so entrenched in the ways of growth that a further tripling of earnings in the next 10 years (or about the same rate of growth as enjoyed in the past ten) may be considered about "par for the course." Again if the company has developed to a point where the probability of tripling its value in the next 10 years involves only about half as much risk of not so growing as was the case ten years before, the stock might be just about as attractive an investment today (i.e., the ratio of what can be made from it in contrast to the risk of this not happening) as it was when at somewhat greater risk it offered ten years ago the chance of twice as much gain in value.

A sophisticated investor would conclude that, on the basis of abstract principles and if the odds as I presented them in regard to Pioneer were presented correctly, then Pioneer 20 years ago, ten years ago, and today might be equally attractive investments. However, he would be totally uninterested in this general conclusion. What would interest him would be that which was the most attractive investment for him, with his particular investment needs and goals which are possibly quite different from those of some other investor who might consider the matter.

My personal belief is that the total resources at an investor's disposal may be a considerable factor in determining which class of investment is most attractive for him. If he has only a very few thousand dollars and no prospect of getting more, he should make a frank and realistic decision. He should realize that at the probable rate of growth for most low-risk investments it is quite unlikely that in the course of his lifetime these few thousand dollars will ever amount to enough significantly to change his standard of living. Therefore, he should decide one of two things. Does he want this fund as sort of an inflation protected nest egg to buttress him or his family against some unexpected future financial emergency? If so, he should confine his purchases to the best of the low-risk institutional type stocks, analogous to Pioneer at 36 times earnings. Or does he recognize that these are intrinsically "surplus" funds anyway and that he has enough other assets to protect him against such emergencies. Then, particularly if he is young, he may well decide if outstanding business people in a promising venture come his way that he should run the sizable risk involved in the type of almost incredible gain that can and does come when financial community recognition of a formerly unknown management causes a great increase in earnings to be multiplied by a dramatic change in price-earnings ratio.

For the larger investor, the choice is far simpler. He already has enough assets significantly to affect his living standards right now. Therefore, being in a fortunate position which, however, might be jeopardized by heavy investment losses, he should largely confine his investments to a mixture of stocks resembling Pioneer as it was ten years ago and Pioneer as it is today. However, depending on a whole series of variables such as how wealthy he is (i.e., how much he could lose without fundamentally affecting his living standards) and how eager he might be to make further spectacular increases in his wealth (i.e., such factors as his age, the degree of his desire to build up important nest eggs for his children, etc.), he might well decide to place some minority portion of his holdings in the type of situation comparable to Pioneer in its earliest stages. In any event, whatever the individual investor's policy may be, he can make his specific decisions more wisely if he understands the factors involved. If he realizes the generally overlooked but basic fact that changing price-earnings ratios are an investment force comparable in significance to changed earnings in bringing about major changes in stock values, he is in a far better position both to appraise the possibilities of a particular situation and to determine whether that situation is one fitting his needs.

This brings me full circle back to the point where I started these comments. Of all the reasons found in a typical sample of Wall Street comments about why this or that stock should be bought, it is surprising how very rare is the appearance of the most important of all: "Here is a management starting to prove itself capable of developing the type of growth enterprise that will eventually win institutional acceptance, yet so far the price-earnings ratio fails to indicate financial community awareness of the quality of the management." If the facts behind such a statement are accurate, such a management will in time unlock the basic formula for the greatest of investment success—a major increase in earnings vastly enriched by a major increase in the price at which each dollar of those increased earnings is valued in the market place.

However, to unlock this treasure trove of value, such a statement has to be accurate in its facts as well as general theory. As explained elsewhere in this book, a low price-earnings ratio, unaccompanied by a corporate management capable of bringing about a high price-earnings ratio, is usually an investment trap, not an investment bonanza. Management must actually be outstanding. Just to be called outstanding is not enough. As certain high officials of a great Boston trust company have stated—and in Boston investment trusteeship is a major industry—in evaluating a common stock, the management is 90 per cent, the industry is 9 per cent and all other factors are 1 per cent. While this statement is not and was not intended to be mathematically provable to the fraction of a per cent, it summarizes the approach that, capitalizing on the matters discussed in this section, provides the key to how the greatest increases in common stock values come about.

3

You and Where Your Investment
Business Must Go

A TOTALLY UNEXPECTED side effect of the publication of *Common Stocks and Uncommon Profits* was the insight it gave me into what matters have most worried investors during the past two years. This is because, almost from publication day, I began receiving visits, phone calls, and particularly letters from people previously unknown to me. Most of them had questions of one sort or another they desired to ask. These questions were of many different kinds. But the comment and question I have been asked about as often as all others combined is this: "I keep looking for someone in whom I can have confidence. I cannot find anyone who seems to have real knowledge of the stocks he recommends. I want to pay for this service. Can you tell me to whom I should go?"

Even though this question keeps coming to me from every section of the country, I do not mean to imply that the investment business as now constituted is not satisfying the needs of many investors. Some of these may be living in a fool's paradise. Nevertheless, in one or another subdivision of the investment field, many others have beyond doubt found capable people who are properly taking care of them. However, the amazing number of people who do not seem to be able to find what they consider suitable investment guidance is, I believe, a clue to possibilities of radical improvement in the basic methods of the investment business.

I at first hesitated as to whether an analysis of what is now wrong with this business as it is being conducted, and a discussion of how this will probably eventually be remedied, properly belongs in a book addressed primarily to investors. I have decided that it does. If, as I believe, an important segment of all investors feel they are unable to find the type of help they are seeking and for which they are ready to pay, it is probably of some interest to them to understand why their problem has developed. Furthermore, if through understanding this, they can also better judge for themselves which type of currently available investment service comes closest to meeting their desires, these matters then become of much more interest.

I feel rather certain the matters covered in other sections of this book will be affecting investors all during the 1960's. The changes I am about to portray may also come about during this period. In contrast, while I believe these changes in the financial business will come eventually, I am unable to be precise about just when this will be. The reason for this lies in the general prosperity of the investment industry as it is today constituted. I think the generally rising trend of stock prices that has prevailed for many years has partially concealed a vast amount of slipshod work by many who undertake to guide others in regard to their investments. This same rising trend of prices has enabled many in the industry who are doing good work—and possibly a considerable number of others whose work is mediocre—to earn quite substantial sums for themselves year after year. As long as things are so prosperous, there is not the inducement to attempt radical improvement. There is a strong tendency to feel that: "As long as everything is prosperous, why rock the boat just because there is a chance of even greater profits through quite different methods?"

This does not mean that major improvement can come only if a prolonged bear market altered the general prosperity of the investment industry. Pioneering financial leaders may at any time use their ingenuity to develop the techniques that in time will dominate finding the bonanza investments of the future. It does mean that, while I can point out where the investment business must go, I cannot estimate whether it will get there in two years or twelve.

The first step in understanding this whole matter is to recognize clearly what nearly all investors want from those in the investment business. An extremely small minority of all stock buyers (other than professional investment men) feel competent to manage their own affairs and merely want brokerage service. But the overwhelming majority are interested in one thing virtually to the exclusion of all else. This is to do business with someone having enough knowledge about the securities he recommends so that in a reasonable period of time these particular securities will do approximately what their adviser claims they will.

It is surprising in this day and age how reasonable, or perhaps I should say how sophisticated, most investors are in this respect. There are still some people who want their investment adviser to tell them what stock will go up three points this week or who think it is the basic function of an investment man to tell them what "the market" is going to do. Fortunately, the number of such people seems to be steadily decreasing. What most investors want is someone with a thorough enough knowledge about the stocks he is recommending so that when he says a dividend is safe it actually is safe, or when he says a stock should go up in a reasonable time it does go up considerably more and not less than the general market. This basic matter of being right on the majority of recommendations is almost the sole interest of those buying stocks on the advice of others, regardless of whether it be the investment counsel, the brokerage, or the investment banking segment of the financial business with which this stock buyer deals. It is equally true of those who place their funds in an investment trust or the trust department of a bank. In such cases, the customer primarily desires those handling the activities of such institutions to know enough of what they are doing so that on balance the stocks they buy perform as they were expected to when purchased.

This matter of performance is almost as important to the investment man himself as it is to his clients. Someone in the investment business may have the manners of an oaf and the personality of a clod. But if he can select stocks that perform outstandingly and do it with reasonable consistency, one client will bring another and that one will bring several more until, after a while, he will have more business than he can handle. In contrast, the nicest, pleasantest, and most hard-working gentleman in the world will always be on the ragged edge of solvency if he depends on advising investors for making a living and is nearly always wrong in the stocks he selects. From the standpoint of anyone in the business of advising about or selling common-stock investments, the record of successes and failures of prior recommendations is probably more important than all other factors combined in determining the degree of present day success.

In view of this overwhelming importance of being right to the investment man as well as his clients, it is surprising how many individuals and investment organizations appear to spend so little of their time checking and rechecking the soundness of the purchases they are suggesting, and how much of it in trying to sell these inadequately investigated securities to their clients. Even less time is spent in attempting to perfect the method best suited to making as sure as possible that a recommended purchase be an attractive one. Yet the difference between a better means of selecting outstanding investments and a poorer approach to the same objective can in as short a span as ten years make the difference between a fortune and a fizzle to both the investment man and the investor he is guiding.

Methods of Investment Evaluation

Let us not make this common mistake. Let us examine in a general way the successive steps that over the years have been developed to improve investment results. In this way, we can begin to understand the strength and the weakness of methods now available. If we understand the weaknesses, we will know both what to guard against and the nature of the improvements that will come in the future.

As recently as 30 years ago, the accepted method of judging attractive common stocks was to examine published balance sheets and earnings statements in great detail. Decisions were then made based solely upon this accounting type of knowledge and upon such general ideas about the nature of the business as any man in the street might know about the company's product line. Trying to select an outstanding investment in this way is about as sensible (and has about the same probability of being successful) as attempting to pick a lifetime partner in marriage with absolutely no other knowledge about a prospective husband or wife than his or her name and a couple of posed photographs. With great good luck, a successful marriage or a brilliant long-term

94

investment might be attained in this way. However, with so many of the basic traits of both the lifetime partner or the stock completely unknown, the danger of a harrowing mistake runs rather high. Although several other factors contributed to the Holocaust, the staggering losses of the great 1929 to 1932 bear market gave eloquent testimony to what can happen to those who rely solely on this method in selecting common shares. This period taught an important segment of the financial community that much more work was necessary if common-stock investment activity were to be successfully pursued.

Out of the troubles of the great depression came the next big step forward in the art of judging successful common-stock appraisal. This was the contacting of top corporate officials to ask them questions affecting the investment status of their company's shares. It was in the 1930's that the various societies of security analysts began to appear. These in turn brought about the day of the plant visit. It also brought about the return visits of the corporate executive to the financial centers to tell groups or associations of financial men about the characteristics of the companies they managed.

This was all helpful. It gave those taking the trouble to contact management a better picture than before of various points of relative strength and weakness in particular companies. However, by the end of World War II, it began to be apparent that this too was not enough. Something more still was needed if enough of the mediocre and weak investments were to be consistently eliminated and a high percentage of important winners selected. Something more had to be done if the investment man was really to know what he was doing.

Then began another major step forward in investment technique. For lack of a better term, in my *Common Stocks and Uncommon Profits* I call it the "scuttlebutt" method. It is taking advantage of the vast mass of information about a particular company that is nearly always known by those outside the company's own organization, but, with whom it deals or has dealt. Customers, vendors, competitors, and research scientists working for government or universities, as well as former employees, usually know an amazing amount about the points of strength of companies with which they have done business. More important, they know about the points of weakness as well. Any one or two of such informants may be highly prejudiced and misleading in what they have to say. However, if anyone who has had some practice in piecing together information in this way contacts enough such sources of information and makes clear to each what he wants to know and why, a surprisingly clear picture will emerge of the enterprise about which he is trying to learn.

Why is getting information in this seemingly round-about fashion so important? It is because only in this way can someone not connected with a corporate organization get a sufficiently well-rounded picture so as to know what information to seek when top management of the company being considered for investment is finally contacted. Such a top management may be most straightforward and may answer all questions with complete honesty. Yet of his own accord and unless he is asked, how can any high-ranking officer of such a company be expected to volunteer important data about his company's weak points? Would, for example, a corporate treasurer, in an interview with an investment man reveal unasked that the great sums the company was spending to maintain some brilliant research scientists were being largely wasted because the personal relationship between the director of research and the vice president of sales was so bad that these costly product development activities were largely being devoted toward producing quite ingenious products, but ones with such small potential markets that they could never be of much benefit to stockholders? Of course, important information of this sort would never come unsolicited. For one thing, the corporate treasurer would take no chance of becoming embroiled with one or both of his fellow officers. On the other hand, if the treasurer saw that the investment man already knew of the situation, he might, in answer to a direct question, use quite guarded language, but he would probably convey a rather accurate implication as to whether the report were true. He might also furnish the answer to an even more important set of questions about this matter. These questions would be: "Are steps being taken to correct this situation? If so, what are they?"

It is not only in regard to learning highly confidential data of major investment significance, such as this that "scuttlebutt" prior to contacting a management is of such basic importance. Nothing matters more in determining the long-range prospects of a company than the overall efficiency of its top management team. In most companies of a size sufficient to warrant investment interest, this may mean a group of as many as five or six key men. Only the occasional investment representative who as yet has no financial interest in a company but is merely investigating its possibilities will enjoy sufficient prestige with management so that arrangements will be made for his meeting all or even a majority of these key men. The one or two he does meet may be well above or well below the average calibre of the group. Unless he has already prepared himself with sufficient "scuttlebutt" about each member of the group, he can hardly help judging the efficiency and status of the whole management from his impression of the one or two executives he does meet. Miscalculations of this sort can be extremely costly when an attempt is being made to distinguish a magnificent investment from a run-of-the-mill one. In contrast, if sufficiently prepared by "scuttlebutt", an investment man who has heard numerous comments concerning a particular corporate officer being unusually able or comparably incompetent can specifically request meeting him. If he does so, he will have the tremendous advantage of knowing exactly what he is trying to verify or disprove.

It is for reasons such as these that this technique of first extracting much of the information available from those who deal or have dealt with a business—and only then contacting top officers of that business—yields such vastly better overall results. In no other way will most investment men be able to find the real weaknesses of many seemingly strong companies. To do all this admittedly takes time. However, the profits are so great for those who are able to invest an important part of the funds they manage in companies whose shares go up tremendously faster than the market as a whole that it should be obvious that the financial reward for time efficiently spent in this way is an unusually rich one.

If then this "scuttlebutt" method will do so much, does it represent the ultimate in the technique of successful investing under existing economic conditions? I believe it has a major element of weakness. In time (but I do not know how much time) this will be cured by a still more advanced technique. This technique will revolutionize the investment industry. In so doing, it will solve the problems of many investors who now seem unable to find where to go to seek investment help.

What is wrong with this "scuttlebutt" method, and why will something better eventually replace it? It is much too slow. One individual working alone may take months to get the minimum background information he should have. It is no simple matter to ferret out the individuals outside a particular company who will know the most about the strengths and weaknesses of that company. It is sometimes equally difficult to find good sources of introduction to all of these people so that they will give an investment man their timm and so that they will be sympathetic toward his inquiries. Geography also raises further problems. Many of those who are the best potential informants may not be in the investment man's home area. There then will occur the obvious difficulties of trying to cross-check with those who are far away additional bits of information as the inquiry develops. Furthermore, it generally is true that the greater the distance the more difficult will be the task of finding good sources of introduction to the desired informants.

Unfortunately, at the breathtaking speed of today's technological and financial developments, events will not always wait upon this leisurely course of investigation. All too often, while the necessary work is being done, others will have recognized the possibilities of the prospective investment. The stock under study therefore may have advanced to a point where its appeal is vastly less than when the study was started. Meanwhile, in a period when so much of the greatest investment possibilities are tied in to complex scientific advances, the investment man may have run up against technologies so complex that he becomes lost in a welter of highly technical claims and counter claims. He may find that he does not have the educational background to make intelligent decisions.

The complex techniques that have been laboriously but nevertheless successfully evolved in the research laboratories of our outstanding industrial corporations point the way to what in time will happen in developing improved techniques for selecting outstanding common stocks. No longer do many of our important inventions and new products result from a single genius working by himself. Rather, they come about by the teamwork of a group of people, each with a different scientific discipline and background. In modern industry, an important new product or process, for example, is much more likely to evolve from the combined labors of five men than of one. There might be a chemist, a physicist, an abstract mathematician, a production engineer, and even a biologist or a representative of the sales department. It is the cross fertilization of the ideas of each upon the others—the ability of the group to call on the special knowledge of each—that alone makes possible much progress in a world where many of the less complex advances have already been made.

However, it should not be forgotten that this type of cooperation does not come easily. Men of such diverse backgrounds are not likely to have entirely compatible temperaments. Their having similar outlooks and objectives are even more unlikely. Consequently, teamwork in the real sense of the word is not easy of accomplishment or always attained. Only the hard way, after repeated trial and error, is industry learning how to produce leadership that can blend diverse temperaments and educational backgrounds into teams that are productive of major practical accomplishments.

Now let us go back to the financial business. Today some of our largest and most successful investment bankers, brokers, and investment counsels have on their staffs real or supposed investment experts, each specializing in a particular industry or group of industries. These men are nearly always located in one city, usually the head office of the company for which they work or of which they are a partner or officer. Depending on such factors as their relative innate abilities and upon how much they use variations of the "scuttlebutt" method, they produce investment results that vary enormously one from another. Unfortunately, some of these "experts" still have a tendency to wander from management to management, depending mainly for their information on little more than what each company will volunteer about its own operations. However, all who appraise common stocks, from the most skillful to the least, are slowed down in their work to the degree that they cannot be traveling all the time. Furthermore, they have to do most of the work in their own specialty unaided by and unchecked by others.

Adroit management will in time accomplish teamwork in "investment research" comparable to what has been done in industrial research. A different and incredibly more efficient system will arise. No longer will there be, let us say, one electronic specialist based at a home office in New York who makes two trips a year "around the country." Instead there will be one such man in New York assigned to that area which might extend from New York State down through Western Pennsylvania and as far as Northern Virginia. His job will not be just confined to getting information about the electronic companies located in this particular region. Rather, it would be to gather all information available in this territory (this necessarily must include some knowledge of the strength and weakness of a company's competition) about whatever electronic company might be under study at the moment, regardless of where that company might be located. Similarly in New England, in California and in the other main centers of electronic activity, such as the Chicago-Milwaukee-Minneapolis area, there would be other members of the same team. If these were people of the right calibre, each would have developed in his own backyard enough friends, associates and contacts so that a vast amount of background data and opinion could be developed quickly through contacts that had already been established. Nor would there be any reason why members of such a group necessarily be limited to working merely in one industry. The amount of time saved each individual through being relieved of having to make extensive calls beyond his own geographic area would easily make it possible for these same people to cover a considerably broader field of industries within their own geographic region than many such experts do now.

The advantages of such a system would extend far beyond the obvious one of making it possible to do in days what now takes a corresponding number of months. Such a system would rely on cross-checking with customers, competitors, vendors, etc. beyond anything now practical with "scuttlebutt." With the number of investment people involved, the personal prejudices of any one of them would have correspondingly less chance of producing the wrong answer. In other words, it would not alone produce quicker answers and more of them. More importantly, it would also produce a bigger percentage of right answers. In the investment business, it is only the right answer that pays off. All others are a drain on the profits the right answers produce.

However, if such a method has tremendous potentialities in theory, getting worthwhile results from it would produce correspondingly great difficulties in practice. The number of highly competent people in this field is not great. It might be difficult to get enough of them together to set up a balanced organization. Only trial and error would reveal all the pitfalls that could then occur. For example, one member of the group might have such prestige and be so respected by his associates that, with no one planning it that way, his views would generally dominate. Yet under such a system, his judgments might not be nearly as good as under present-day methods. This is because he no longer would be having the personal contacts with all the managements on which he was passing judgment. Many such companies would be located beyond his own district. In time, I believe this type of problem will be solved and the investment business will develop a technique for furnishing its clients with the right recommendations for buying, holding, and selling common stocks with an efficiency undreamed of now. However, so much in the way of proper coordination will have to be learned in the early stages of such a development that, at first, it is entirely probable that such a system, in addition to being far more expensive than today's methods in its total payroll costs, might in its preliminary period produce rather disappointing results.

At this point, the parallel between what lies ahead in the investment business and what has already happened in the field of industrial research is very close. Modern research laboratories are vastly more costly for their corporate backers than the older method of brilliant individual investors working by themselves. Furthermore, just assembling groups of research experts with highly divergent skills does not assure eventual financial success. It only assures heavy immediate expenses. But the history of many of our most successful corporations shows that under skillful guidance these tremendously costly modern research outlays can be an engine for producing an ever-increasing stream of profits beyond the wildest dreams of a former generation of individual inventors. The transition did not come overnight. First two or a very few people of divergent skills and trainings started working together until gradually the technique of modern industrial research developed. Similarly, the switch in the investment business from the present-day lone expert wandering all over the country to teams— each with its friends, contacts, and major sources of information in each principal geographic area—will not come at one given moment. A few able people working in different areas on the same problem (not just comparing notes after their individual work is finished) will begin to get the right investment answers so much quicker and get so many more of them than those using existing methods, that, in time, competition will surplant present ways of arriving at investment decisions.

What in time will happen in the investment business will closely compare with what is now happening and will continue to happen in the air freight business. The all-cargo jet planes that will become familiar in the 1962 to 1964 period will be much more expensive to buy and will cost far more for each hour the plane is in the air than the old DC-4's. However, they will be able to carry a great deal more freight. Because of their greater speed, they will make many more round trips each week. Therefore, they will be able to move each pound of freight at a cost per ton-mile vastly lower than that of the DC-4. This in turn will make possible the moving of vast tonnages by air that would never have used air transport under the rate structure of the DC-4. It will open up major sources of growth and new business for those with the huge amounts of capital and the complex organization needed to handle these new jets. Similarly, giving proper service to clients under the methods that in time will develop will probably be so costly that only the larger firms now in the business or some of the smaller ones working together will have the capital to compete. Yet the job done will be so much more efficient that the cost per satisfied client will be as much under today's wasteful and inexact methods as will be the airfreight costs of 1964 to those of 1958. As more and more people find it relatively simple to get investment advice from those who really know enough about the inside workings of the companies whose stocks they recommend so as seldom to be wrong about them, the total number of investors and the amounts they place in common stocks will grow spectacularly. I do not believe it possible to encounter the number of people from every section of the country who keep telling me of their inability to get truly informed investment advice and reach any other conclusion.

A better understanding of why so many of today's investors are having so much trouble finding where to turn for proper investment advice can be obtained by observing the hodge-podge of illogical and overlapping ways in which the investment business has grown. An even better understanding is available if we go one step further and examine how most of these major subdivisions of this business, in actual practice, act quite differently from the way they might be expected to in theory. In making such a study, we should keep certain basic concepts constantly in mind. These are:

(1) That the one thing and the only thing almost all investors want from any subdivision of the investment business with which they deal

is correct advice on what investments to buy, which ones to hold, and which ones to sell.

(2) That almost anyone in the investment business that gives preponderantly good advice of this sort will find that his business will grow and grow and grow. Conversely, those whose advice is generally poor will not have a growing business. They will usually be constantly on the ragged edge of trouble because they will steadily be forced to exert major selling effort in an attempt to acquire new clients to replace those they are always losing.

(3) That the one sure way of giving investment advice that will be preponderantly to the benefit of those seeking it is to know all of the major facts about any common stock being recommended for purchase or retention. Even more to the point, if this advice is to be outstandingly profitable to those following it, it is necessary to know of important changes for the better or the worse that may be affecting these companies, before these facts are generally known to most of the financial community and certainly before they get reflected in current earning statements.

There are at present roughly four major subdivisions to this tremendously important industry of taking care of that part of the nation's savings devoted to common-stock ownership. These might be termed investment bankers, stock brokers, investment trusts, and investment counsel. As will be seen presently, the lines between them are anything but clear cut. However, let us attempt to see how each, in theory and in practice, measures up to these three basic concepts of investment performance vital to the best interests of both the client investor and the investment firm with which he deals.

First, let us take the investment counsel. In theory at least, here is a group that should measure up well in regard to these three basic concepts. Their sole function, the basis on which they get compensated, is to act in the interest of the investor client. They do not have a vested interest in recommending the purchase of a few securities they already own, as does the investment banker. They do not have a vested interest in the amount of buying or selling done, as does the broker with his dependency on commissions. Why are there so many investors who seem to have so much difficulty finding a satisfactory investment counsel?

Actually, there are around the country various investment counsel (some are called professional trustees) who are doing an excellent job in measuring up to these three fundamental concepts. As in any other large group, there are some who are not, primarily because of personal incompetence. These are people who never should have been in this field in the first place. However, I think there is a third and extremely important group whose work fails to measure up to what it might be and to what I believe investors should have a right to expect, largely because of their work methods and possibly their size. Many investment counsel are relatively small firms. If the working hours of their personnel (exclusive of purely clerical personnel) were analyzed, I think it would be rather revealing. A breakdown might be made of the number of hours each week spent in four different categories. These might be termed (1) Seeing clients or prospective clients, talking to them on the telephone, or analyzing clients' individual investment lists; (2) Reading publicly available corporate financial statements, financial periodicals, or attending formal meetings of societies of security analysis. In all of these instances not only is the same information available to the entire financial community but most of it is highly slanted in favor of the corporation which is providing the news source. Unfavorable aspects of a company's affairs are usually toned down or completely omitted; (3) Interviews or telephone conversations with corporate officials about their own company's affairs, and (4) Seeing or talking to informed people about matters of investment significance in companies other than their own but with which they are familiar.

All too many investment counsel seem to spend the bulk of their time on matters in the first category, with steadily decreasing amounts in the second as compared to the first, the third as compared to the second and, particularly, the fourth as compared to the third. Yet over 30 years of experience in the investment business has convinced me again and again and again that it is only the time spent in the third category, reinforced by a great deal of time in the fourth (particularly in the early stages of investigating and buying into a company) that can produce an impressive batting average of highly profitable investment decisions. By bunching their clients' holdings in a few properly chosen companies, investment counsel are in a uniquely favorable position to win the loyalty of the management of such companies and, thereby, to keep themselves well informed from that time on.

Now let us turn to the largest segments of the investment business: the stock broker and the investment banker. I take the two together because, while historically they started as completely different entities, there are few, if any, investment banking firms today (at least in the field of common stocks, which is all that concerns us here) who are not also stock brokers. There are some brokers who never act as investment bankers but most will take investment banking positions or at least participate in selling groups when they see a profitable opportunity to do so.

For those of you who may not be familiar with these terms, this might be a place to pause for a few definitions. An investment banker is a merchant of securities he already owns, just as a wholesale or retail bakery sells dough products belonging to it. A company may desire to raise money through selling additional shares of stock, or a large stockholder may desire to dispose of part or all of his holdings as a block. The investor banker will pay the company or individual cash for these shares, and then will attempt to wholesale or retail them. If they go up while he is doing this, he makes that much extra profit. If they go down he has that much less profit or a loss. In any event, until he sells them, like any other merchant he is running the risks of changing value of his inventory.

A stock broker, in contrast, is purely the agent of the buyer or seller, as the case may be. He gets an order to buy or sell. On an exchange, for listed securities, or in the "over-the-counter" market, for others, he matches this order at the best price he can get against someone else who is offering the shares he wants to buy or bidding for those he is trying to sell. Since he is purely an agent, he has neither the capital costs nor the risks of the investment banker who carries his own inventory. At least in theory, he does not have to compensate a salesman who will retail this inventory. Therefore, a stock broker's commission is quite small in relation to the total value of the purchase. For example, the New York Stock Exchange commission for buying 100 shares of a stock selling at 50 is $44, or less than nine tenths of one per cent of the principal involved. In contrast, for a listed stock, an investment banker might legitimately charge two and a half to three times this much as his "spread" for handling a block of the same shares. For the stock of a company first being introduced to the financial community, he might charge as much as from 5 to 15 per cent.

Of course in a new issue of this type, his charges must cover the various heavy legal expenses he incurs in regard to Securities and Exchange Commission (SEC) registration, as well as compensation for the risk that he may not get the expected price for a heretofore unknown security.

I have already pointed out the investor's theoretical disadvantage in dealing with an investment banker or stock broker, rather than with an investment counsel. The investment banker is a merchant trying to sell his wares, so it does not seem logical that he can give as disinterested or as good advice as would the buyer's own agent. The stockbroker makes his money on action, that is, on buying and selling. Therefore, it would seem there would be constant pressure to trade in and out, whereas it is the heart of successful investment to stay with an unusual stock for many years, if not a lifetime. More money has been lost by stockholders' selling an outstanding stock on a small profit instead of holding it 25 years and obtaining, say, a 3,000 per cent gain, than from all other foolish investment actions combined. For reasons such as this, it would look, at least in theory, as though the investor wanting advice, help, or management should stay away from investment bankers, stock brokers or, as is so often found, the combination of the two in the same firm.

In practice, it does not always work out this way. This is because many of these firms, particularly the larger ones, have some advantages that may offset these disadvantages. There is a quite close relationship between most of our larger corporations and a particular investment banking firm in exactly the same way there is between these same companies and a commercial bank. In other words, when they need more permanent capital, they look to one particular investment banker to raise it for them through the sale of securities, just as when they need temporary capital they do not go to just any bank for a loan but to the particular bank to which they are close and which understands their affairs. Because there is a close and continuing relationship between so many major companies and one or another investment banking firm, many of the larger investment banking houses have a great deal of knowledge about a particular group of companies. Frequently they have a partner on the board of directors. This type of contact can produce investment recommendations that can be of real value. Similarly, many of the larger stock brokers—entirely aside from when they are acting as investment bankers—have enough of their clients' money or the money of their own wealthy partners in a particular company, so they, too, may have much this same type of inside knowledge. Many stock brokerage houses also hold some significant directorships among the partners or officers.

Meanwhile, this matter of the significance of the vested interest of the investment banker in peddling his own merchandise or of the broker in recommending needless transactions for the sake of the immediate commission involved may vary tremendously between one financial house and another. It varies even more between different individuals within the same firm. There are many in the financial business who have not lost sight of one of the three basic concepts with which this discussion started. This is that if they perform well for those who came to them for financial advice, their business will grow. Otherwise it will not. These people—who may be just as eager to boost their own earning power as their more short-sighted co-workers—will give far greater weight to whether a particular move seems to be to the client's genuine interest than they will to whether there is either an immediate commission or an extra large commission in it for themselves. They do so not because they are unmercenary, but because they have enough long-range judgment to know that to be most successful themselves they must do well for those they advise. They know that only time will produce a scoreboard of their work which largely governs how much or little business they will be doing some years hence.

All of this means that from the investor's standpoint, under present-day conditions, finding the right investment man upon whom to depend is not primarily a matter of whether his adviser's firm be investment counsel, stock brokers, or investment bankers. Actually, so scrambled have the lines become between these once quite different activities that some of the largest financial houses are now performing all three functions. Because certain investment bankers who also hold memberships on the major exchanges have valuable pipelines for obtaining significant investment information from these older activities and have supplemented such sources of basic investment data by establishing a sizable group of security analysts to obtain more data, they have set up their own investment counseling service along with their other activities.

This type of development is entirely logical and, I believe, points the direction toward which the financial business must go. The stock broker's business has changed radically in the last 30 or 40 years. Prior to World War I, most stock purchases were made by wealthy individuals for speculation, that is, in large lots to sell to someone else for a quick profit. In those days, the broker was largely an order taker. Any advisory function he might render was largely in the way of passing on rumors, tips, and individual pieces of inside information that might be colorful enough to provide one sharp move in the affected stock. Providing the background of thorough knowledge and close contact with the management necessary to obtain the tremendously greater profits of major long-range growth was well beyond the broker's functions or the interests of most of his customers. In those days, a stock broker really acted as a broker in that speed in filling an order, secrecy, and nimbleness in executing it were all of major importance in filling his customer's needs.

Today, the average customer is a long-range investor of moderate means. He is buying in amounts of one to 500 shares rather than one to ten thousand. He cares not an iota whether one broker can rush the order to the floor of the stock exchange 30 seconds faster or slower than another. What he wants is someone who has enough knowledge of what he is doing so that he can get dependable advice on what to buy, how long to hold it, and when, if ever, to sell it. For the growing number of people who desire to do this on a long-range, not short-range, basis, this is essentially the investment counsel's function. This is why so many stock brokers, consciously or unconsciously recognizing that the nature of their business has changed, are to varying degrees attempting to perform as investment counsel. Some charge an extra fee for this, others do not. In either case, they are recognizing something basic. This is that under today's conditions what most investors want is competent investment counseling service, and the man who will get the business is the one who can perform this service best regardless of what he calls himself, or even if he be a salesman peddling stocks in the inventory of his own firm. What matters is how well such stocks are chosen and whether the adviser is competent to keep following them and thoroughly to know about them after they are so chosen.

At this point, those of you who have not been able to find an investment adviser to your satisfaction (and I am constantly being reminded your number is not small) may agree with everything I have said but feel an utter sense of frustration. You may admit it can be helpful to know where the financial business is trending, and how some years from now the problems of people such as yourselves may be solved. However, your real interest is right now. Your problem will not wait for some indefinite time in the future. You might well say, "All I have learned from these many words is that whether an investment man call himself an investment counselor, a stock broker, or an investment banker has nothing to do with whether or not he is someone I can depend on for sound investment advice. This is all negative. What I want is to find not what does not matter but what does. How does all this help me?"

Five Steps for Selecting the Right Investment Counselor

To answer this, I am about to state five specific steps which an investor might take in attempting to select a competent source of investment advice. However, first I purposely went "the long way round." I believe the reason for this will now become apparent. For example, by explaining the three successive stages through which the technique of selecting outstanding stock investments has progressed in the past and by showing the fourth stage that will come in the future, I have tried to provide a background that will enable an investor better to understand how to take some of these steps for himself.

The five specific steps that might be taken by an investor seeking to find someone in the investment business upon whom he can genuinely depend are:

Step 1. Divide all investment men who are being seriously considered as a source of investment advice into two classes. Those who are fundamentally more interested that a particular transaction be to your long-range benefit than they are in the fee, commission, or profit they will make from that transaction, and those for whom making this fee, right now, is the larger part of the motive behind the specific move they are proposing. Eliminate at once anyone who does not clearly fall in the former group. How can one determine this? Those who are good judges of human nature can probably determine this pretty well from preliminary conversations and certainly after observing how and why a few transactions are proposed. Others may have to fall back on what they can learn about this from those who can be contacted that are already being served by this same man, that may know him socially, or that may know him through also being in the investment business.

Step 2. Ask any prospective financial adviser about his basic investment philosophy, that is, what he is going to try to do for you and how he proposes to go about it. Eliminate anyone whose long-range objectives are different from your own. As my *Common Stocks and Uncommon Profits* is essentially little more than a summary of my own philosophy of proper investment and the one which I believe is most desirable for most (though not necessarily all) common-stock investors, there is no point in repeating all of that here. However, I should say again what I said in that book: While I believe this to be the most desirable way to profit from common stocks, it is not the only way that has been successful or that will be. What is important is not that the investment man you select agree with my long-range goals and methods for attaining them, but that he has definite ones of his own and, most important of all, that they agree with yours.

Step 3. Ask for specific details of how the man you are considering or the organization behind him gets the data he uses as the basis for making his investment recommendations. Find out what he or his organization is doing to keep in touch with what is going on inside the companies whose stocks he recommends you to buy, not just now, but after you have bought them, and while you are holding them. See how carefully he or his associates watch the management factor rather than depend largely upon published financial statements after such statements (which are results, not causes) are available to the entire financial community. Remember it is knowing important facts before they are known to the financial community as a whole that is the greatest source of important profits or the avoidance of important loss. Never forget that a brilliant investment mind acting upon meager and inadequate knowledge will produce results far inferior to an ordinary but reasonably competent investment man who has full knowledge of the significant facts about a company at a time when most others do not. This is why the nature of the sources of information is so important. This is why it is so vital that what I have called "scuttlebutt" be used, except only when an investment man is so unusually close to the management of a company that he can depend upon it for a completely balanced picture of favorable and unfavorable developments—something that usually only develops after years of close association. Otherwise, while the facts an investment man learns from a company management may, of themselves, all be accurate, he has no way of determining if there may not also be other matters that counterbalance or more than counterbalance them. It is why one extremely large and highly successful investor recently told me he had stopped a number of so-called "security analysts" from calling on him. He said, "These men just go from company to company and repeat to me what the managements, to which they are not particularly close, tell them. I have found such unbalanced stories can be quite dangerous."

In this all-important matter of checking a prospective investment adviser's sources of data, do not confuse quantity for quality. I am reminded of a rather amusing incident that occurred in my own office about a year ago. A representative of a sizable stock-broker investment-banking firm from another section of the country called upon me. He told me of the amazingly large number of security analysts his firm employed and of the number of extremely worthwhile special reports they made. I assured him that should they provide me with any ideas I could use he would not go unrewarded in regard to brokerage business. He offered to leave me some of their reports: Only one was of a company about which I have rather thorough information. I selected this report and a few others each written by a different so-called specialist. I was totally unimpressed with the one on the company I already knew. It told about what anyone might know who occasionally called on the management and had a rather superficial knowledge of that company's affairs. I then took another of these reports, one on a company of which I have little knowledge, and asked a friend in that company what he thought of it. He showed it to several of the company's top officers. All agreed with him that it showed just about the degree of knowledge of the company that an outsider might have attained who had made a casual study of it and nothing more. It did not go beneath this surface at all. I decided I did not want to get involved with anyone in the investment business that seemed to be doing this sort of superficial work. At the risk of seeming rude, I decided it would waste the least amount of everyone's time if I told the representative just this on his next call. Nevertheless, because I did not want to hurt the feelings of someone whom I had judged to be genuinely sincere, I was a little apprehensive when this man returned. After expressing my thoughts as tactfully as I could, I was astonished to see him grin from ear to ear. He told me that he had reached identically the same conclusion concerning the firm he was with, saw no future with those who supported their contact men with hack work, had already resigned, and had called on me not to do business but to ask my opinion as to an outstanding investment group to which he might apply for a job!

In short, when talking to a prospective investment man, be concerned by the quality of the work available to him, not its quantity. You may not know enough about any company to be able to judge the quality of one of his reports for yourself, but you may (as I did) have a friend high enough up in such a company to do this or get it done for you.

Step 4. If you already own a group of securities, see whether a prospective investment adviser has equally positive opinions about whether you should sell or hold each of them. No one can have access to such an endless amount of real background data that he can be an expert on all the stocks listed on the various exchanges or commonly traded over the counter. Therefore, when confronted with a list of stocks not previously bought at his suggestion, an honest investment man frequently has a tough problem. He can leave his new client in stocks which have a good reputation but about which he is not adequately informed. On the other hand, he can be frank with his client, tell him that he can only be responsible for investments he really knows and leave it up to the client whether he wants to switch the stock about which neither of them has adequate knowledge (and which may nevertheless be an excellent investment) into something which may be no better but which the investment man is in a position to watch intelligently. Usually the investment man who is most frank about what he does not know is the one who has thorough knowledge about something else. The man who in the investment field pretends to know everything about everything is the one who can be quite dangerous. Similarly, never expect an investment man to be qualified to pass an opinion on all possible common-stock purchases. The most casual awareness of how much knowledge is needed to warrant a buying recommendation for the stock of a single company should make the reasons for this obvious.

Step 5. Learn what you can of the record of any investment man under consideration. Eliminate those whose performance appears to have been poor in relation to the action of the general market for the period under study. In this connection, keep in mind that some of the most spectacularly successful common stock investments may take as long as several years before they commence to prove themselves in the market. Therefore ignore, one way or the other, any record of performance that is of less than three years' duration. Also, do not ask a prospective candidate for handling your investments to give you references in this connection unless you know him quite well. It is inevitable that he will do better for some people than others. It is only human nature that he will refer you to some for whom he has done particularly well. However, if you can find people whom he has served over the years, what they have to tell you may be extremely illuminating. Then, if the record is not good but otherwise you are impressed with both the man you are considering and the investment house behind him, go into the matter a little further. Sometimes an investment man's record will appear poor, primarily because the client partly follows rather than fully follows his advice. Thus, some investors commit the major financial folly of being unable to resist taking small profits. Against all advice, they grab a few points' gain and are sold out of a brilliant investment long before it triples or quadruples. Hence, they have no large gains to far outbalance the occasional loss that is inevitable with any common stock adviser. To blame an investment man for this, when it is done against his advice, is of course ridiculous.

Is it more important to learn something of the record of the particular broker or salesman, or of the firm with which he is connected? This depends. Some investment firms keep the closest control on what they allow their people to recommend. I believe more and more will follow this policy as time goes on. In contrast, others take great pride in exposing their people to all sorts of information but leave it up to each as to what he will do with such data once he has it. In the former cases, it is the record of the firm which is significant and in the latter, the individual's. In most cases, if you ask outright, I believe you will be told with complete frankness which policy is being followed.

Although I have listed this matter of "checking the record" as the fifth and final step in selecting an investment adviser, I perhaps should have listed it as Step 1. I did not do so because I wanted particularly to emphasize the matter of immediately eliminating anyone so short-sighted as to be more interested in the commission he will make from you right now than in whether you will significantly benefit from what he suggests. However, it is entirely logical that your first step in selecting a competent investment man is to find out from friends as to who, or what firm, has served them well for a long enough time to be of significance. Those that show up well from such an investigation would be logical candidates to consider further. In this sense perhaps what I have listed as Step 5 should be considered as Step 1.

There is a more serious charge that might well be raised against the course of action I have suggested for those who do not know where to turn for investment help. There are many among leading investment counsel firms, stock brokers, and investment bankers who could pass these tests with flying colors. However, the matters on which I suggest you focus your attention give a distinct advantage to the larger investment counsel firms, the big brokerage houses, and the giant investment bankers. They are the ones more likely to have the personnel, the memberships on key boards of directors, and the channels of investment information of greatest value to the investor. Is there no place in the investment picture for the small local firm with only a small personnel?

This is a charge to which I am personally rather sensitive because I have strong feelings about the importance to our nation of protecting small enterprises from big ones, whenever the social and economic costs of so doing are not prohibitively high. I have endeavored to follow this policy in practice and not just be philosophic about it. For example, it is my normal custom to go considerably out of my way to purchase from small independent merchants who know me as an individual and will try to take care of me if sometime I may need their services, rather than buy the same article at the same price from some giant chain or department store group. On the other hand, in other fields there is another side to this matter. Many years ago, I paid for a small part of my college expenses by selling wholesale groceries in my spare time to quite small, independent grocers. The supplanting of some of these rather high-priced and quite unsanitary food outlets in the economically poorer districts by clean, low-priced chain stores is not an unmixed evil. I believe that whether the small is entitled to survive against the large should be judged individually in each situation.

In regard to stock brokers, investment counsel, etc., I think the overriding or most fundamental consideration is obviously this: What system will produce the greatest profits and smallest losses for the investor-customer? So great are the social evils and the individual problems when the savings of the individual get lost or diminished through incompetence or lack of knowledge, that any other basic standard is unthinkable. Under today's conditions, the larger investment firm, *if properly organized*, probably has a slight competitive edge because it can afford more specialists to investigate and keep track of investments, has more contacts with top corporate management, etc. However, in my opinion, so great are the variations in skill and efficiency between different organizations in the investment business, and so small the present advantage of the large firm that, today, many small stock brokers and investment counsel are still doing a much better job than some of their larger competitors.

When the art of appraising common stocks develops into its next stage of considerably greater cost and vastly greater efficiency of common-stock analysis, the advantage of the well-managed large firm, of course, becomes considerably greater. Sizable numbers of mergers and acquisitions will come about in all phases of the investment business just as economic necessity has produced them in so many other lines. Even then, however, there is no reason the small investment firm need be doomed—provided it uses ingenuity combined with good judgment in choosing associates from other areas. Then, as today, there will be nothing preventing such a firm from selecting a larger organization not located in its own area and becoming affiliated with it in a subscriber or some other relationship. There will be nothing to prevent a number of smaller, geographically diversified, and independent financial houses cooperating to give the clients of each good investment service. The basic fact that in selecting common stocks—

two recommendations that later prove to have been outstanding is far more desirable than ten pretty good ones—is another factor limiting the advantage that the larger investment house would normally have.

Rather than the small investment house, the one that will have trouble as the 1960's progress is the one whose members are "too busy" to take the time needed for the proper investigation of the common stocks they recommend. All too often, you hear the comment "We just do not have the time to check a company any further than asking one of its officers about it." In the generally rising markets of the 1950's, such methods were good enough frequently to "get by." But the very extent of the rise of most stocks in the 1950's makes the 1960's a period where a considerably greater order of diligence and skill will be needed if the same sort of pleasing results are to be accomplished. The investment man or investment house that is "too busy" to do all that is necessary to take proper care of the investor may find itself in the investment climate of the 1960's in about the same position as the farmer who planted the same crop year after year and was "too busy" to fertilize his fields.

Perhaps you have noticed what may seem like an oversight in these comments. I mentioned there were today four main subdivisions of the investment industry, each trying to serve the needs of the investor. I have discussed the investment counsel, the stock broker, and the investment banker. Up to this point, I have said nothing about the group that in the 1950's had by far the greatest growth of all. These of course are the investment trust.

I purposely reserved comment on this group to the last. This is because I believe whether they grow or shrink in investment importance depends much less on their own actions than the degree by which, if at all, the other investment industry groups improve their own standards of performance to take care of the needs of investors. With their great emphasis on diversification, most investment trusts, as I have already pointed out in another section of this book, have an enormous built-in bias toward average results. In a period such as the 1950's when many investors felt frustrated in their effort to get through other channels, the type of investment advice they wanted—this diversification, with its seeming promise of above average safety—had great appeal. If in the 1960's many common-stock investors continue to be unsure of where they can go to find advisers who thoroughly know about the stocks they recommend, the tendency of the investment trusts to produce a "somewhat around average" result will continue to have great appeal. On the other hand, when other groups in the investment industry develop techniques for upgrading the quality of investment service, this great diversification with its tendency to provide only average results will have considerably less appeal. In short, I believe the great growth of the investment-trusts is partly an indication of lack of confidence upon the part of many investors in their ability to find high-grade investment service elsewhere. If that feeling changes, one of the big markets for investment trust shares may disappear.

However, I think there is another reason why investment trusts have had this great growth in the past ten years. The bulk of this growth has been in mutual funds. These mutuals normally charge the buyer enough of a "spread" over the liquidating value of the trust to make possible the payment of a big enough commission to the salesmen to in turn make it worth his while to sell the mutual shares in rather small amounts. Spurred on by the economic possibility of selling their shares to those of modest means, the investment trust people have done a magnificent merchandising job. Taking a leaf from the phenomenally successful history of the life insurance industry, the investment-trust salesmen have gone among economic groups that had never before been significant stock buyers. Like the life insurance people before them, they have attained a magnificent volume of business in this way.

The other branches of the investment business have not been able to take comparable advantage of this selling technique. The salesmen for the investment banker (or the over-the-counter security house where the spread between "bid" and "ask" permits of a greater sales commission) have come closest to doing so. However, the activities of this group do not lend themselves to transactions of less than a few thousand dollars each, nor have they generally been provided with the mechanism to enable customers to buy on the installment plan. In contrast, the stock brokers, through devices such as the New York Stock Exchange monthly purchase plan, do provide a means for small investors to pay for common stocks from each month's savings. However, as already explained, the normal stock broker's commission is such a tiny per cent of the amount invested that there is not enough margin to permit brokers' representatives to go out and take the time to sell the small customer in the way the investment trust representative can do. Finally, most investment counsel charge a fee of only about 1/2 of 1 per cent per annum of the principal placed in their charge. Many of them feel that $100 thousand of assets is the very minimum for any single account, if they are to be in any way compensated for their effort. So they, too, have not extensively tapped this mass market.

Why are these brokerage and investment counsel fees so small? I believe primarily because enough of the advisory work produced has been of such poor grade that the average investor is hesitant to pay more. But suppose the investor becomes convinced there is real quality to the work. While my own experience may not be typical since I do not serve the general public, I have found that once the investor feels rather sure he is getting results there is no reluctance whatsoever to paying much higher fees. Why should there be? If over a long series of years an individual or an organization has rather consistently produced results 50 per cent better or 100 per cent better or 150 per cent better than, say, any of the recognized market averages, why should any investor object to paying a fee that could run many times the current standard investment counsel or brokerage fees and still be but a quite minor fraction of the results obtained?

If I am right that as the years go on it will cost the financial house far more immediate cash outlay to get the basic data properly to handle the investor's common-stock holdings, but that there will be even greater improvement in the quality of the job done, it seems entirely logical that there will be a sizable increase in the fees charged for doing it. I believe the relatively recent trend of certain key investment-banker stock brokers to charge investment counsel fees superimposed on their regular brokerage charges is the forerunner of what will develop on a larger and larger scale. Provided (and this provision is basic) that the quality of the service is good enough to warrant the charge, I believe this trend is greatly to the best interests of all concerned. As the trend develops, it should reach a point where the fee is big enough to warrant salesmen going out and attempting to sell quite small stockholders on the merits of their services. If this happens and the general public becomes genuinely convinced of the worth of the investment service—something unlikely to happen for long unless the service intrinsically deserves this appraisal—it might provide major competition for investment trusts in one of the places where they are now the strongest. It might also provide a tremendous increase in volume for the security business as a whole. In so doing, it would also increase the overall demand for common stocks.

To the investor who may again feel I have spent overmuch time on what will happen in the future, whereas his immediate interest is right now, I would point out that there is one major matter concerning him right now that he can learn from all this. This is that there is over a span of, say, five years, such tremendous differences between the market action of one stock and another that, if an investor can be sure of able guidance in his affairs, whether he pays a small fee, a larger fee, or a still larger fee for this guidance becomes of litle comparative importance. Proving this is just a matter of simple arithmatic. But how can the investor be reasonably sure of the quality of the work involved? To help on this matter, I have included the five steps we have already discussed for selecting the right investment man. Beyond this I can only say that in today's specialized world, one of the key measures of success, sometimes even of survival, is being able to pick the right expert in a field in which we are not expert ourselves. Nothing may be more important to the very existence of a loved one than selecting the right doctor. How do those untrained in medicine select him, or, for that matter, the right lawyer, the right architect, or the right plumber? I am afraid some of us will always use less care or be less shrewd in making what may prove key decisions along these lines than others. Some will always take the so-called specialist who happens to be nearest at hand and then wonder later why he always seems to be less "fortunate" than his neighbor.

Because I have heard it so often, I know the reaction some of you will have to these thoughts. Of course, you will say, I am ready to pay a higher fee for top-notch investment work. I can readily see how that will pay me. But I just do not have the time to investigate a lot of possible investment experts so as to select the right one.

Actually, in today's investment world (a few years from now this may be quite different) paying a higher fee or even an investment counsel fee at all is no safe insurance of a higher quality of work performed. My observations lead me to guess there is surprisingly little correlation in many places between the fees charged and the average long-term results being attained.

However, for those who do not now have investment connections to their satisfaction and who claim they do not have the time to make a thorough search for a suitable one, let me say this—There are very few things in this world for which we cannot find the time if we believe those things are important enough to us. If you doubt the importance of this one, make the following simple test: Put an alphabetical list of the stocks listed on the New York Stock Exchange before you. The simplest way to do this is to turn to the page in any large metropolitan newspaper furnishing the latest stock exchange quotations. Put a pencil in your hand. Next, in the manner of children playing "pin the tail on the donkey," close your eyes and bring the pencil down to *any* point on the page. Let this selection be a purely random one. Then, eliminating all preferred or preference stocks, take the next 20 common stocks in alphabetical order from that point on. After allowing for stock dividends, split-ups, etc. (most stock brokers would be willing to make this computation for you if you find it too difficult to do for yourself) notice the price at which each of the 20 common stocks sold five years ago in relation to where each is today. In an average year, you will then see the most astounding variations. Some will be down to about half their price of five years ago. Most will be up or down 20 to 40 per cent. However, a few may have doubled or quadrupled and one or two may well be up a thousand per cent or more! This amazingly large variation between the course of one stock and another was recently expressed in a different way when it was pointed out that while the average level of the Dow Jones averages in 1959 was about three times that of 1946, about one third of all stocks listed on the New York Stock Exchange in 1946 were selling at a lower price in 1959 than they were then.

In short, depending on which common stocks you buy and hold, five to ten years can bring about increases or shrinkages in their value vastly greater than that of the market as a whole. Under such circumstances, can anyone afford to hold common stocks at all if he does not take the time either properly to handle them himself or to find someone who can? Just how valuable does any investor consider his time to be, if he is "too busy" to learn the basic principles of investments and the investment industry when stakes such as these are involved? Only in this way can he help himself to find the right investment connections if he is not yet fortunate enough to have them. Just because some years from now it may be considerably easier to get outstanding investment advice than it is today is certainly no reason for not making all the greater effort to take advantage of the best of the facilities now available.

4

Trivia but not Entirely

IN THE FINAL ANALYSIS, even the most successful common stock investing consists essentially of three things, and three things only. These are: (1) Choosing one or more stocks to buy that in the future will rise far more than the market as a whole, (2) Knowing approximately when to do such buying and (3) Knowing when, if ever, to sell. However, to do this properly requires a great amount of background knowledge concerning the affairs of the company or companies in which investment may be made. It also requires some knowledge of what, in another section of this book, I have called the investment community's momentary psychological attitude toward the particular class of stock being considered for purchase. None of this vital background material is normally attained without the successful investor or his investment adviser acquiring some skill in knowing what to look for and spending a great deal of time looking for it.

As though this were not enough, there are a number of other matters of some, but considerably less, investment significance which are frequently being presented to investors for their consideration. I believe too much time and thought spent on such considerations is harmful chiefly because it tends to detract from giving as much consideration as might otherwise occur to the investment factors that matter far more. On certain of these subjects there is a quite considerable amount of confusion upon the part of a large number of investors.

In this section of this book, I am attempting to discuss several of these matters of varying degrees of investment significance, but regarding all of which this general confusion is rather extensive. One of the most important of these subjects is the investment significance of mergers.

WHAT ABOUT MERGERS?

I have attempted to emphasize again and again that the investor desiring to obtain major profits over a period of years can best do so by investing solely in companies which give strong indications that their earnings will grow far faster than those of American business as a whole. It also has been pointed out that a steady upward trend in a company's sales is an essential background condition for this. It is not the only essential background condition, since a growth in sales without a corresponding increase in per-share earnings is of no use to the investor whatsoever. Without such a sharp upward sales trend, stockholders occasionally enjoy a short-term benefit from a one-time major jump in profits due to a management finding ways to increase efficiency markedly. Within a relatively few years, however, the limits of what can be done in this way will largely be attained. Consequently, the type of investment bonanza that results from per-share profits spiraling decade after decade, both calls for and grows out of corresponding increases in sales. For this reason, a major and consistent upward sales trend is often regarded as the first clue to an unusually attractive investment.

Nothing will cause a company's sales to increase more quickly or more spectacularly than the acquisition of one or more operating units. Furthermore, such acquisitions are usually accompanied by optimistic reports, that are at times well founded in fact, of how putting these growing companies together will decrease the operating costs (thereby increasing the profit margin) of each of them. One such way that is possible, though not very likely, is that the acquired operation can be run by the top management of the acquiring unit without that top management having to be expanded to take care of these additional duties. This would result in a lower management cost for all concerned and could expand profit margins. Another possible savings that looks nice in theory but only occasionally occurs in practice is that manufacturing costs can be lowered by combining production facilities. This would thereby reduce the burden of manufacturing overhead. Far more often, worthwhile savings in mergers materialize from hoped-for economies in sales and distribution costs. Frequently, a small company finds it a major burden to support a sales force adequate to cover its potential market merely to sell a small product line. If a larger company is already selling a number of other products to the same customers, it can handle this additional line, too, at almost no extra cost. Of course, if the larger company is selling to a different set of customers, this type of expected savings is not so likely to materialize.

Another way in which a merger can produce great benefits does not come from this type of immediate savings in cost, be they in general overhead, in production, or in sales. Instead, it comes from the general improvement in the entire operation that occurs when a highly efficient management takes over a company that has heretofore not been nearly so well run. Over a period of several years, enough ways can often be found to increase the profit margin of the acquired concern so as to build up its total profits to a point that will make a magnificent return on the original investment. At times, sales of the acquired concern can be increased importantly as well. Some of the most worthwhile of all acquisitions have been cases where even before the merger, the research or engineering department of the dominant organization has figured out a way radically to redesign one or more major products of the acquired concern so as spectacularly to broaden the available market.

Important savings at times also come from purely financial benefits. A large acquiring company may have a credit rating sufficient to enable it to borrow readily at 4 per cent interest. It may acquire a less entrenched corporation that, as a somewhat less secure borrower, has had to pay 6 per cent. A merger makes possible an immediate refunding operation that reduces the smaller company's interest charges by 1 1/2 per cent.

With all of these and other possible advantages to acquisitions and mergers, why hasn't the tendency to merge and to acquire been even greater than the high rate of such activities that recent years have produced? Should not a considerable part of the time of the ablest managements be spent in seeking opportunities along these lines? Should not the investor eagerly seek the company that is constantly growing through acquisition?

Perhaps the matter can best be put in proper perspective by a football comparison. Taking to the air—that is, attempting gains through long forward passes—will, if successful, gain a team far more yardage far more quickly than will carrying the ball on the ground. But if unsuccessful, the danger of interception—that is, of a major loss in yardage—is also tremendously greater when a team depends primarily on forward passes than when it does on carrying the ball.

Mergers and acquisitions are exactly the same as forward passes. If they can be executed successfully they will cause a business to progress with far above average speed. They can be dazzlingly successful. Their very nature, however, carries sizable inherent risks that can result in less earnings rather than more. Far more important, they can so weaken a corporation that in the years ahead it will prove a less rather than a more attractive long-range investment.

Of course, there is one limiting factor to the danger of acquisitions that does not exist in the case of a forward pass. Any forward pass, if intercepted, can mean a major setback to the team that lost the ball. In contrast, if a company only occasionally acquires other units that are much smaller in size than it is, such acquisitions prove disappointing, and the cost may still not be great enough seriously to detract from the investment appeal of the large acquiring corporation. Of course, the reverse of this coin is that such relatively minor acquisitions are also likely to make only minor contributions to the betterment of the much bigger corporation when they are successful.

Why do mergers and acquisitions carry such a high degree of risk? In almost all cases, the seller, who has operated the business for years, knows much more about it and its weak spots than does the buyer. As one brilliant corporate president once told me in speaking of major acquisition his company had made through merger, "It is only after you have married the girl that you find out about the false teeth and wooden leg." In this case, the "false teeth and the wooden leg" referred to plants in far worse physical shape than the acquiring company had believed and a dangerous situation in regard to both the morale and the depth of junior executive talent of which the acquiring company had been almost totally unaware. Because of the unusual abilities of this particular company, it eventually did overcome these difficulties. Several years and many million dollars later than originally anticipated, it did obtain for its stockholders the great long-term benefits that had been expected from the merger. Nevertheless there still remains unanswered the "$64 question" of most mergers. Could not this same unusually competent management have done even better for its stockholders if in the ensuing years it had devoted to other purposes the talent it took to work out these far worse than anticipated problems? I do not know the answer to this question, but I do know that a slightly less resourceful and determined management could well have turned what had previously been (and still is) a magnificent long-range holding into a quite unattractive investment solely because of this one merger move.

However, in certain types of mergers and acquisitions there are even greater dangers. One of these is the personnel friction that mergers frequently can produce. When mergers take place between two companies of about equal size, there may be bitter competition between most of the top corporate teams of each for the various jobs such as controller, vice president of sales, or director of research. Only one man from either organization can fill these vacancies. Instead of a team working together, this can easily produce so much personnel "infighting," jealousy, and outright "knifing" that efficiency just disappears in a maze of the worst type of personnel feuds and vendettas. This type of thing can wreck the investment status of the best corporation.

Even where one of the merged organizations is clearly dominant, personnel problems, unless handled with far more care than frequently occurs, can make the acquired company much less valuable to the acquiring company than might have been anticipated. The same executives whose ability might have contributed most to the value of the acquired company have probably over the years developed great skill in getting on comfortably and well with the chief executive for whom they had been working. Now almost overnight, the center of authority has passed to someone they hardly know. He may be located hundreds of miles away instead of just down the hall. Uneasiness and insecurity are bound to occur. Unless handled skillfully, this can mean the loss of extremely valuable talent that may be quite costly to replace. Even if handled skillfully, enough uneasiness is almost bound to occur during the early days of acquisition to cause some loss of efficiency.

A major merger between companies because of the personnel problems that are sure to arise might well be compared to surgery for the individual. Some time after it happens, if all went as planned, it may make the patient very much better. If it doesn't go as planned, it may make him very much worse. But whether it attains the anticipated longer term benefits or not, in the short-term period immediately after happening, major mergers, like major surgery, will make those undergoing the operation temporarily weaker rather than stronger. If the merger changes a smooth management team to one that becomes a hotbed of internal friction, it may leave the merged companies permanently weaker than they were before.

Each merger is slightly different from all others. This is true in regard to the degree of benefit it can cause if successful. It is equally true in regard to how much risk the investor is running if the merger proves a disappointing one. Are there any general rules or standards that the investor may use as guideposts in a matter which can affect the future of his investment as much as this sort of thing can? I believe there are and that they may be summed up about as follows:

(1) There are three main sources of danger to investors from mergers or acquisitions. These possible dangers should be kept in mind at all times, both by managements considering acquisitions and by stockholders in companies where such matters are under consideration. These are (a) that the struggle for occupying each of the top jobs (Controller, VP of Sales, Research Director, etc.) in the combined organization will so engross and disturb most key personnel that former smooth-working teams will degenerate into a hotbed of internal infighting and friction, (b) that top mangement will get involved in so many problems in fields with which it was not previously familiar that it will find itself unable to carry on with its former efficiency, and (c) that because the seller nearly always knows more about his business than the buyer, the surviving company will have acquired a unit with faults far worse than allowed for in the price of acquisition.

(2) Mergers or acquisitions that help integrate a company backward seldom involve a sizable degree of risk for the stockholders involved. These are combinations that enable a company to get a captive source of some of its raw materials, component parts, or other supplies more advantageously than could be done before. The advantage may be because these needed supplies can be made more cheaply by the using company than they can be purchased from others. It may be because, if the using company produces them itself, they will be made more carefully so as better to meet the company's standards of quality. However, in any event, the benefits of such a move can be pretty accurately estimated in advance. Vastly more important, such a move by

its basic nature does not usually open up the Pandora's box of any of the three dangers mentioned in Rule 1. There is seldom any internal struggle for power since the acquired personnel fit into their own niche and neither conflict with most of the functions of the acquiring company nor do the acquiring company's personnel represent job hazards to them. Furthermore, the field is one that top management of the acquiring company probably knows rather well, so that top management is not liable to become involved in new problems too burdensome for it to handle. Similarly, because top management knows the business well, it is not liable to be excessively out-traded in its purchase price. On the other hand, such acquisitions, while at times genuinely worthwhile in their benefit to the acquiring company, are seldom of tremendously beneficial importance to the stockholder of that company. They usually are of minor significance to him, one way or the other.

(3) With one exception, from the stockholder's standpoint, acquisitions that integrate forward, that is, that give the acquiring or surviving company a captive customer outlet, may be judged by the same set of standards that were stated in Rule 2 for companies that integrate backward. This exception happens when a management makes the mistake of acquiring one company that competes with a number of its other customers and fails to allow for the loss of most of its sales to what were formerly customers but are now competitors. Such a move can be very costly. However, in fairness, it does not always arise solely from mergers or acquisitions. At times, a company's existing organization will create a new product line that competes with its own customers. Nearly always the results are highly undesirable.

(4) When a larger corporation acquires another company that is tiny in relation to the size of the acquiring company, the risks to the stockholders of the large company are usually quite minor. Even if the small new acquisition becomes completely worthless, the resulting dilution in the larger company is not of sufficient importance significantly to affect the investment status of the larger company. On the other hand, even if the small acquisition turns out to be a highly satisfactory one, it normally is too small to make much difference either. However, occasionally this is not

true. This is when the tiny acquired company has a new product line which can be developed into an important new product field for the bigger company, or when it has one or two outstanding individuals who can make major contributions to the acquiring company's management. Acquisition of this sort can be not only among the least hazardous but also the most profitable in the entire field of mergers.

(5) For reasons directly related to the hazards outlined in Rule I, mergers or acquisitions have the greatest prospect of being a success when they are between companies in similar lines of business that have been aware of each other's activities for years and that thoroughly understand each other's problems. Conversely, the greatest chances of a costly failure occur when a merger or acquisition happens relatively quickly between two companies in quite dissimilar lines that were previously only vaguely aware of each other.

(6) The most successful overall record on acquisitions has usually been made by companies that are not constantly seeking such acquisitions but that only make them very occasionally when all measurable factors seem overwhelmingly propitious and when the acquired company is in a field closely related to the existing company's activities. The occasional deal of such a company is usually a good deal for the stockholder because the acquiring company "only does what comes naturally" and is not straining to be making "deals" all the time.

(7) Conversely, there may be a quite high degree of investment risk in a company that as a matter of basic management policy is constantly and aggressively trying to grow by acquisition. The investment risk, for reasons tying directly into the matters discussed in Rule I, usually becomes much greater when top management does not confine these activities to lines rather closely related to its existing business but is willing to go into a seemingly endless series of unrelated lines. This becomes even more hazardous when a management takes on several such acquisitions in widely differing fields in a short period of time. There are many who will disagree with this, but it is my own belief that this investment risk is significantly still further increased when one of two conditions exist in a company's organizational makeup. One is when the top

executive officer regularly spends a sizable amount of his time on mergers and acquisitions. The other is when a company assigns one of its top officer group to making such matters one of his principal duties. In either event, powerful figures within a company usually soon acquire a sort of psychological vested interest in completing enough mergers or acquisitions to justify the time they are spending. This causes the very "straining" that is the exact opposite of the type of thing covered in Rule 6.

(8) For reasons that both tie into Rule I and closely parallel the rules for individual investors when acquiring their own personal holdings, the least desirable acquisitions are those where a not particularly attractive business is acquired at a very low price in relation to existing assets and past earnings. The most attractive acquisitions have frequently been those where a high price has been paid for something that thoroughly fits into the needs of a business. Companies that would otherwise have been a magnificent opportunity for stockholders have a number of times been made quite unattractive by a management with one good line of great intrinsic strength and potential, acquiring several other weak or run-of-the-mill types of business. Usually, this is done with the explanation to stockholders that by diversifying the company's activities, the stockholder's position is being strengthened! When this happens, the previous steady upward trend of the price of the company's shares sometimes comes to an abrupt and perhaps permanent halt.

(9) The greater the number of completely different industries in which a company is engaged, the greater the strain on management. A surprising number of the most successful companies have confined their activity to one broad industrial classification, such as chemicals, electronics, or paper products. However, a few other quite successful companies have been able to engage with great efficiency in two or occasionally three quite different industries. Furthermore, in today's complex technology there is no clear-cut line as to where one industry ends and another starts. A large part of what General Electric makes, for example, is electrical, but do these electrical lines, different as they are, represent one industry or several? For reasons like this, it is impossible to make a hard and fast rule about where the danger

point is when a company becomes too diversified. The speed with which a company has diversified its activities may be even more closely related to the dangers to the investor than the number of lines involved. This is why mergers or acquisitions other than between companies of vastly different size (as discussed in Rule 4) in quite different lines of business should be studied with the greatest care and greatest suspicion.

For some years, the stock market has more or less consistently valued companies in several widely diverse lines of business at a lower price in relation to their earnings than companies with activities confined to one or at most very few lines of industrial activity. This is probably a sound rule. If so, is it not also sound policy to evaluate at an even lower ratio of market price to current earnings companies that have recently taken on major acquisitions in fields in which they had not been engaged? Should not such lower evaluation prevail at least until the managements of such companies have demonstrated that they are capable of measuring up to the far more difficult job of "riding more than one horse" at the same time?

Mergers then may be summed up as matters the investment significance of which can vary enormously, one from another, depending on the nature of each. The really big ones, I believe, usually contain far more pitfalls to the stockholder than they do promise. But there is a relatively new although related field of business activity. This is the formation of jointly controlled companies. Here no merger takes place, but two or more established companies, nearly always with diverse technological backgrounds, join together to form a new company managed jointly by its several parents. Starting with such fabulously successful companies as Dow Corning and Owens Corning Fiberglas, joint endeavors of this type have been sprouting all over the economic map in recent years. The great majority have been successful. Many have been outstandingly successful.

The reason for this type of growth is not hard to find. As industry is getting more and more technologically complex in its nature, new commercial possibilities open up which may be well beyond the technical ability of one company but not beyond the combined skills of two or more companies that possess scientific know-hows largely unrelated to each other. Furthermore, at times, one or more of the founding companies may not possess the technical background but will have a supply of raw materials or a knowledge of markets of great importance to the new enterprise. The sizable amount of capital frequently required is an additional factor that has at times played a part in the formation of such jointly owned companies.

The sensible business logic behind the formation of such companies is not the only reason why so many have been successful. Also contributing is the fact that so many of the parent companies have unusually competent managements themselves. This means that they have able people to transfer to the new enterprise. The new company starts off without the dangers of inexperienced managements, the factor that handicaps so many otherwise promising young ventures.

Has the success of so many of these jointly owned companies brought a proportionate increase in the market price of the owning companies' shares? In general, I believe, it has not. That portion of the profits of the jointly owned companies that gets passed to the parents in the form of dividends gets valued at the same price-earnings ratio as the rest of the reported earning power of the parent companies. But, I believe, except in rare cases, investors give a great deal less weight to the owning company's share of the profits that are retained in the jointly owned company than they do in the earnings that are retained in the owning company itself. This means that earnings that are retained in these jointly owned companies for their further growth do not have the same favorable effect on the price of their parent company shares as do the same proportional amount of earnings retained in either of the parent companies to aid in their further growth.

The reason for this may not be as illogical as, at first glance, it would appear. Intelligent investors are satisfied to have the managements of their companies make the decision as to what percentage of their companies' earnings are passed on as dividends and what percentage retained in the business, because they have confidence the management can make a decision in this respect in the best long-range interest of all concerned. If they did not have this confidence, they would presumably sell their stock. But when their earnings are retained in these jointly owned companies, they are not completely under the control of a management which they know and in which they have confidence. The management in which they are investing has to get the approval of others, or at times make some compromise with others, before they can proceed on such matters. Therefore, the assets in the jointly owned companies seem one step further removed from the stockholder. To this degree such assets are that much less desirable than the assets of their own company. By this degree the retained earnings of the jointly owned companies are that much less highly valued.

Is there a solution to this problem—a means by which earnings of these jointly owned companies could be made as desirable to the stockholders of the companies that own them as are earnings of their directly owned companies? I believe there is a rather simple solution. This is for the practice to spread that occasionally has already been seen when these jointly owned companies grow and may need additional capital. Occasionally, they have had to raise this capital by offering some shares to the general public. This resulted in a public market for shares of these jointly owned companies. Groups of investors then develop who have appreciation of and loyalty to the managements of these jointly owned companies rather than to one or another of their parents. The owning companies could if they so desired convert part or all of their holdings of a jointly owned company into cash by selling their shares at or near the current market price.

Wherever truly outstanding management exists, following this still rare practice would create a situation where the real value of these jointly owned companies would soon be reflected in the market price of the owning company's shares—something that all too frequently does not now occur. Future retained earnings of the jointly owned company would in time be reflected higher market quotations of first the retained company's shares and then those of the owning companies. This would accomplish the desirable end of making retained earnings of the jointly owned company as valuable to the stockholders of the parents as are the retained earnings of the parent itself.

Certain financial people would quarrel with this conclusion. They would point, as in the closed-end investment trust field, to the substantial discount that the shares of certain companies regularly sell to the price at which the shares they own can be liquidated in the open market. They would claim that if these now closely held shares of jointly owned companies had a public market, this same type of discount would prevail and the real value of the jointly owned company would not flow through to the price of the owning company's shares any better than before. I do not believe this to be necessarily so. I think these discounts below the liquidating value of liquid assets to be an indication of two things. In the case of investment trusts, they somewhat reflect the cost of the investment trust doing business. The shares of such a trust are held by investors to be worth as much less than the liquidating value of those shares as the overhead of the trust takes away from the income of those shares. To this must be added what I believe to be a discount (or premium) from this "adjusted" liquidating value to allow for the financial community's degree of lack of confidence (or of confidence) in the ability of the management of the particular trust to operate in the best long-range interest of its shareholders. In the case of Lehman Corporation, for example, where over the years the management has done quite well for its shareholders and where seemingly the financial community has every confidence the same group of people will do equally well in the future, the shares customarily sell not at a discount but at a premium from the liquidating value. Similarly, if an outstandingly well-run operating company owned an interest in an equally well-run jointly owned company with an established market for its shares, the investor can be sure the market price of such quoted securities would to a considerable degree be reflected in the market price of his shares.

If, then, it would be so relatively simple to make this ever-growing number of jointly owned companies more valuable to the stockholders of the owning companies than is now the case, why have not more of them issued stock to the general public? Why have investment bankers, usually not slow to exploit profitable fields of activity, failed to urge these companies to do further financing through public stock issues? The reason lies in the way so many in the financial community have completely misjudged and over-rated the importance of stockholders' voting rights. Let us consider this matter.

VOTING RIGHTS AND PROXY FIGHTS

In most corporations, common stockholders have the right to cast one vote for every share they own. It is their votes that elect the board of directors. Legally, the board of directors is the top source of corporate power. It appoints all key officers including the president. It also determines most major policy.

For these reasons, this right to vote appears on the surface to be something of real importance and value to the investor. All the superficial trappings of the financial community would seem to confirm this. Thus, in the detailed prospectus that the Securities and Exchange Commission requires be published for most new security issues, there are set forth what the Commission considers to be the most significant facts concerning such issues. Any variation from the standard pattern of voting rights is always explained in great detail in these prospectuses. Similarly, many magazine articles and some books have been written on the rights and wrongs of various aspects of this same subject. The Gilbert Brothers, for example, have risen to national prominence for their many years of rather spectacular crusading against certain corporate practices. Not all, but much of the reforms they advocate pertain directly or indirectly to stockholders' voting rights.

Nothing I am about to say should be construed as indicating any belief on my part that even in the field of voting rights much of what reformers such as the Gilberts advocate is not entirely proper. In some instances, such as their advocating elimination of boards of directors with staggered terms of office in the few corporations still maintaining this management protecting device, their contentions seem extremely proper. What I am about to try and show is why, for investors who handle their affairs in accordance with sound investment practice, this whole matter of voting rights is quite unimportant.

I believe the basic confusion on this matter arises from a natural tendency to draw a close parallel between two things that are quite different. One is the importance to a citizen in a democracy of having and using the right to vote on the affairs of his nation and his locality. The other is the significance of the same function for the stockholder. What is overlooked is a major difference between the two processes. A citizen has a vital self-interest in utilizing his right to vote with all the judgment at his command. He should help select the best possible (or at times the least bad) of available alternatives both as to personalities and issues that may be up for decision. Modern history is full of examples of the sad conditions to which entire peoples have sunk when the great majority of them have become indifferent to the importance of such matters. However, the reason why these political matters are so vital is that there are so many different ties holding the average family to the nation in which it has lived. Even when political conditions become almost intolerable, it is still no easy decision to pick up stakes (assuming it is not a criminal offense to take your stakes along with you) and move somewhere else.

Contrast this with the corporate stockholder. For the most part, he is not born with a particular stock in the manner that an individual acquires a nationality at birth. He can and should select shares of companies with managements that meet his particular standards of conduct. Even in the case of those who inherit securities (or the many times when an investor may find he has bought into a corporation with whose management he is dissatisfied), he can dispose of his holdings and switch to a management of his choice with relative ease. Because of this, I believe the investor who has used even a modicum of judgment in selecting the stocks he now owns should almost invariably follow a basic policy in regard to his voting rights: He should either support the management completely or sell his shares.

I am well aware that this statement runs directly contrary to the thinking of most of those who have chosen to speak out on the subject of corporate voting rights. Who has not heard this type of comment: "No matter how good a corporate management may be, if it needs stockholder approval for something which the stockholder believes to be undesirable, it is not only to the stockholder's interest but actually his duty to vote against it. The stockholder who sells his shares in a poorly managed company rather than join in a proxy fight to obtain a better management is dumping his mess on others instead of making the effort to clean it up himself. He deserves to miss out on the profit that will be his when a better management results in the shares selling at higher prices."

Arguments of this sort are not new. At first glance they seem plausible. Let us examine them more closely and see if they will then still make sense. Let us do so first from the standpoint of the stockholder's own self-interest and then from that of the general public good.

First, let us take the case of the stockholder who has great confidence in and respect for the management of his company but now finds himself in disagreement with some particular thing the management is proposing to do. Since two intelligent people will seldom agree on everything, it is hardly surprising that sooner or later some particular proposal will come along which the shareholder would prefer the company not doing. Nevertheless, he does not consider this proposal so bad that he would want to get out of an otherwise highly attractive picture just because it is enacted. Such a proposal might be a merger, a change in capitalization, the election of a new member to the board, or perhaps some sort of stock option or new executive compensation plan.

In view of the investor's confidence in the overall excellence of his company's management (if he doesn't have this view perhaps he should ask himself why he is holding the shares at all), I think the first thing he should ask himself is this: "How sure am I that my view is right and the management is wrong on this particular matter? After all, the management is likely to be considerably more informed about some aspects of any matter they propose than am I." If the management is sincere and able to start with, should not the stockholder be ready to review his thinking to at least make allowance for the possibility his views may be ill founded? However, let us suppose the stockholder is still convinced that the management's proposal is a bad one but, as is usually the case, not so important that he would want to sell out of an otherwise attractive situation because of it.

If so, we come to the heart of the matter. Is it in any sense wise for shareholders to try to throw around their weight in minor matters to curb the desires of a management that has been doing an outstanding job for them? I think by examining basic practices of management itself we get clear evidence it is not. No large company ever built up an outstanding management team which did not delegate authority to those who were performing well. Otherwise, junior executives could have no opportunity to perfect themselves from actual experience, to mature, and to grow. As long as such executives perform within the framework of general corporate policy and produce the desired results, they are allowed to make their own decisions. This happens even though at times top management might do the job somewhat differently. If it is important that top management restrain itself and give those beneath them some freedom to act, which means at times to learn from their own mistakes, as long as they do their overall job well and produce outstanding results, why should not shareholders use the same restraint and permit the same freedom of action to a top management that is also performing outstandingly? I believe any other course of treatment to an outstanding management will, if it is successful, produce sufficient resentment and internal strain that it is apt to cost the stockholders far more than they might lose through the enactment of an occasional unwise proposal.

However, let us now take a more extreme case. This is where the shareholder has been quite happy with his investment, but the proposal to which he is opposed is so undesirable that, if enacted, he would prefer to sell his shares. Such a matter does not occur very often, but it can happen occasionally. Before deciding to cast his vote against such a matter, the stockholder should ask himself two questions. The first is: Is there any significant chance of defeating the proposal? The second is: If the management is supporting something this bad, is it not probable that its judgment or its morals have deteriorated enough below what I had believed was the case, so that even if this plan is defeated, other highly undesirable propositions will be initiated by them just as this one was? The chance of the answer being yes to the first question and no to the second is rather remote. Yet unless these answers fit the facts, it would seem obvious that from the standpoint of the individual investor he is better off selling his shares and waiting for a really outstanding investment to become available than he would be remaining in one where either he could not block a thoroughly bad proposal or, if he could, he would be faced with the probability of having to fight this sort of thing more or less continuously in the future. Nothing so takes a management's mind off the far from easy tasks it needs to be doing than internal wrangling with its shareholders.

Fortunately, the number of cases where outstanding managements make proposals that place shareholders' interests in major jeopardy is extremely small and provokes few proxy fights. Most proxy fights occur when an established management has not had an outstanding record. The result is that either important shareholder groups generate an internal revolution, or some outside group sees a chance to gain control and attempts to convince the owners of a majority of the outstanding shares that it can do better. Here is the stuff of which most of the really spectacular proxy fights of recent years have been made. Before the average shareholder (who is not going to get a high-salaried job no matter who wins) becomes too partisan in any proxy fight, he might well reflect on a few investment fundamentals. If a poor management has long been in control, the greatest attrition is usually in the junior executive ranks. Younger men of ability will drift away to places where opportunity for promotion is greater and where new ideas and suggestions for doing things better will be welcomed rather than frowned upon. Hence, even if the stockholders overturn the existing poor management and place thoroughly capable people at the top, it is often a matter of several years before the lower executive ranks can be first recruited and then trained to a point where noticeable improvement in the overall performance record can be established. In the meantime, there is always the danger that the new management is not as capable as appeared the case during the proxy fight, so that not much fundamental improvement will take place at all. Perhaps the newcomers are merely a group of glib opportunists who saw a chance of talking themselves into high-paying jobs. For all these reasons, I believe that when a proxy fight results from clear evidence of something less than outstanding management, the investor usually fares best who does not get himself involved but sells his shares and looks around for a well above-average situation in which to place what is left of his original investment. Perhaps he should watch his former company with the thought that two or three years later enough time may have elapsed so that if a genuine management upgrading is taking place, the first tangible signs of this are starting to appear. Then a real buying opportunity could be in the offing. In any event, once the initial flurry of excitement is over, I can recall few times during the past twenty years when a public proxy fight for control was followed by market performance over the next several years noticeably better than that of common stocks as a whole. Perhaps this is further indication that shareholders' voting rights may be far more important to those who like to "pop off" or flex their legal muscles than to those whose main concern with common stocks is to make money.

But if from the selfish standpoint of the stockholder's immediate interest the wisest course is nearly always to sell his shares if he does not believe he has a management so good that he can consistently support it, how about his actions from the standpoint of the public interest? If stockholders "rubber stamp" their approval to whatever management asks, will not they be removing the strongest restraint to possible future management abuse? If they believe a management is faulty and a better one has offered itself for stockholders' approval, don't they have a moral obligation to their fellow shareholders to retain their shares and vote for a change?

Again, I believe looking a little below the surface will show that the generally accepted answer to these questions is not the correct one. This is because shareholders' voting rights are such a clumsy and inefficient method of getting things done. The number of publicly owned companies which in any five-year span experience a change in management because of a proxy fight is but a tiny percentage of all publicly owned corporations. Similarly, the number of management proposals that have been defeated because of stockholders casting an adverse vote in instances where the management itself has not been overturned, is, I suspect, probably even smaller. This is because management, particularly weak management, knows it may be under attack and prepares to entrench itself accordingly. It can usually—through purchasing stock, making alliances with big shareholders, or through any number of fairly well-known devices such as voting trusts—so buttress itself that it is largely invulnerable to anything but an attack by some other well-financed group that makes similar alliances. Here again, the comparison so often made between shareholders in a company and citizens in a community completely breaks down. Political experts tell us that in the United States even the strongest of entrenched political machines have seldom been able to command over 20 per cent of the effective vote, a tough hurdle for unorganized citizens to beat, but one which an aroused citizenry can get past. However, in corporations which are entities from which most of us can break our ties with an ease not available to citizens, those in power can frequently tie down over 50 per cent of the vote, so that they are unbeatable.

However, if the voting weapon is often a weak one to bring pressure on sub-standard management, stockholders possess another vastly more powerful force which can make itself felt. This is to act as their self-interest demands in the first place, and, if they don't like the management, to sell their shares and keep away from the stock. A management that is sufficiently hard-boiled and self-centered can ignore bitter minority votes against it. On the other hand, persistent stockholder selling directly affects the managers in their own personal fortunes, in the fortunes of the allies they depend on to stay in power, and in the operating results they attain. They are seldom indifferent when continued stockholder selling reflects itself in quotations for the shares at a far lower ratio to earnings than exists in the case of competitors. This persistent evidence of investor disapproval will make any further financing the corporation may have to do far more costly than for its better regarded competition. Furthermore, and striking close to home, it results in the net worth of the managers themselves if they own much stock in the corporation (or of those they depend on for support if they don't own enough stock to keep them in power) to be but a fraction of what it would be if they enjoyed the good will of the investment community. This is something that may really hurt those that are legally invulnerable. It is far more likely to change management policy than a few adverse votes.

In short, the investor who sells out of a poorly run company, who helps depress the price of such shares, and contributes to unfavorable investment regard for the management is doing so purely to better his own position. Nevertheless, he is bringing real though perhaps unconscious pressure upon that management. If enough others do the same thing, here is a real force. On the other hand, the investor who keeps his shares but votes against management proposals, even when joined by many of his fellows, usually is tilting his lance against a windmill. He accomplishes little or nothing toward building up his economic position. Perhaps this is why in spite of all the talk about voting rights and all the space they are given in such things as the prospectuses of new stock issues, the "bloodless verdict of the market place" puts so little tangible value upon them. If you doubt this, look up the various cases in the past 40 years where two stocks of the same corporation have sold side by side, each exactly like the other except that, because of voting trust arrangements or some other legal device, one stock failed to have the effective voting power enjoyed by the other. Almost never has the voting stock showed any consistent greater market value because of its voting rights. Frequently, the two classes of stock were, so far as quoted value went, completely interchangeable.

Perhaps the creed of the successful investor concerning this whole subject might be: If you look below the surface you will see there is no real validity to the idea that there is any basic similarity between the relationship of the shareholder to his corporation and the citizen to his locality or nation. Ignore the nature of corporate voting rights for they have little to do with the investor's future fortune, one way or the other. Concentrate on outstanding management for this is what produces the results that count. When you have found such management, support it regularly with your proxies whether you favor every single move proposed or not. Do this just as you would go along with the program of any other expert you trusted who, through abnormal skill, was producing unusual results for you. As in the case of your doctor, your lawyer, your plumber, or any other specialist you select, if your opinion of them changes significantly for the worse for any reason whatever, don't get in endless arguments with them but get rid of them and get someone else who is better.

SHOULD YOU BUY OR SELL STOCKS BECAUSE OF U.S. ELECTION PROSPECTS?

We have been graduated from a college quite some years ago and have drifted far away from knowledge of student body or alumni affairs. We find ourselves in the football stadium as the "big game" starts. Our college is playing its traditional rival. We have never met a single member of either team. Actually, we have no real knowledge of the background of any of the squad. Nevertheless, as the band strikes up the familiar martial music and at the sight of jerseys in the colors we have long thought of as our own, we become emotionally completely partisan. That those wearing the uniforms we think of as our own might be a bunch of young punks whose services are being pretty much paid for by a group of extroverted alumni would probably seldom cross our minds. It is *our* team. It suddenly becomes a major concern of ours that they do well.

Today, social scientists have shown that the ties which so many of us have with one or the other of our two great American political parties are not so different in their origin from the influences that make normally inactive alumni so partisan at an athletic contest at which the old school colors, its song, and its customs are obtrusively on display. It has been shown that such factors as the state in which we grew up, the neighborhood in which we grew up, the neighborhood where we now live, our racial background, our religious background, and the economic class with which we tend to identify ourselves are like powerful ropes tending to pull us toward supporting candidates of one political party or the other. Soon, though we may claim to be independent in our thinking, we find ourselves becoming more and more politically partisan to the point of accepting some of the extreme claims of the party of our choice. We do this to the point where it is quite liable to influence our investment decisions.

Many people will ask if, after all, giving great weight to the prospects for the political party of our choice is not a basically sound investment policy. The actions of government can have a tremendous impact upon the value of common stocks. Therefore is it not wise to buy when those in whom we have confidence are in power? Should we not sell if there are prospects of victory for the party about whose objectives we are concerned?

To answer this question, let us start from a common basis of understanding. This is that there can be no question about the power of government to alter the real value of common-stock holdings. A government ready to lower the standard of living of an entire people in order to gain certain hoped-for social objectives in which its leaders ardently believe could seriously and adversely influence the value of good common-stock investments. Conversely, a government far wiser than any administration we have witnessed in recent years might significantly enhance their value. No one can deny what governmental influences can do. This is not at issue. What is at issue is whether in the United States of the recent past or in as much of the foreseeable future as the United States continues such as it is today, the victory of one party over the other is apt to be of sufficient importance to warrant changing investment decisions from what they otherwise might be.

There are many investors whose belief on this subject runs about as follows: The Republican Party is primarily the businessman's party. Republicans understand and are sympathetic with the problems of business. The Democrats draw their strength from groups many of which are jealous of and hostile to business success. Therefore, when the Republicans are in office business is safe. Common stocks should then be held. When the Democrats come to power, the common stock-holder will suffer.

There is another group of possibly about the same number of voters. This group has far less wealth and possesses very much less (but still a little) influence on the stock market. Their beliefs lie in exactly the opposite direction. Because the great depression that reached its low point in 1932 came under a Republican administration, they believe that the Republicans are the party of depression and the Democrats the party of good times. They conveniently forget, if they ever knew, that other major depressions came under the Democrats. They are convinced that when the Republicans are in power stockholders and everyone else must keep worrying about constantly reoccurring bad times. When the Democrats are in power everyone can feel safe.

I believe that in the United States as it is today (at some future time it may be quite different) just as at any time in the recent past, there has not been a genuine basis for either of these beliefs. The view that the Democrats have any special formula for preventing depressions or that they have done any better than the Republicans in this regard seems so at variance with demonstrable facts that it appears pointless wasting much time discussing it. The contrasting view, however, that stocks should be bought and held when Republican prospects look bright, is so much more widely held among many groups of stockholders that it may be worthy of somewhat more detailed discussion.

It is probably true that in his background thinking the average Republican office holder is somewhat more sympathetic in his views about business than the average Democratic office holder. However, for many years there has been no sharp line of cleavage in this connection. Senator A, a Democrat, who defeats incumbent Senator B, a Republican, may well be far more antagonistic to business than was Senator B. However, three states over, another Democrat, Senator C, similarly defeats incumbent Republican Senator D. Here we find Senator C to be more favorably inclined toward the businessman's viewpoint than was Senator D. Furthermore, because he is a member in good standing of the majority party, he may be far more able to put his ideas across.

However, there is a basic trend of modern American politics far more significant to the stockholder than the individual sympathies of Senators A, B, C, or D. This is that the great mass of American voters are strongly inclined toward moderation. They are opposed to both the extreme right and the extreme left. It is not with whom the office holder sympathizes but what he does that is important. What does he do in his effort to be retained in office?

The typical Republican once elected starts to make all sorts of slight moves toward the left in an effort to attract support from this dominant center and to prove he is not a "creature of big business." He may not in his heart like some of these moves. Nevertheless, he makes them. A series of anti-trust actions well beyond anything seen in prior Democratic administrations—moderate further "social give-aways" at the expense of the economically efficient classes and a tendency to give strong priority to individual as against corporate tax relief—are a few signs of this trend in recent years.

What does the typical Democrat, once elected, do to attract support from the much-sought-after and usually dominant moderate voter? He sometimes talks rather strongly against "big business," but he advocates relatively little that is dangerous to legitimate American enterprise. His tax views are surprisingly moderate. He probably outdoes his Republican counterpart moderately, but only moderately, in the number of additional "socialistic give-aways" he genuinely wants furnished to the economically weak at the expense of the economically efficient. When hard times do appear, he may be even more solicitous than his Republican brethren in trying to relieve the strains of business.

These background conditions may not last forever. Sooner or later basic public opinion may change and the great majority of voters may not realize (as they seem to today) that it is only the amazing efficiency of American private enterprise working under the free profit system that is making possible the seemingly unbelievable feat of both steadily advancing the living standards of every major class in the nation and at the same time assuming one of the heaviest defense burdens that any free people have ever been called on to face in time of peace. The vast mass of American voters, possibly more by deep-rooted instinct than conscious thought, seem to recognize that it is only the leaven of private profits that produces the enlightened self-interest that causes an entire people to be constantly increasing their efficiency and producing these results. If this viewpoint changes, then the fundamentals of modern-day politics may change. Party politics may then become very much more important to stockholders than now is the case. As yet there is fortunately not the least sign of this, however. Until it happens, the investor who sells good holdings because he doesn't like the partisan political outlook may be duplicating the unfortunate results of a number of quite wealthy and previously highly successful Republican investors back in the early days of the New Deal. They were so fearful of the new administration that they ignored the brilliant opportunities of the period. Among other things, they completely miscalculated that the mildly unfavorable aspects of some of the legislation to which they were so opposed were far outweighed, so far as common stock ownership was concerned, by the inflationary aspect of certain other legislation to which they were also opposed. This same combination of influences might again prevail in about the same proportions if a mildly anti-business administration should be elected into office in the future.

It can be quite misleading to an investor to reach the easy conclusion that every member of Congress who wears the same party label as his own is a tower of strength. Similarly, every member of the opposite party is not a consistent source of danger. To illustrate this, let us examine what I believe to have been the most vicious piece of business legislation to become law during the past quarter century. This was the so-called "excess profits" tax, a plausible sounding title its backers arbitrarily attached to a quite vicious tax to help hide its real nature. The reason this particular levy was so much more harmful than most was that it singled out for special penalty those who were conducting their business affairs well, were building up new industries, and creating new job opportunities. It gave relative competitive advantage to the inefficient company that was doing little or nothing to build up the economy. To anyone in a position to watch closely the influence of this tax on better-run enterprises, it soon became apparent that its day-to-day influence on corporate decisions was largely to blunt the normal tendency of better-managed companies to fight waste and inefficiency. Since for these companies the government was paying such a large share of increased expenses as long as the tax continued, there was a constant tendency to be extravagant. It even had a bad effect on labor relations for, rather than try to work matters out with employees, a large part of the cost of a strike would in effect be shifted to the government.

This tax originally had had its main support from the so-called liberal wing of the Democratic party. With the advent of a Republican administration in 1952, many investors assumed that Republicans would be solidly against such a tax. This proved not to be the case. When the new administration called for its temporary extension, not on the grounds that it was a good tax but that the revenue was needed, a surprising number of Republican congressmen shifted their position. Meanwhile, and perhaps more surprising, certain of the more liberal Democrats who had seen the ills wrought by this tax in their own states had also shifted position and had completely lost their former enthusiasm for such legislation. With party positions frequently shifting and so many divergent personalities and viewpoints within the same party that party lines are seldom solid, as long as the great mass of American voters maintain the middle-of-the-road viewpoint they do today, actual or prospective party victories or defeats will continue to be an unsound basis for the making of long-term investment decisions.

If under existing political conditions these purely party victories or defeats should be without influence in long-range investment planning, do they have any significance from the short-term or timing viewpoint? Let us suppose that for the more basic reasons advocated in other sections of this book, a decision has already been made either to buy or sell a common stock. If this decision has been made fairly close to election day, a slightly better price can usually be obtained by keeping the following in mind:

Those with wealth sufficient to influence the course of stock prices overwhelmingly appear to believe that a Republican party victory makes stocks more valuable and a Democratic victory makes them less valuable. However, because presidential and congressional elections are so much in the limelight and because professional opinion (as reflected in the betting odds, for example) on the outcome is nearly always correct, the stock market for many years has consistently, in short range, over discounted the election news prior to the day of actual voting. This means that excepting only the very occasional time when a genuine upset occurs, the market the day following a national election will go sharply in the opposite direction from what most people expect it to. In other words, if as nearly always happens, the election goes as professional politicians expect, on the day after election the whole market goes sharply up if the Democrats win and sharply down if the Republicans do. Thus, for example, the day following each of Franklin Roosevelt's four landslide elections stocks went up sharply. Similarly in 1946, when for the first time in eighteen years the Republicans took control of both houses of Congress in an election sweep that was also generally expected by the professionals of both parties, the following day witnessed a very sharp one-day break. Keeping these facts in mind and hastening or postponing election-time transactions accordingly can well make a few extra dollars for those who, for other and sounder reasons, are planning to make such transactions at about this time of year.

How about the occasional time when a genuine election upset occurs, that is, when the results do not go according to the betting odds and professional political opinion? Then a Democratic victory seems to cause some further fresh selling and a market which would have gone down. This is exactly what happened the days after President Truman's surprise election in 1948—probably the only genuine presidential election upset of the twentieth century. On the other hand, when the Republicans benefit from a genuine upset, real fireworks on the upside can be expected the following day. This was about what happened in the congressional election of 1954. The Democrats were expected to sweep the elections, taking congressional control from the Republicans by a significant margin. However, Vice President Nixon sparked some efficient last-minute campaigning that minimized Republican losses in the East and virtually stopped them in the West. The Democratic margin in Congress was unexpectedly so tiny as to be negligible. The result was a few days, not just one, of sharply climbing prices.

Compare what has happened on the day after elections when upsets have occurred with what has happened when they have not. A rule emerges just as easy to follow as the far more fundamental one of not making investment decisions because of party election results unless and until the political climate changes sharply from that which has prevailed for many years. It is that if you are going to buy or sell around election time anyway, be guided by which party is favored to win in the betting odds. If it is the Republicans, do your selling just before election day and your buying at least one full trading day afterwards. If it is the Democrats, get your buying done prior to the election but wait for a post-election rally before doing your selling. If it is the Democrats who are expected to win and an upset should occur with the Republicans showing unexpected strength, you may find your following this timing rule has been surprisingly worthwhile.

5

Major Growth
Industries of the 1960's

I BELIEVE IT extremely important that the investor desiring to
get the maximum long-term gain from his funds thoroughly understand
some of the points I am about to mention in this chapter. However,
I believe it equally important that he realize the limitations of what
understanding these matters will do for him. Reading this chapter will
not just by itself tell the reader the name of the occasional investment,
purchase, and retention of which can build a personal fortune. As a
matter of fact, while it may possibly be aside from the subject at hand
at the moment, I do not believe that reading this or any other book can
automatically do this. The element of the time that must necessarily
elapse between when a book is written and when it is read would
by itself tend to make ridiculous much possibility of a book being a
source of worthwhile information on exactly which particular stock
to buy.

There might be a close comparison between the benefits an investor
would and would not obtain from reading this chapter and those a
fisherman might receive from studying a fishing guide to an area new to
him: Reading even an outstanding fishing guide to a region of mountain
streams and lakes could not possibly automatically assure obtaining a
spectacular catch of fish. This is because even the best printed fishing

guide cannot tell you exactly where a particularly prize fish will be at any particular moment. Similarly, by the time a reader may have read about a particularly choice investment, its situation, like the fish's location in the stream, may have changed considerably. If enough others have already been told about an attractive investment, the price may well have advanced to the point that a purchase will not offer an opportunity for nearly as spectacular percentage appreciation as it did a year or two before or might a year or two hence.

I think examining the parallel between our fishing guide and what I am going to attempt to do in this chapter is worthy of further consideration. We have discussed what a fishing guide will not do, but what about what it will do? It will show the particular bends in particular streams, the special lakes, and even the section of shoreline of such lakes where fishing is apt to be the best. Equally important, it will show what type of fish are most apt to be caught in what places. Possibly most important of all to the newcomer to the region, it will show where certain types of fish are almost surely not to be found.

There are a number of industries loosely associated in the public mind with growth, just as to a newcomer the banks of a number of streams might bring thoughts of fishing. However, I suspect that the types of investment that certain of these industries yield in contrast to others vary far more from one another than do the species of fish found in one stream compared to those in another not far away. Understanding these relationships will, I believe, help the skilled investor in pinpointing the areas (i.e., industries) which he wants to investigate in order to find exactly the type of investment he may be seeking. It should be equally helpful to the many investors who realize they do not have either the time or the background to manage their own investments and are sensibly depending on professions in the investment business. It should help them to appraise the work of these professionals and to understand what their present or potential advisers are trying to do for them.

With these objectives, let us look at some of the major fields in which so-called "growth" stocks are frequently sought and are occasionally found. Let us try to go a little way beneath the surface to see how different some of these industries are from others. This in turn will show why these variations produce completely different types of investments. It will tell what to look for in order most fully to exploit the occasional opportunity that does come along.

THE CHEMICAL INDUSTRY

Let us start with the chemical industry. Without getting too involved in precise definitions, I am going somewhat arbitrarily to assume that for investment purposes this consists of companies the main business of which is to take elements or relatively simple molecules found in nature and rearrange these chemical building blocks to form very much more complex materials having special properties or characteristics that make them of economic interest. This admittedly arbitrary definition would exclude lines like the sulphur producers and the fertilizer companies on the grounds (with which they might disagree) that from the standpoint of investment characteristics the chemistry involved in their principal activities is not sufficiently complex. It would also exclude the pharmaceutical manufacturers on the equally arbitrary grounds that their tremendously complex chemistry and a completely different economic background makes them investment-wise an entirely different industry with an entirely different set of investment characteristics.

Companies falling within this definition have, over the past 50 years, provided some of the most spectacular records of success of any in all American industry. In fact, so closely are the ideas of the chemical industry and unusual investment success interwoven in the mind of the average investor that to many the chemical industry is one of tremendous promise to those who would "get rich quick." Their imagination is stirred by the great successes of the past. It is even more stirred by reports, many of them quite realistic, of even more colorful new products soon to be introduced that can hardly fail to contribute to still more sales growth and further profits. They visualize this industry as sort of a magic conveyor belt. One end starts with a number of test tubes out of which come endless new miracle products. As these colorful and exotic products travel down the conveyor belt to the ultimate consumer, they automatically and endlessly pile up ever higher profits for the fortunate companies that make them.

Nothing in my opinion is farther from the truth than that the chemical industry is one of America's great get-rich-quick industries.

Actually, It is not a get-rich-quick industry at all. In direct contrast, it does something quite different. This is to provide what may be the best opportunity of any available to the American investor in modern times to get rich at a rate that is "slow but sure." Let me explain and support this statement.

As is so often the case, the statistics will vary somewhat depending on exactly which set of figures may be used. In general, however, comparisons of the sales curve of the chemical industry with that of industry as a whole show that in the United States over a longer period of years the chemical industry has been growing somewhere between two and one half and three times as fast as the approximate three per cent per annum growth rate of general business. The ever-increasing tendency of the industry to spend more and more on research and development, reinforced by concrete evidence of a significant number of new and exciting products in varying stages of laboratory development, give strong assurance that this rather favorable ratio of chemical industry growth to total industry growth will be at least maintained for quite some years in the future. There is some prospect it might even be bettered. Therefore, since all companies in an industry never grow at the same rate, it is just a matter of simple arithmetic that the fastest growing companies can better the industry average (of at least two and one half times three per cent per annum or seven and one half per cent per annum) by enough of a margin to moderately exceed the average growth rate of ten per cent per annum which some financial authorities consider the minimum for true growth stocks. Such a sustained growth rate will prove highly gratifying to almost any investor. It will not, however, usually produce the sensational year-after-year rise in share prices that has been witnessed by certain stellar stock market performers in certain other industries such as electronics, where average annual growth at the amazing rates of from 25 to 40 per cent a year have been maintained by leading units in their respective fields.

There is another reason entirely aside from the rate at which markets may be expanded, that is rather sure to limit the internally generated growth of even the fastest-growing of the leading chemical companies to a rate somewhat lower than this sensational 25 to 40 per cent growth rate sometimes found elsewhere. This is the unusually large amount of capital needed to finance most types of plant expansion in this industry.

Even with the most skillful of chemical engineering techniques, it requires about one dollar of new plant to produce each dollar's worth of additional product. This is true for nearly all of the so-called "heavy" or "basic" chemicals which are the starting points for the industry's complex production technology. It is also true for a large part of the generally more profitable intermediate and end products. This in itself is a factor tending to limit the growth rate in well-run chemical companies. There is an ever-present problem of financing further growth without diluting much of the benefits through the sale of stock to others. This calls for most of the expansion being financed through retained earnings or borrowings. While this can be very profitable if the right new products are launched and the still greater earnings from these can in turn finance still further new products in a sort of endless growth by "super compound interest," nevertheless, there are obvious limitations on the top per cent that a company can grow each year when expansion requires this much capital for each dollar of additional sales.

Furthermore, there is another way in which this high cost of needed plant combines with the industry's complex production technique to tend to limit how quickly (but not how surely) the leading units in the industry will grow. A new product, with large potential markets, is conceived in the laboratory. This in itself usually takes several years at a minimum. Then the company must take all possible steps to avoid the risk that would result if the huge sums needed to construct the required plant were to be placed in a, as yet, new and untested production process. Therefore, a pilot plant is constructed. Frequently, a small pilot plant is built first in order to make the process work under the simplest of operating conditions. Then, after all adjustments have been made to obtain optimum results from the tiny pilot plant, a large pilot plant is erected, adjusted, and tested for many months under varying conditions of performance. Even now that the go-ahead signal has finally been given for full commercial production, this new end-product plant, in normal times, is still quite a long way from being started. It will require large amounts of special intermediate chemicals that in turn can only be made from huge amounts of basic heavy chemicals. Frequently, neither are fully available in the needed quantities within an area close enough to the required plant site. So these basic chemical plants must be built, established, or enlarged before there is any point in completing the new end-product plant. Since at every step the new plant must be put through the difficult start-up phase as it goes "on stream," all of these things usually result in many years having passed from the time when a major new chemical product looks exciting in the laboratory until it starts to be offered commercially. Then comes the additional time needed to convince the average potential customer of its merit.

However, if all these things are major obstacles to an investor getting rich quickly from an outstanding chemical investment, they have offsetting characteristics helping him to get rich surely. With the exception of a few highly specialized fields, the huge capital sums required have tended to prevent new companies being organized to compete in the chemical industry as they have in most of the other more rapidly growing segments of American industry. These heavy capital requirements, however, have not prevented already established large companies in other industries entering the chemical field in sizable numbers in an attempt to participate in the lush growth that appeared to lie ahead. What has happened, I believe, is worthy of the closest study. Contrary to the views of many in the financial community, I believe it is highly reassuring to investors in the better old-line chemical companies. Certain petroleum companies and certain rubber companies with production techniques in their own lines quite similar to those of the chemical industry have been highly successful in building up a chemical business, particularly in areas chemically quite close to their own raw materials. This is at least partly balanced by the success certain old-line chemical companies have had in obtaining their own raw materials and power supplies by becoming oil and gas producers. However, even for some of the petroleum and rubber companies that some years ago had quite ambitious chemical plans and for many, but not all, of the host of other companies from many industries that started entering the "glamorous" chemical field, I think the results have been far short of the expectations. The complexity of the production techniques is but one of the barriers that arose. Keeping research productivity high and selling to so many different types of customers frequently proved harder problems than originally contemplated.

Today the dust is settling on the large number of companies that in the years immediately following World War II attempted to "move in" on the chemical industry. I believe certain conclusions are becoming increasingly clear. Such competition, particularly from former chemical industry customers operating captive plants, can be quite effective in certain basic or heavy chemicals such as ammonia or styrene. This is particularly true when no important co-products result from the process, where one customer can take a plant's entire output (so that no major selling problem is involved) and where the production technique is of a type that an engineering firm can be found which will guarantee a "turn key" job—that is, one where the construction company will guarantee that the plant will perform as specified and will train its customer's employees to operate the plant once it is running. For products that fall in this classification, I suspect future growth will be divided among more and more producers and the narrower profit margins of recent years are here to stay.

However, once you leave these less-complex basic products and get into the more complex activities that are the heart of much of the activity of the most outstanding chemical investments, the competitive picture changes drastically. Here many products are co-products of each other. You must find outlets for all, a problem sometimes solved by selling to many lines, and sometimes only by researching still newer products to use up some of those being produced in surplus. Not only getting in front but staying in front in both chemical engineering and chemical research becomes tremendously important. I believe only a few of the relative newcomers to the industry have been able to keep abreast here, and even this does not represent as much additional competition as might appear, for some of it was done only by merger, that is, with the aid of already established chemical units. I would venture the opinion that while the chemical markets will continue to grow at least as rapidly in relation to the economy as they have in the past, greater realization of these problems will cause no repetition of the rush of outsiders to enter the industry that was witnessed in the latter part of the 1940's. Therefore, the companies able to maintain their competitive position during the past ten years should do at least as well in the coming decade.

This, of course, only applies to chemical companies with broad enough diversification in their product line. They alone are protected by the law of averages. If a competitor's technological advance obsoletes one segment of their product line, it would only affect a small part of the total business. This would in all probability be more than offset by competitive gains from the company's own new techniques benefiting other of its products. In this industry, a specialty company can occasionally have a sensational growth, such as that enjoyed by the Thiokol Chemical Corporation with the advent of government demand for solid chemical fuels for rockets. However, the investor should always remember that specialty companies can be subject to equally sharp reverses through no fault of their own if an ever more rapidly changing technology should suddenly pass them by.

In summary then, the past decade again gave proof under unusually severe conditions of a basic investment factor that the entire history of the modern chemical industry has demonstrated. This is that a large and diversified chemical company (to become outstanding in its field) must correlate a great number of technical skills with a high order of business judgment in order to produce an ever-increasing number of more complex but chemically somewhat interrelated products. Once it becomes a leader in this sort of thing it gets "know how" in so many divergent activities that it is a rather difficult matter for outsiders to gain enough mastery of all of them at the same time to be able to break into the field on even terms. This means that once a diversified chemical company gets in the forefront of a number of fields it will probably stay in front provided it does just two things: (1) Its technical proficiency must advance at least as fast as that of the particular subdivisions of the industry in which it is engaged. (2) It must retain good business judgment. With basic policies and philosophies of conduct firmly entrenched in certain of our leading chemical enterprises, both these developments appear rather sure to happen for a number of the industry leaders.

Now what is the special investment significance of all this from the standpoint of someone considering investing in the chemical industry? It is that in the chemical industry it is surprisingly easy to select the most attractive company or companies for long-range investment. The record of the past is available. The characteristics of the technological leaders and of the low-cost producers can for the most part be learned without much difficulty. Therefore, which stock or stocks to buy presents little difficulty. This is in sharp contrast to the situation that occurs in most of the other industries offering the investor unusual promise of growth. In most such lines of business, selecting the right stock to buy is a very much more difficult matter.

However, from a practical standpoint, the unusual ease with which the investor can find the chemical companies that are almost certain to grow spectacularly in the future does him surprisingly little good. This is because since finding these companies is easy for him it also is easy for many other investors, too. As a result, these outstanding investments normally are bid up to prices that discount this growth quite a ways ahead. This is why the leading chemical stocks usually sell at such relatively high ratios to their earnings.

Much has been written, quite a bit of it obvious nonsense by people of little vision, concerning the "danger" of buying chemical stocks at the high price they usually sell in relation to earnings. While temporary market declines can come at any time and cause short-term losses on such investments (or on any other investment for that matter), certain chemical shares come as close as any investment can to assuring at least some significant long-term gain. This is because the probabilities are so strong that their steady growth will continue. Nevertheless, there are two things to keep in mind before making such purchases in normal times.

One is that there are a number of other chemical companies with an intrinsic quality varying from slightly lower to a great deal lower than the most attractive companies in the industry. With the tendency of many investors to look around for something "almost as good but not quite so high," such stocks frequently tend to sell at or nearly at the same ratio to earnings as the industry leaders. Such purchases may be somewhat dangerous for there may be much less assurance of the growth needed to support a high price-earnings ratio. Once evidence appears that this growth rate may not be attained, a sharp drop in the price-earnings ratio is a probability. This can mean a permanent loss in the investment. The other thing to remember whenever one has an urge to buy a chemical stock at these prices is this: While buying the best of the chemical stocks will, after enough time, almost surely produce some sort of profit, by using a little self-discipline it may be possible to invest in these attractive companies to produce a vastly greater long-range gain.

This brings us to the major difference from an investment standpoint between buying the leading chemical equities and most other outstandingly attractive growth stocks. Just because selecting the best chemical stocks is relatively so easy, the factor of "what to buy?"

becomes of somewhat less significance and the matter of "when to buy?" or of timing becomes a matter requiring the greatest judgment.

Leading chemical stocks become ideal to buy for major long-range appreciation, at such times as the development of a major bear market has tended to make the glamour fade from nearly all stocks. This is particularly true if the economic reason behind the bear market is the appearance of a business recession or depression. The reason for this is somewhat more basic than just that most stocks are likely to be in a buying range at such a point. It lies in the economics of the chemical industry itself.

In good times, influenced by the general good feeling which customarily breeds too optimistic conclusions, investors tend to be carried away by all the important new products coming from this industry. They reach the false conclusion that the chemical business is depression proof. This is quite wrong. Since plans must be made far in advance to provide production facilities for these new products (as well as to take care of boom time demand for old products) the long lead time needed in chemical production results in new products having little influence in preventing the industry from being overexpanded. Traditionally, there is always too much production capacity whenever the business curve unexpectedly dips down. Nevertheless, in every boom, the investment myth that this industry's growth rate makes it depression resistant seems to spring up once again. The result is usually temporary disillusionment. The best of chemical equities go down about as fast as far poorer quality stocks when the depression first strikes.

However, just at this time of disappointment when the typical stock-broker's bulletin is rediscovering that chemical earnings are cyclical, the peculiar economics of the chemical industry again take hold and a buying point for the right stocks has been reached. This is because, with an average growth rate at least two and one half times that of general industry (for the best chemical companies it will be, of course, above this industry average), other new products will be coming along as well as new uses for old products. Since much of the raw materials for these new products will be the same basic chemicals and intermediates which a company is already producing and for which it currently has excess capacity, it starts utilizing parts of this excess capacity rather quickly. Earnings then start coming back a good deal faster than for industry in general. In other words, the real significance of the chemical industries' growth rate so far as business depressions are concerned is not that sharp downswings do not occur. It is that they are shorter and that new peaks are reached sooner than for industry as a whole. This means that the downturns in price may be fairly short for the best chemical equities. Taking advantage of these can bring the investor an unusually fine type of investment that will grow for many years, yet which is bought at a price that will show him a striking gain on the capital invested.

As I write these words, optimism rides high in the business and financial community. Almost everywhere is a feeling that either there will be no depression at all in the "golden 1960's," or if there is one it will be so light and short as to preclude need for worry. If the deep gloom that pervaded many in trade and industry and many more in the financial community during the short depression that bottomed in the spring of 1958 is not forgotten, the very fact that the business decline proved so much less severe than was generally anticipated seems to make the American public just that much more certain that depressions are no longer a cause for worrying and good business is here to stay.

Without repeating most of what I have tried to say on this subject elsewhere, economic history shows us repeatedly that such views are highly dangerous. Economic downturns seem an inherent price we must pay for the many advantages of free competitive enterprise. They traditionally come when least expected. The less they are anticipated, the greater the effect they may have on the price of common stocks. Furthermore, nothing in all the "built-in economic stabilizers" of which so much is heard gives assurance against a depression—these things merely give promise that such a depression will be relatively short. Therefore should, sooner or later, at some time in the 1960's a typical recession appear and strike like a bolt from the blue, it can almost be taken for granted that in the stock market the Dows, the DuPonts, or any other outstanding chemical unit will at first go down along with the rest. Those who then act and acquire such shares will have attained at bargain prices not the type of investment whose growth will be among the fastest of available common stocks. Instead, they will benefit from a slower but highly desirable growth rate enhanced by an unusual degree of surety that such growth will actually happen. For investors with the judgment to then hold such purchases through the temporary interruptions that future depressions will from time to time unexpectedly cause, such stocks give strong likelihood of once more proving magnificent long-term holdings. They have done this again and again and again in the past.

There is another type of background situation that at times presents itself for favorable timing of buying opportunity in choice chemical stocks and which is largely independent of judging the business cycle. This is taking advantage of the market decline that sometimes happens when earnings are reduced by the temporary high costs that are usually incidental to (1) an abnormal amount of placing new plant on stream and (2) the special sales cost frequently resulting when the new products thus introduced are first offered. To someone in close enough touch with the affected management, this can provide an unusual chance to buy a magnificent long-range investment at a considerable discount but at little risk.

This type of opportunity is sufficiently lucrative that it is worthy of close study. Usually, when a spectacular new plant is being built or an important and colorful new product is about to be placed on the market, a considerable amount of buying occurs in the affected stock by those whose enthusiasm has been aroused. Much of this buying is frequently speculative in its nature. It comes from those who understand little of the technical problems involved but expect a quick and easy profit. When month after month losses from costly alterations to the new equipment replace the anticipated profits, such holders become frightened and tend to dump their shares. At first, the decline is moderate as other investors tend to take advantage of these "bargain prices." However, as technical troubles continue, more and more stockholders become frightened. The word spreads that the management is "in deep trouble." The stock sinks lower and lower. Often it fails to recover more than a tiny part of the drop until many weeks after the technical problems have been solved and enough time has elapsed to get several months of profitable earning figures from the new plant. Of course, such buying opportunities are far more likely to occur in smaller chemical companies (or companies in the chemical processing industries) than in larger ones. Usually, for the largest companies, costly start-up of one new plant will have a much smaller impact on total earnings because so many other plants are operating profitably at the same time.

An almost classical example of this type of buying opportunity occurred in the shares of the Beryllium Corporation of Reading, Pennsylvania, during much of 1958. For some years, this company had enjoyed a profitable and growing business in the field of making a beryllium copper alloying material and in fabricating this material into wire, rods, strip, and other forms which its customers would then make into finished parts and other products. As the field showed growth prospects and the company appeared to be in a strong competitive position, the stock usually sold at a rather high ratio to its earnings. Then beryllium metal, which from a production standpoint is quite a different matter from the making of beryllium-copper-alloying material, began to have exciting prospects, both in the atomic and the aviation industries. In 1957, this company and one other each received a five-year contract from the Atomic Energy Commission to deliver beryllium metal of an almost incredibly high state of purity. The Beryllium Corporation bought an old locomotive roundhouse at Hazleton, Pennsylvania, and started to install the necessary equipment. The shares, which had been selling in the low to middle 1940's, rose to a high of 59 1/2 on the prospects of what beryllium metal could mean to this relatively small company.

Shortly thereafter, the stock market ran into the sharp decline that preceded the 1958 business slump. If there had been no beryllium metal excitement, Beryllium shares would undoubtedly have sold down moderately anyway. This was because the old-line alloying business, although remaining fairly profitable was, like most all other raw material and component suppliers, definitely affected. However, from the relatively stable manner in which sales and earnings from the Reading operation were maintained, such a decline would probably have been of fairly modest proportions.

Instead, however, in the frantic months that were to follow, the management was faced with problem after problem in this newest venture. One unexpected technical difficulty after another had to be investigated, diagnosed, and solved. All of them took money. Most of them took time. Month after month, in the first half of 1958, the huge losses at Hazleton came very close to overbalancing the depression-reduced profits from the established business, with the result that the first half statement showed the company doing very little better than breaking even.

During this period, among certain stockholder groups, the prior years' optimism had given way to deepest pessimism. Nobody could give a firm estimate of when this costly period might end. Each time it seemed over, some new trouble would arise. As usual, there were those who began to doubt if the problems would ever be properly solved. Meanwhile, to complicate matters still more, something else was happening that is quite common when radically new products are being launched. The near-term demand for beryllium metal was proving quite different from what it had appeared to be when the venture was started. The requirements for atomic purposes were proving far less than originally estimated. While it was also true that the airborne requirements were promising to become far greater than at first anticipated, this did little or nothing to dispel the gloom for the atomic demand that was immediate, while much of the airborne demand was still conjectural and, at best, somewhat in the future.

In the face of all this, the stock reacted about as might be expected. By the end of 1957, the stock had broken 30. All during the first six months of 1958 it sold in sizable quantities in a range between there and about 24, most of it close to the lower figure. Of possibly even greater interest and also rather typical, for some time during the second half of that year, when conditions at Hazleton were clearly on the mend, so great had been the bearishness that many stockholders seemingly were still lacking in confidence that the company was really conquering its production problems. In the face of ever more encouraging reports about the possibilities of beryllium metal for defense purposes, many shares were still available in the low 30's. Even though the alloy end of the business was now flourishing, by the year end the shares had only recovered to the 38 to 39 level. This was actually just under where the shares had been before the metal venture first became a factor in the market price! Some investors recognized that all that had happened was nothing more than what so often occurs in getting a plant requiring a new and involved technology to function properly. They bought either in the 24 to 30 range when these problems were at their height or took less risk and bought in the 30 to 40 range when these problems were well on the way to solution. They did something more than merely acquire an investment that was to show them a rather sharp price gain in the immediate future. At bargain prices, they bought into a situation that might grow and grow with a whole new industry.

With the steady increase in the tempo of technology in many fields, this sort of opportunity, for those who will take the trouble to get the facts and not be stampeded by the emotional reactions of Wall Street, should be even more frequent in the 1960's than they were in the past decade. The faster the pace of technology, the more such opportunities there will be.

There is still one additional way that I believe major long-range profits can be obtained at minimum risk in the chemical industry. So far, only investments have been considered in companies that are generally recognized as the most attractive units, in other words, companies that for some time would have been considered by informed sources as having unusually able management. However, in the chemical industry as in any other, companies can occasionally be found which in the past would have qualified well in regard to some phases of management capability, but rather poorly in regard to others. Then along comes a new management which, building on the stronger points of the old, starts developing a company capable of a much higher overall performance. In any industry, this can open up an opportunity of real investment interest. In the chemical industry, with its special appeal of great probability of comfortably above-average growth at below-average risk, it is of even greater interest. This is because it may open up a chance for what the investor should always be seeking in a chemical stock purchase: To participate in this great probability of above-average growth in a well-run company without having to pay a tremendous premium for it.

Because opportunities of this type are so appealing, they usually are followed by a quick run-up in market value as more and more investors recognize them. Such a rise, of course, is no reason for selling, for such a company with its improved management should by its nature now grow for years ahead. However, it does mean that the most unusual part of the buying opportunity may be over.

In this connection, the sharp rise that took place in the stock of the Nopco Chemical Company between July 30, 1958, and March 31, 1959, is rather interesting. After allowing for stock dividends, these shares approximately doubled in nine months. Part of the rise was unquestionably triggered, not by a changed investment appraisal of management capabilities, but by the ending of the costly period of getting a new product on stream, much as was described in the Beryllium

Corporation instance. As typically happens with establishing production facilities in a technologically new field, the cost of starting Nopco's exciting new rigid and flexible urethone foam lines was greater and ran over a considerably longer period than originally had been anticipated. Now that these lines were starting to show a profit instead of a loss, the stock began making the normal response. However, I believe, the size of the rise represented something well beyond this. Some time before, a new and unusually capable president had been chosen. Various management changes took place. As usual, considerable time elapsed until tangible evidence started to accumulate that real progress was being made. As new trends became more obvious, however, key people in the financial community began feeling that here was a relatively small chemical company with a management of a calibre they had not previously suspected. I believe this changed management appraisal, more than any other single factor, produced the ensuing sharp rise.

A larger chemical company, The Food Machinery and Chemical Corp., enjoyed a similar doubling in price over somewhat the same period. This also was seemingly due largely to the financial community's upward reappraisal of the management factor. It is a particularly interesting example, because it shows the extreme impact on stock prices of a changed attitude about a stock by the large institutional buyers, a matter which, as discussed elsewhere in this book, promises to have greater and greater influence on stock prices as the 1960's progress.

In the period from about 1934 to shortly after the close of World War II, the Food Machinery Corporation had been one of the outstanding performers of the entire market. While—probably because of their confidence in top management—a small minority of institutional buyers continued to be enthusiastic, this stock during the next ten or twelve years was shunned by many more. This decline in status could largely be attributed to the company's chemical activities most of which were initiated by acquiring other existing units in the immediate postwar years. During all this time, the machinery divisions were generally held to be outstanding low-cost producers with an internally generated growth rate assured by the company's brilliant developmental engineering and sufficient to make these activities a highly desirable institutional holding. In contrast, the abnormally low profit margins of the chemical operation, which in sales represented around one half of the total, was considered sufficiently below institutional standards so as to make the combined enterprise of little interest. Obsolete plant, low employee morale in certain of the chemical divisions, and absence of the emergence of new and exciting products from company research were all considered supporting evidence that this poor profit margin would continue.

New and unusually able personnel were moved in to handle these chemical problems. As usual, for several years, the betterment that was taking place under the surface produced very little effect on stock prices. The money that management was beginning to save through greater efficiency was being fully balanced by vastly greater expense for research, etc. Therefore, the real strides that were being made were not particularly apparent. By the second half of 1958, enough of the rather amazing management job began to show through to begin to stir investment interest. As 1959 progressed, it began to be realized that a quite outstanding chemical operation was emerging.

In the case of Food Machinery as in the case of Nopco, those who recognized ahead of the financial community what was happening within management were also able to find a way of participating in the steady growth of the outstanding chemical companies without paying the usual premium that customarily high price-earnings ratios cost investors when they attempt to participate in that growth. Furthermore, in one way, finding these fundamental improvements in management is the least difficult way of all to accomplish this aim, for in such instances the improvement in share prices seldom takes place as new personnel are placed in positions of power but some time later as the results of their work begin to be felt.

The investor or his adviser should be extremely sure of his ground, however, before reaching the appealing conclusion that a lower-grade chemical company has experienced enough real management improvement to warrant a significant upward rating of its investment status. Companies that do not have the finest records are sometimes a bit prone to claim they have changed their ways. I recall several years ago one well-known chemical company which did not enjoy one of the most enviable records in the industry for growth of sales and earnings. It was about to do some financing. Some of the officers held meetings with financial groups around the country. Much talk was then heard of all the changes and improvements that were starting to occur. Some excited buying of the stock occurred shortly thereafter. I believe most of these buyers subsequently sold out at a loss when it became reasonably obvious that few fundamental changes had happened at all.

THE ELECTRONICS INDUSTRY

Now let us turn to another major area in which investments with even more sensational long-range rewards occasionally can be found. This is the electronics industry.

From an investment standpoint, there are only two important traits that the chemical and electronic industries have in common. They both have a virtual surety of tremendous growth ahead. In both, this growth will come from pushing forward the frontiers of scientific knowledge through successful research and development. Beyond this, in their investment nature, the two industries are as different as are the polar regions from the deep tropics.

This comparison of the electronic industry and the tropics is not as far-fetched as it might appear to be at first glance. Here is an area where annual growth rates are maintained year after year that elsewhere in the financial world would be incredible. The best electronic companies can and do grow at from 25 to 45 per cent a year. Project such a curve forward a few years and figures start to appear that would stir almost any long-range investor to a high pitch of excitement. But as in the fierce competitive struggle in a tropical jungle, many of these exotic growths can fade about as quickly as they bloom.

Many influences help to bring about this tendency of electronic companies to leapfrog ahead of each other with breathtaking suddenness and at times to fall back just as quickly. One factor is the importance of defense contracting, with the vagaries of huge individual contracts at times shifting from one company and its suppliers to another. Even more important is the nature of the technology, which not only is advancing with incredible speed but which in important (though not all) subdivisions of the industry does not lend itself to giving any assurance that the company ahead today will necessarily be ahead tomorrow. It is too easy for the designer of one circuit to copy and slightly improve on the designer of another.

Contrast the chemical and electronic industries and additional reasons for the somewhat slower growth rate but much higher relative competitive security of chemical companies becomes apparent. In the chemical industry, as I have already pointed out, most major companies are highly pleased if they can get one dollar a year of additional output for about one dollar of new capital spending. But in most phases of the electronic business, mechanization is so much less important that each dollar of additional sales only requires about 20 cents of new plant and equipment. Occasionally, this can be done for as little as ten cents on the dollar. This means that it takes relatively little capital for a newcomer to attempt to break into many (though by no means all) of the subdivisions of the electronics industry. Furthermore, batch or job-lot manufacture usually occurs in these areas of low-capital cost so that an efficient newcomer making such electronic products as certain types of special-purpose tubes can frequently make them as cheaply as the giants of the industry. This is a far cry from the millions of dollars so often needed as the minimum requirement of a newcomer endeavoring to compete in a major chemical process and the huge volume similarly required if the newcomer is to have as low a production cost as the established producers. Finally, the restraint on new competition resulting from many products being co-products of each other— so common in the more complex ends of the chemical business—is almost unknown in electronic manufacture. In short, with relatively low capital requirements to get started, small volume manufacturing common in many parts of the industry, and the ever present hope of getting started on a large government contract, it is hardly surprising that both entirely new enterprises and established companies in less exciting lines of business continue to enter this industry in impressive numbers.

With, then, an investment background whereby electronic stocks have far greater possibilities for major gain than do the best of the chemical equities but also have equally greater risk from competition, the emphasis on what to look for shifts considerably from that which we considered in regard to the chemical industry. The factor of timing, that is, of "when to buy" becomes very much less important. So much growth can occur so quickly if an electronic stock has the right product and the right management that (unless the price of the stock has already fully discounted these two things) any time at all, even the beginning of a major bear market, can be the right time to buy a really "right" electronic stock. But the factor of which stock to buy (often a relatively easy thing to determine among the major chemical companies) becomes not only vastly more important—for the losses can be staggering if the wrong company is chosen—but also vastly more difficult to do.

In general, there are two basic matters to attempt to appraise in trying to select electronic stocks that will prove outstanding. One is how fast will the company grow if it maintains its anticipated share of the total demand for its type of product. The other is how probable is it that will be able to maintain this growth and not have its growth curve unexpectedly upset by competition leapfrogging ahead of it. In the wild bull market experienced by electronic stocks in the closing years of the 1950's, it was the first of these matters that received almost undivided investor attention. However, the inherent nature of certain products and certain companies gives them a strikingly lower risk factor in regard to this second matter of sudden competitive upsets than exists for many other enterprises existing in the exciting electronics field. As the 1960's progress, I believe the unhappy experiences that will overtake unwary investors in certain of the glamour electronic favorites of the late 1950's will cause this second factor to be considered even more important than the first. In my opinion, an electronic stock should qualify highly on both matters to be worthy of investment interest. If it does so qualify, I think the 1960's will again confirm what was so dramatically demonstrated again and again in the second half of the 1950's—the profit from such a stock, if bought before its strong points get known to the entire financial community, can surpass the wildest expectations.

This is a period when it is pretty generally known that even a relatively modest investment placed in an Ampex or a Texas Instruments somewhere around the mid-point of the 1950's would, by the end of that decade, have laid the foundations for financial independence. Perhaps the bare financial history, as exemplified by increases in the market value of shares of this type being recorded in the thousands rather than the hundreds of per cent is too well known. The emphasis has been on the breathtaking gains made by these electronic stocks. Possibly, the emphasis should have been on what it was about a few electronic stocks such as these that resulted in such handsome rewards for their owners, while many others more closely resembled the brief course of a rocket. They may have moved at a quite spectacular pace for a short period of time, but it was a one-time performance.

Because selecting the right electronic stock prior to its becoming a general market favorite is so hard to do but so rewarding if done right, I believe it appropriate to devote a rather considerable amount of space delineating some of the characteristics that I believe should be present to give the greatest possible chance that the stock selected will be one of the big electronics winners of the future. Of course, this whole matter of electronics stock investment (or stock investment in any other industry for that matter) could be summed up accurately, if somewhat inadequately from the standpoint of helping the prospective investor, by saying that it is the best managed companies that will make the biggest strides. Naturally this is true, particularly in as competitive an industry as electronics. Even strong patent protection and outstanding engineering would be unable for long to make continued forward strides if a high level of business efficiency in the major phases of good business management were absent. But over and beyond this, for what particular aspects of good business management should the investor look if he is to spot the electronic investment with the sensational future?

I believe the following are some of the characteristics of particular importance in this connection:

(1) *Does the company have a research organization capable of keeping ahead in its particular field rather than of just being ahead at the moment?*

I believe the record of the Texas Instruments Co., which has become one of the classic examples of successful electronic investment, is a particularly good example of the importance of this. A few years back, this company took the lead in the commercial development of the silicon transistor. In view of the fact that at that time the company's total resources were but a tiny fraction of those of some of its giant competitors, many questioned if Texas Instruments could long keep the lead it then enjoyed. However, by making continued further research and engineering progress from that point, the company appears to have been able to keep many of these competitors in the unhappy position of constantly straining to get to the position where Texas Instruments was, only to find that at just about the time this goal was attained, this relatively small Texas producer had again moved forward to a new position. Then the catching-up process needed to be repeated all over again. This has resulted in this once small semi-conductor producer continuing to maintain a significant percentage of one of the most rapidly growing fields in all American industry. As the semi-conductor business is gradually becoming mechanized and as standard patterns of distribution are forming, the industry is going through the inevitable cycle of shaking down from many small and relatively inefficient producers to a few surviving large and efficient ones. This means that this quite small company of only a very few years back has maneuvered itself into the fortunate position of being one of the strong surviving units, thereby justifying a price for its shares considerably higher in relation to its current earnings than was the case when it was thought to be just another struggling small company in a field that was glamorous but not necessarily profitable. It is this combined effect of both steadily-improving earnings and steadily-rising price-earnings ratio that has produced the great rise that has been witnessed in the price of Texas Instruments shares.

Texas Instruments is, I believe, a particularly good example of the significance of another factor that is vital if research and engineering alone are not strong enough to put an electronic company in front but to keep it there. All of the very high order of talent employed by Texas Instruments and all of the many millions of dollars spent on research would not by themselves have produced the results attained. To this was added a correlation between the research groups and a comparable high degree of skill in selling or marketing so as to steer the research activity toward those phases of the semi-conductor business which would have greater rather than narrower sales potential in the years ahead. In semi-conductors as in many other phases of electronics, the field is growing so rapidly that it would be impossible for any one company to explore and research products for all the fields in which its specialty might apply. The company with the judgment and the teamwork within its personnel to steer the research group toward those specialties with the larger rather than the smaller future markets will get far more ultimate benefit from its research dollars. It will also have far better prospects of staying in front of competition, if only because it will probably be expanding its volume of output the most rapidly and will enjoy the savings in production cost per unit produced that larger production runs usually make possible.

While close coordination between research and marketing (or market research) can have a great effect in improving the overall research results, in many subdivisions of the electronics industries the efficiency of the coordination between research and those engaged in the day-to-day problems of both production and sales can be almost as important. It is not enough to make a better gadget than the market has yet seen, for it is rather probable others will soon also be making similarly improved gadgets. The developmental engineers who work closely enough with the salesmen in the field to know just how the design can be improved so that in addition to greater basic efficiency it will also have greater appeal to the customer's foibles and prejudices and will have a decided advantage over the company which designs products solely on the basis of engineering criteria alone. Similarly, the company that can design a product with a comparable basic engineering and customer appeal but which is easier and cheaper to manufacture will have a noticeable price advantage over the competitor whose lack of close coordination between production and research results in higher-cost products.

Actually, if there is any one trait which, I believe, more than any other characterizes continued successful corporate research activity, whether it be in the electronic industry or any other, it is this matter of coordination or teamwork. Today's technologies are usually sufficiently involved so that pioneering industrial research efforts call for a group of people not with one scientific background but with many. A theoretical physicist, a mathematician, an inorganic chemist, a metallurgist, and a solid-state physicist may all be equally involved in trying for a breakthrough in developing one product. Meanwhile half a dozen quite different experts may be needed for a sister project being carried on by the same company. How well these men work together is likely to be the most decisive factor in the results they accomplish technically. However, how successful they are for the stockholder is not only dependent on how well these technical experts work together, but how well they can work with more prosaic business people in sales, production, market research, and particularly top management. Under the conditions of modern-day industry, moderately able people who can work together will usually outperform the genius or geniuses who act like prima donnas.

Conversely, the top management which is broad enough in its outlook to recognize and cooperate with the legitimate aims of its technical personnel will usually produce results for its stockholders far beyond those unable to see beyond the immediate profit interests of their research projects. A sizable number of top technical people are fundamentally more interested in making technological progress and in winning status among those trained in their own specialty than they are in making money. A management that recognizes this and goes out of its way to support one of its researchers making a significant scientific contribution when the researcher knows the management sees little near-term payout in the project, will, if it handles its research properly, usually get a magnificent long-term return for its actions in greater teamwork and productivity from its entire technical personnel. In something where teamwork and enthusiasm are so great a factor in success as occurs in corporate research, the management that can skillfully direct its research workers and still maintain a high degree of loyalty and drive is the company that year after year is likely to continue to progress.

If these are the things for which the electronic investor should look, in regard to research activities, what are the pitfalls he should avoid? In my opinion there are two quite common mistakes against which he should be on his guard. One is he should never buy a stock just because some outstanding scientist, such as a Nobel prize winner, has joined the company and is about to do great things for them. Modern industry just doesn't work that way. The newcomer may be the greatest expert in his field in the world, but if he does not have the support of above-average people not only in other specialties but in such more prosaic fields as market research and production, the most he is likely to do is make a one-time spurt in the company's affairs. If, for all his technical skill, he proves to be deficient in the qualities needed for teamwork, instead of even a one-time spurt he may prove solely a source of major expense. Many an investor has regretted his impetuosity because he bought shares on hearing that the great Dr. X or Professor Y had joined a company, but failed properly to check on how well he was fitting into that company or even if the company had provided him a suitable place in which to fit.

The other common investor mistake in regard to research is to buy shares simply because a company is showing that it is spending a lot on research, either per share of stock or per dollar of annual sales. In the first place, unless the most careful accounting adjustments are made, these figures for comparative purposes can be quite misleading. One company will include a lot of costs as research expense that another will consider to be sales engineering or possibly even direct production costs. In recent years, since top managements have learned that many in Wall Street give considerable weight to how much per year is spent on research, there has been a regrettable tendency by some companies to charge everything possible to this account. But even if the accounting adjustments are all made, there is an even more fundamental reason why depending on such figures can be very costly to the investor. Probably in no phase of a business (except possibly advertising) is there as much variation from company to company, between what goes in as expenses and what comes out as benefit to the stockholder, as there is in research. Over a ten-year span this variation may vary up to as much as three to one if only the best run companies are included. If run-of-the-mill companies are compared to some of the best, this "productivity of research" factor would vary between companies by many times this amount. Obviously, a stockholder is interested in the long-range benefits he will get. Yet in the very phase of company activity where these benefits bear the least relationship to what they are costing him, stockholders weigh the research appeal of a company not on what it is doing or will do, but on how much it spends! The characteristics to be investigated in appraising the attractiveness of electronic investments will show why, in the electronic field particularly, giving much weight to such simple mathematical ratios as anything but the crudest sort of guide can lead to quite misleading conclusions.

(2) *Has the company a sound product ratio between related defense and civilian business?*

One thing which should never be forgotten by the investor in any electronic stock is that 49 per cent of the business of the entire industry comes directly or through subcontractors from the United States government—nearly all of it for purely military applications. Furthermore, if cold war conditions remain, there is every prospect that this tremendous demand will not only grow but grow importantly. Engineering advances made not just in the field of long-distance missiles, but in the somewhat more conventional weapons for fighting local or "brush" wars, call for more and more electronics. Meanwhile, most of such advances call for more sophisticated and therefore usually more expensive electronic systems than the weapons they displace. Therefore, in military electronic markets, companies with unusual engineering and production capabilities have open to them opportunities for building up tremendous sales volume.

However, from the investor's viewpoint, military business is usually much less desirable than a comparable volume of civilian orders. There are a number of reasons for this. Possibly the least important of these is that profit margins are usually lower. This is not unreasonable as the large volume that can at times be attained permits enough total profit to offset the lower margin on each dollar of sales.

One of the basic disadvantages of military business is its instability. It would be so much to the advantage of the overwhelming majority of citizens of all major countries if the arms race could be ended and real trust re-established between East and West that there is always the hope that sooner or later a means can be found to bring this about. Should this ever happen, the largely military supplier would find himself almost out of business. However, ignoring this possibility, which does not seem too promising in the present state of world tensions, military business still has elements of instability far beyond those usually found in the civilian field. Contracts not only can be but frequently are cancelled almost without warning, "for the convenience of the Government." The ever-increasing technological pace of electronic procurement makes it probable that this sort of thing will increase rather than diminish as one contractor works out on the drawing board a weapons system that makes an existing one obsolete and therefore useless.

Contributing to this general instability is the extreme difficulty of building up in Government business anything corresponding to the "good will" that is so common in civilian trade relationship. If a valued and regular supplier has made a mistake in his cost estimates and is losing money on an important contract, it is relatively common among enlightened private companies to make an appropriate but legally unnecessary contract adjustment. This is not charity on the part of the company paying the higher than legally necessary price. The good will produced will usually produce rich dividends some other time when the buyer is in a jam for supplies and needs help. Similarly, most individual consumers develop loyalty to a brand name or to a retail outlet which satisfies them and which they continue to patronize. In contrast, continuing to deal with a particular supplier simply because he has gone out of his way to render special service in the past is frowned on in military procurement if someone else submits a slightly lower bid on the same item. The tendency of the military to rotate tours of duty—so that the procurement officer with which a company deals today may be gone tomorrow—further increases the difficulty of building up any good will or loyalty of lasting value. Most military contractors must take into account the possibility that important parts of their business may stop at any time.

There is another and as yet not generally recognized factor that is making military business increasingly less desirable to the electronic investor. This is the accepted military practice of expecting that developmental engineering or research be done by private industry at little or no profit. The theory behind this is that, if properly done, the developmental engineering will in time lead to important production contracts. Enough worthwhile profit will then be made on these large-volume production orders so that the company could readily afford to do on a non-profit basis that part of the work for which the government received no actual hardware for its money.

This custom of doing the designing on a no-profit basis and making the profit on production became widespread just before and during World War II. It worked well at that time. This was because in those days the bulk of military hardware was represented by ordnance items such as tanks, rifles, shells, etc. and by manned airplanes. By today's standards, the total number of engineering manhours required to develop each new weapon were relatively small. In contrast, the quantity of weapons required was enormous. Consequently, the ratio of engineering done to hardware bought was relatively low.

So rapid has been the pace of change in the past decade and a half that the weapons and technology that would be used in warfare today are probably more different from those of World War II than were those of that recent period from those of the armed knights and lightly armed yeomen of the middle ages. This makes completely obsolete the still continuing custom of expecting a military contractor to do his development work at little above cost so that he can make his profit on the production items that will follow. The reason for this is that many of the most modern weapons are so horribly efficient that only a few of them would destroy all available targets. Yet so fast is the pace of development that before even the engineering work is done on one such model another is in the early stages of design that will make it largely obsolete. For a major part of modern weapons systems, the ratio of weapons produced to engineering time has decreased sensationally from World War II days. It has been remarked that in today's armament race it is the engineering and not the weapons that is being stockpiled! Of course there are exceptions to this, for certain electronic components and assemblies may be suitable for many weapon systems with only slight changes. However, on the whole, it means that much military business is becoming less and less desirable to the investor as more and more essentially profitless engineering must be done in order to obtain production contracts with smaller and smaller production runs.

In an age when maintaining engineering leadership in defense items may be vital for survival, from a national standpoint, it is tragic that inertia places all the profit emphasis on what is secondary in importance (production) rather than what is most needed (creative engineering). I believe the fact that civilian business is fundamentally so much more attractive than military business is having the highly undesirable effect of inducing an important segment of the finest engineering and business brains of the country to be spending their time on further perfecting some of the most frivolous of consumer products when the very safety of the nation needs their contributions toward maintaining leadership in the arms race. The dangerous stupidity of such a situation may in time produce changed background conditions. Nevertheless, I do not see the faintest sign of such a change as yet. Until such signs start to appear, the investor desiring to do the best for himself had better form his judgments on the basis of what seems likely to happen, not on what he would like to have happen. Consequently for the immediate future, military electronics business, unless directly related to civilian business, must be considered significantly less desirable than non-governmental business.

From this, it might be judged that the investor desiring to select the electronic stocks capable of producing the most sensational increases in value should confine his interests solely to companies doing no defense business. Actually, this is anything but correct. Instead, the thing to seek is the company doing military business which from an engineering or some other standpoint is closely enough related to its non-government lines so that it is receiving a sort of double benefit from its government work. In addition to such profits as it may make on these jobs for whatever time the government work may last, it also will be building up skills, largely at government expense, that may enable it to develop civilian business of both a more profitable and more permanent nature.

Some companies, through careful coordination of those with various engineering and marketing backgrounds within their own managements, have developed a very high order of skill in selecting the particular types of government jobs that can most help them. Such work can improve their ability to enter and compete in technically related, but sometimes seemingly quite different, types of industrial or consumer markets. It might consist of government research contracts, production contracts, or more likely both. Usually it can only be obtained by being preeminently ingenious and skillful in pioneering the particular field involved. However, when an electronic company can actually build up a valuable body of civilian business knowledge in this way—and not just talk about doing so—it may be considered a promising enough prospect of being an outstanding electronic investment to warrant the closest study to see if it also qualifies as to the other major prerequisites of such an investment.

Many times electronic managements will tell investors with great pride that their business is fairly evenly divided between government and civilian business. This would make it appear as though there were tremendous virtue in such diversification for its own sake. Such diversification—if it lead to no significant nourishing of the civilian end of the business—probably has some net advantage in the way of stability over a less diversified business. However, electronic investors should never forget that for the great investment appeal the two must not only be in some way interrelated but the management must be finding means of using its military skills significantly to benefit its civilian lines.

From the standpoint of the national safety, it is extremely fortunate that today's complex electronic technology sometimes permits this. With the very existence of the United States at stake, it is an appalling thing that our customs and our politics make it more to the immediate interests of our ablest engineers and business men to design an improved model of hair-curler or waffle iron than a new system for jamming and making inoperative an enemy guided missile. These experts will, themselves, own the hair-curlers or waffle-iron design. They will benefit if it is outstanding. The successful missile jammer might do anything from saving the lives of five million people to discouraging a potential enemy from making any attack at all. However, when the engineering of an invaluable defense device has been completed, the rights to the design probably will not belong to the company that created it anyway. After close competitive bidding, the production contract—which under our obsolete theories of military procurement is expected to "compensate for" the almost complete lack of profits in governmental engineering contracts—may go to an entirely different company. Furthermore it is almost certain (after renegotiation) to end up in relatively unstable and narrow profit-margin business with the company that eventually wins out on the production contract. In short, although from the standpoint of the national interest a missile jammer may have incredible value and an improved hair curler little or none at all, the business fact remains that the same amount of business and engineering ability will produce a larger and more secure economic reward in even the most frivolous consumer field than when working for the government. Under such a system, if it were not at times possible to get additional civilian advantages from creative military electronic work, an even greater percentage of our best engineering and management effort might be flowing toward the hair curlers and away from the missile jammers. As a result, it is unlikely that there will be any change in a system which costs the government nothing, since the military work must be done anyway, and which does attract more of the top talent where it is most needed. Therefore, those with outstanding electronic skills are apt in the 1960's as in the late 1950's to have unusual opportunities to make giant strides for their stockholders in businesses where military and civilian electronic know-how are closely interrelated.

(3) *Can the company establish such general acceptance of the technical superiority of an important part of its product line that customers are not inclined to purchase lesser known competitive products just because of price concessions?*

Particularly, although not exclusively, in that subdivision of the electronic industry having to do with the making of instruments, a combination of circumstances will occur that can be of great advantage to the investor. Quality of the product can be of such significance that few customers will want to take any chance whatsoever that some new or secondary brand will not perform as well, simply because this new or secondary producer would sell for, say, a ten or 15 per cent lower price. Since it is seldom possible to break even if much more of a price concession than this is made, larger price reductions are usually hard to bring about against an established efficient producer who probably already has the cost advantage of manufacturing in large volume.

All of these circumstances can exist and will have comparatively little significance to the electronic investor when there are two or more outstanding producers having about equal status in regard to the quality of their products. However, sometimes in the most complex and difficult products to make and service, one producer will get to be considered outstanding for quality. When this happens, the electronic stock involved undergoes a change in status that quite legitimately can produce a considerable upward change in the price at which it is likely to sell in relation to its earnings. To understand this, we should go back to the basic investment characteristics of most electronic stocks. This is that they have much above-average growth potential but also have much above-average risk that competition may, almost without warning, interfere with that growth, even to the point of putting the entire investment in jeopardy. However, in the occasional instance when one company gets such a reputation for quality that it gets harder and harder for others to break in, the normal investment characteristics of an electronics stock begin to change. The growth factor may be as great as ever, but, assuming the management has the sense to take no chance on quality and to maintain its efforts toward product improvement with undiminished vigor, the risk factor becomes less and less. If this happens in a line of business affording unusual growth prospects, it can produce the seeds of a magnificent electronic investment.

The Ampex Corporation which has been one of the most sensational of the electronic investments of the 1950's might be considered an excellent example of this. Ampex is a company that would stand up unusually well when measured against the various other standards of electronic investment that have been mentioned. But, in my opinion, part of the high price-earnings ratio that has characterized Ampex shares can be attributed to something other than the company's tremendous growth rate, good business management, outstanding engineering ability, and good relationship between government and civilian business. In much of its instrumentation line, customers want to take no possible chance on quality. It is difficult for others to make inroads on the company's reputation for quality in regard to these particular parts of its product line. As long as this continues, the prospects are great (in comparison with the usual abnormal risks in the electronic industry) of the company continuing to stay on top in a dynamic field. With the risk of a competitive upset subnormal (again in comparison with most electronic companies), the price-earnings ratio is understandably high.

It is possible that many investors—who seem unable to understand why certain electronic stocks continually sell at what, to them, are such unreasonable prices in relation to their earnings—might avoid serious miscalculations if they kept one basic concept in mind. In as dynamic a field as this one, relative freedom from a major competitive upset can be almost as important as the growth curve in determining a legitimate price earnings ratio.

(4) *Is the company strong in sales and marketing ability?*

Other things can have contributing importance but in any manufacturing business, there are three basic matters, superiority, or excellence of which are the mainstays of an outstanding investment. These are (a) ability to sell and expand sales more efficiently than most of the competition, (b) production ability, that is, to be able to keep making the product better and more cheaply than most of the competition, and (c) ability to handle developmental research not only to aid in steadily improving existing products but to create profitable new products in fields the company is qualified to handle. All this is just as applicable to any other industry as electronics. Therefore, from one standpoint, it may seem illogical particularly to stress sales ability when discussing the peculiar investment characteristics of electronic stocks. However, just as I have included a discussion of research in this electronic series—because research is even more important in this ultra-fast moving industry than is its key role to the investor in many other lines of business—so for a quite different reason I believe that any investor in an electronic security should give even more attention to an electronic company's ability to sell than the very great amount of attention he should devote to this matter in considering other types of investments.

The reason for this goes back to the very large percentage of electronic business that originates with the federal government. I am fully aware that continuously to obtain important segments of such business does take a form of sales ability. However, I believe it to be a quite specialized form of sales skill. Mastery of selling to the Defense Department is not only considerably easier to attain than is outstanding skill in marketing in ordinary commercial channels but, in my opinion, is sufficiently different in its nature that, from a sales standpoint, great experience in government selling does not by itself have any tendency to build up a company's civilian marketing skills.

In other words, in most industries, if a company does not have a strong sales organization it usually does not grow. The shrewd investor is seldom attracted to such companies. They certainly do not often sell at the high price-ratio to earnings found amongst so-called "growth stocks". Yet in the electronic field, such a company, if it has sufficient engineering ingenuity, can grow to spectacular size. It may even, on the strength of its engineering ability, obtain from time to time some significant business from large corporate customers. However, I believe, such companies should be avoided by the discerning electronic investor. Government business is notorious for being "here today and gone tomorrow." In regard to the all-important electronic investment factor of protection against sudden changes in the sales outlook, nothing can be much more important than being in a company that has built up a distribution organization capable of reaching a large number of potential customers when those customers may be desperately needed. Whether this organization be the company's own salesmen or an organized group of distributors such as independent manufacturers' representatives is not important. What matters is that the individual units involved—be they company employees or outsiders—are well selected and trained for the company's particular needs and that the company knows how to get new ideas through to them quickly and thoroughly when new sales concepts are needed.

No armchair examination of balance sheets and earning statements will tell the investor about such matters. Neither will overall statements about the proportion of government to civilian business. Yet few factors are more important in selecting the electronic stocks that will both get out in front and keep out in front in a technologically leapfrogging industry such as this one. Many electronic companies were started and continue to be dominated by individuals of great creative engineering skill. Nearly all brilliant persons of this sort have a keen interest in production as well as in developmental engineering matters. Therefore, the production end of the business seldom suffers from lack of attention and understanding. While there have been some outstanding exceptions, all too many of these unusual engineering minds just do not have the same interest in selling. They do not have a comparably intuitive understanding of how to build up marketing leadership. Because, on the surface, a company with brilliant engineers but an inadequate sales organization can for a time accomplish much for its stockholders in the electronics field, many are prone to continue to overlook the long-range significance of a good selling organization. Over the years, the electronics investor who does not make such an oversight may be rather richly rewarded.

The Pharmaceutical Industry

Another of the major growth fields that promises much to the investor of the 1960's is the pharmaceutical or drug industry. So dramatic has been man's conquest of diseases like diphtheria or polio before which, until comparatively recently, the human race stood almost helpless, that it takes little imagination to see the intense demand that would occur instantly for effective or better remedies against all the ills of the body (and many of the mind) that still scourge both man and his domesticated animals. Here is an industry that in the modern sense only really came of age with the thrilling events that lead to the development of the antibiotics during World War II and the years that immediately followed. This was when the production technique for the making of many of these wonder drugs was perfected to the point where they could be priced at a level that would enable them to sell to a mass market. Because of the huge markets that should quickly follow most key technological breakthroughs in this area, the better-run ethical drug companies have been spending a percentage of the sales dollar that rivals some of the best of the electronic companies in their search for new and improved products. Unless all signs fail, this will open up some lush gains for the alert investors during the 1960's. What are the investment characteristics peculiar to this colorful field?

Scientifically, the drug industry resembles the industrial chemical industry in that through chemical processes it either rearranges certain molecules into others with specially needed characteristics or takes atoms and relatively simple molecules and builds them up into more complex substances having a particular set of desired properties. In other words, even though the molecules produced by the drug industry are frequently larger and more complex than much of the output of the chemical industry, from a technical standpoint the differences between these two groups is rather vague.

From the investment standpoint, however, the situation is quite different. Lying somewhere between the chemical and electronic industries in their investment nature, drug stocks—both in the speed with which they can grow in value and the high degree of risk I believe inherent in most of them—far more closely resemble the electronic group investmentwise than they do the chemical stocks with which they have such close technical affiliation. I have already pointed out how in the chemical industry, once a major product has passed the pilot plant stage, it usually takes many millions of dollars of capital and much time to put into operation the complex series of plants required to make it. Only occasionally can the best of chemical engineering improve on the classical ratio of a dollar of plant for each dollar of annual sales. In the drug business, in contrast, equipment needed for taking care of a nation's wide market can usually be installed quickly and relatively cheaply. Therefore, there are not the serious physical barriers found in the chemical industry to the quick exploitation of a new product and the possibly equally quick decline of a competitive product heretofore enjoying substantial sales.

Furthermore, I believe, though many might disagree, that in a field where swift technological obsolescence can take place at any time, careful examination of the product mix of many of the major pharmaceutical companies reveals that they have considerable less protection against this sort of thing than is generally supposed. A surprising amount of sales in many cases come from a very few key products. Moreover, usually these key products are producing an even greater percentage of the total profit. Therefore, a competitor obsoleting one or two major products can have a quite unhappy effect on the earning power and therefore the market value of these stocks.

While these background conditions appear closely to resemble those of spectacular growth at great risk which I have described for the electronic industry, there are other factors which tend somewhat to limit both this rate of growth and the risk factors involved to something less than the extreme conditions found among electronic companies. For one thing, so far as the United States is concerned, new products affecting human health can not be put on the market until they have received the approval of the Federal Drug Administration. This means that a great deal of clinical data must be submitted, all of which takes time. With enough advance warning competitors may be able to take steps to meet the situation. Meanwhile, it should be remembered that the real market for most drugs is determined by the hundreds of thousands of doctors in the United States and abroad who write the prescriptions. This tremendous number of individuals will necessarily contain a large number of doctors with the type of mind that is always seeking a better way to do things. This segment of the medical community will welcome a new drug that gives evidence of being an improvement. But among the vast number of practicing physicians, there will also be many who, knowing the risks involved in any powerful new drug (for there is usually an occasional patient who for unknown reasons will suffer badly from a drug that has produced no unfortunate side effects on thousands of others), will prefer to stick with the old. Finally, there are the doctors who have used the old drug for so many years that they have gained great skill in just how to administer it. They will hesitate to go to a newer and possibly better drug with which they do not feel at home. For these reasons, it has been the experience of the drug industry that seldom does a worthy new drug ever quickly obtain all of the market to which its merits might entitle it. Similarly, a drug that technically has been completely obsoleted will nearly always continue to enjoy sales that will run on for years at a fairly stable rate, although one naturally far below that experienced prior to the new competition having appeared upon the market.

There is another factor which also makes the competitive pace somewhat less severe than that of the almost unbridled technical competition of some sections of the electronic industry. The average doctor is an extremely busy man. So many new drugs are introduced each year, many of them with such extravagant claims, that he cannot possibly find time to keep informed of all the pharmaceutical developments going on or claimed to be going on in his specialty. He will pick up part of his information on new drugs from technical papers or advertisements in medical journals. He will also probably get part of it from the drug industry's so-called "detail men." These are the sales representatives employed by each drug manufacturer to call on the individual doctor and keep him informed of significant developments in that company's product line. However, most doctors do not have time to see any but a small number of the detail men who would like to call. Therefore, they select the few to which they will give time. Unquestionably, the selection will be partially on the basis of the detail man's personality. It will also be partly on the basis of the doctor's prior opinion of the status of the drug house the detail man represents. This influence tends to give some competitive advantage to the established company with good reputation and a well-organized group of detail men. To a moderate degree, it tends to prevent newly introduced drugs from having as much sudden competitive effect as logically might be expected.

From the investor's standpoint, far beyond just the size and status of its organization of detailed men, the relative ability of one drug company as compared to another to establish a market for a new drug is only secondary in importance to its research ability to create a steady flow of such drugs. With so many and such different types of doctors to whom the marketing men in a drug company must appeal, the techniques involved are neither simple nor inexpensive. If the new drug appears both medically and economically important enough, an attempt may be made to interest the most prominent specialists that can be enlisted to test out the drug and report their clinical findings. These will then be most carefully written up, both in reports to medical journals and in brochures mailed out by the tens of thousands along with free samples. Sometimes a smaller drug company may not only lack all the marketing know-how to extract the maximum publicity needed to obtain the optimum market import. It may also lack even the needed cash.

In summary then, this industry will almost surely have rapidly expanding volume as, during the 1960's, more and more progress is made in finding chemical means to combat sickness and ill health. But what can the investor do to benefit from this in a field where there are a few built-in stabilizers to moderate slightly the risks of sudden ups and downs, but where for the most part the normal order of procedure means that a new discovery by one company can imperil an important market for another?

There are two things the investor can do. One is to buy the shares of only the very best of the large drug companies, ones like Merck or Schering, that combine an outstanding research organization with an above-average marketing ability and which also enjoy unusually high repute in the medical profession. Since the whole field is expanding such companies—with both outstanding research and about as broad diversification as can be obtained in this industry—should find sharp gains from their own innovations will significantly outweigh possible losses from competitive technological breakthroughs of others.

However, here there is both a close parallel and a sharp deviation from the comments I have already made concerning buying the best of the chemical shares. The parallel is that if bought at any time, the growth factor is probably great enough so that, *after enough time*, such purchases of the best of either the drug or chemical stocks may be expected to show worthwhile profit. Here, as in the case of the chemicals, far greater profit will be shown by those who have the self-control to use patience and take advantage of the occasional opportunity for proper timing of such purchases. This brings us to the sharp deviation. The background conditions that will bring the timing opportunity in buying into the most outstanding companies in the chemical industry and the drug industry are quite different. As I have already said, in the chemical industry such an opportunity will usually come with a general business setback. Such a period may prove a relatively poor time to buy an outstanding drug stock. Since the drug business is only slightly affected by general business conditions, investors are likely to value drug stocks particularly highly when the earnings of so many other lines are declining sharply. The result is that depression conditions do not put these shares on the bargain counter. However, other things do occasionally cause the industry to lose investor favor. One is the threat of government interference with the high profit margin many of these companies enjoy in products so vital to human welfare. This sort of thing could easily cause buying opportunities in drug stocks from time to time in the 1960's. Whether they do or not, just as has happened at certain times in the past, a sudden major decline in the earnings of a particular drug company can cause the financial community to realize (as it usually is inclined to forget) that the same thing could happen to others. All the shares in the industry lose favor for a time until the great success of other new drugs causes the whole matter to be forgotten in a new burst of general enthusiasm. Those who keep a sense of balance at such times and buy into the best companies can be enormously rewarded in this dynamic field.

However, for those with more intimate knowledge of what is going on in the research laboratories of this industry, there is occasionally another sort of major opportunity—one that can occur at any time. One or another of the better managed of these companies will come up with a brand new product of sufficient importance to produce a major spurt in earnings. The results can be magnificent if such shares can be purchased before the significance of this development to company earnings is realized in the financial community. The results, while somewhat short of magnificent, can still be substantial if the results are known to the financial community but, as sometimes happens, only a little bit discounted in the price of the shares. Of course to realize such gains, the investor or his adviser must have real knowledge of what he is doing. But he must have this kind of knowledge for consistent outstanding success in any type of common stock purchasing.

OTHER INTERESTING INDUSTRIES

The entire period since World War II has been one of steadily rising wages. With this background, any company which can offer a new product which can pay for itself by permitting the same number of people to turn out more or better work can be of great investment interest. For this reason, no list of places where the more attractive investment possibilities of the 1960's might be found could possibly be complete without mention of the machinery industry.

The fundamental basis of an outstanding machinery company is no different from that of an outstanding chemical, electronic, or drug company. In each case, it is the degree of superiority in production, in sales, and in research that together play the major role in determining how spectacular the success of the investment will be. However, within this overall framework, there are two matters to which the investor should give unusual consideration when investigating the possibilities of nearly all machinery companies. They are just as applicable to that important segment of this industry, which tends to facilitate the work of those who keep records and which is often called the office equipment industry, as they are to the companies that make equipment that will turn out more things on the production line.

The first of these is how ingenious is the company in constantly improving on its own products so as to make its customers eager to replace former purchases. With a few important exceptions, the machinery industry does not have the advantage enjoyed by many other lines of business. These other lines can be assured of constant repeat business from existing customers because their products are either used up almost at once (as with foods, chemicals, or paper) or must be replaced after a somewhat longer but still fairly limited time cycle (such as with textiles, paints, or tires). Certain types of machinery which by their nature are constantly jiggled or bumped as they move from place to place do wear out after a given amount of use and need to be replaced within a pretty definite time cycle, even though this cycle is rather a long one. Automobiles are, of course, the most important example of this group. However, most of the output of the machinery industry is designed to be used in one spot and is not subject to these special stresses and strains. While key parts or components will wear out and must from time to time be replaced, most such stationary equipment can be kept functioning long periods of time by the replacement of a few essential parts. This means that most machinery manufacturers can depend on only two markets for their sales. One is expansion of the industries served, so that their customers will want more of the same equipment. Only occasionally is a machinery maker fortunate enough to be serving an industry that can consistently give him a growing market based on expansion alone. Therefore, nearly always for a growing market he must depend on the other and usually far larger source of sales which is developing equipment that will either do a job cheaper than existing machinery now does it or do this job better. This is why determining that machinery companies have personnel that are capable of being continuously creative and ingenious in their product design is of such vital importance if an investment in this field is to yield anything more than a one-time spurt in value.

The other matter to which prospective investors in almost all ramifications of the machinery industry should give special attention is the company's ability properly to service its products once they have been sold. While most types of machines will run a tremendous length of time unless they are constantly jiggled or bumped, very few of them will run for long without occasional special attention when some part starts wearing out or gets out of adjustment. Many machines are so complicated that the user may not be able himself to do what is necessary at such times. Servicing such machinery at widely spaced geographical locations, many of them far from the factory, may be both difficult and expensive. However, if not properly done, such a lack will frequently produce sufficient customer ill-will to jeopardize the basic health of the business. In contrast, if well done, this servicing can not only be a means of keeping the customer close to the company from the standpoint of further machinery sales. It can also be a source of steady and profitable income both through servicing fees and the sale of spare parts. It can also be a means of discouraging new competitors from entering the field, since proper servicing greatly adds to the initial cost of entering the machinery business. For all of these reasons, close study of the service set-up should be a key matter for anyone considering an investment in the machinery industry.

With considerable reason, the economically newer metals are regarded by most investment experts to be a growth field. Since its commercial debut over 60 years ago, aluminum, the first of these to become an economically significant industry, has continued to grow decade by decade. This growth has been far more rapid than that of American industry as a whole. Every sign points to a continuation of such above-average expansion. Magnesium, the next of the "light metals" to appear, has enjoyed similar rapid growth. It has equally exciting prospects for the next ten years. In the second half of the 1950's, first titanium, then zirconium, and later beryllium began to attract investment attention as special needs in the growing fields of atomics, aviation, missiles, and chemical processing indicated significant markets for the unusual properties of one or another of these metals. Tantalum and particularly columbium may well be added to this list some time in the 1960's if more is learned about how to produce them more cheaply and fabricate them more easily. Who can say what additional metal or other substance, today of little commercial significance, may be urgently required in the technology of tomorrow? Who can say which may be a vehicle for magnificent investment?

I suspect by this time many of those who may read these words are well ahead of me and already are aware of what I now want to point out: the limitations of too much reliance on the nature of an industry in determining the attractiveness of an investment. This is because there is no clear-cut line of demarcation between industries. Frequently, it is purely a matter of arbitrary assumption whether a financial classification is made for a quite large industry, such as food processing, or whether it is broken down into more significant smaller segments, such as the meat processing industry, baking, or fruit and vegetable canning. Of greater importance to the stockholder trying to determine the investment characteristics of a particular industry is the fact that there is nothing but the vaguest of no-man's land as to where one industry stops and another may commence. To examine this further, let us go back to the three key words in the last sentence of the preceding paragraph. These three keys words are "or other substance."

From the investor's standpoint, there is no fundamental difference whatsoever in the investment characteristics of the development of such a substance as yttrium, which as one of the rare earths would automatically be classified by the financial community as part of the chemical industry and, say, aluminum, which most Wall Street sources would consider as part of the metal, not the chemical, industry. Both substances are chemical elements. Both are brought to a commercial product by purely chemical processes. Of greatest significance to the investor, in both processing is so much more complex than is the digging of the ore containing either yttrium or aluminum from the ground (which is mining) that the basic ways in which a company engaged in either of these two fields would act as an investment would far more closely resemble each other than would an aluminum company resemble the characteristics of a typical mining company such as most copper, zinc, lead, or silver producers.

However, here an even further qualification is necessary. Under today's conditions, the mining and refining of copper bears little resemblance to the chemically vastly more complex processing of the aluminum or magnesium industries. Therefore, investmentwise it is only the integrated copper company and then only insofar as the fabricating end of its business is concerned, that bears any close relationship to the aluminum or magnesium company at all. But this difference may not always be true. For some years, with varied commercial success, new chemical processes have been tried out to produce some of the economically older metals by quite different processes. Should such methods eventually prove economically successful, the investment characteristics of some of the older branches of the mining industry might become quite different from what they now are. For all practical purposes, certain companies that we today think of as mining enterprises some years in the future might become chemical companies instead. In short, not only are the borderlines between the investment characteristics of one industry and another far from clear cut, but in an era of rapidly expanding technology such as is sure to occur all during the 1960's, the boundaries that exist today may be quite different from those that exist tomorrow.

If then there is so much that is purely arbitrary in the industrial classifications into which the financial community is so prone to divide investments, is there any point to spending so much time on the varied characteristics of different industries? From the standpoint of getting the very most from each investment dollar, I believe there is. In the case of the stock of the International Business Machines Corporation (IBM), for example, it is a purely arbitrary matter whether these shares are classified as (1) part of the electronics industry, (2) part of the machinery industry, or (3) in their own subdivision as the office equipment industry. What does matter is that in considering the possible attractiveness of these shares the investor understand the importance of both constant ingenuity in developing better machines (for this type of equipment does not wear out quickly) and of servicing, both of which are of particular importance in appraising any type of machinery stock. It is equally important that the investor knows how IBM qualifies in regard to some of the matters to which particular attention should be given in regard to electronic stocks. I refer to the four matters specifically mentioned in the discussion of that industry (i.e., ability to keep ahead in research, interrelation of defense and civilian business, susceptibility of product line to achieving such customer acceptance as to give some freedom from price competition, and ability to sell). Of course, none of these matters relieves the investor of his responsibility (to himself) to determine how IBM or any other investment qualifies in regard to any remaining attributes of a well-managed company, such as ability to produce efficiently and ability to handle its people wisely. However, understanding the investment characteristics of the industrial background does pinpoint quickly (1) what to look for and (2) the type of investment that is there, once these characteristics are determined.

Because the financial community pays so much attention to the accepted growth industries, some of the outstanding investment opportunities lie not in the heart of these industries but at their edges. Thus, for example, just before the opening of the present decade, that is, in the last 15 months or so of the 1950's, investors started to become aware of the long-range potential of a small New Hampshire company called Miniature Precision Bearings, Inc. The chief investment characteristics of this company were about as follows: The company was the largest and one of the lowest-cost producers of a line of miniature or tiny ball bearings. The superior quality of these tiny bearings as against larger or conventional size ones appeared to open up prospects of above-average growth for years ahead. Not only did they fit into the general concept of miniaturization as it was developing in many places but their advantages in missiles made it appear certain that regardless of which of the many competing weapon systems would temporarily be the last word, more and more of these tiny components would be used. Meanwhile they had already made possible such important civilian developments as the high-speed dental drill. Therefore, their future was not tied exclusively to armaments. This factor was further reinforced by the company having in the early stages of commercial production an equally interesting and patent-protected larger type of bearing that was not tied to defense at all. Because of the obvious market potential of these miniature bearings a number of other companies including some very much larger of the old-line bearing manufacturers were endeavoring to compete in this field. However, production ingenuity and quality control had enabled this small company to maintain itself as by far the largest supplier—a happy position which manufacturing skill, marketing skill and mastery of the special metallurgy involved gave promise of continuing.

Here was a company in the not always glamorous metal working industry that had a growth factor closely tied in with the more colorful electronic and machinery fields. Key to the investment appeal of the stock is the difficulties of the technology involved. If it were relatively easy for others to equal or surpass the leading suppliers in meeting exacting customer standards in this field, Miniature Precision Bearing stock would have had little investment appeal. Because it was not easy and because, in both company philosophy and management personnel, the company afforded strong prospects of staying in front, 1959 saw a real opportunity of growth investment in this enterprise. As manufacturing technique gets more and more complex in the 1960's, more of such opportunities should present themselves. The key factors to watch are, secondarily, the amount of growth ahead for the product, but, primarily, the degree of probability that the company on top today will continue to get its proportionate share of the market as the industry grows.

These comments are not meant to furnish a complete list of all the industries in which the great investment opportunities of the 1960's will arise. I doubt if anyone knows enough of all the facets of American business to warrant even the crudest attempt to do this. I am positive I do not have this degree of knowledge. However, before concluding, I do want to mention one other large area in which I believe significant opportunities will continue to appear. This is the company that furnishes a service rather than a product and works itself into a position where most everyone turns to it rather than others for that particular service. The examples I will cite from the past are companies that have furnished that ever-more-important raw material of competitive business—information. Opportunities that arise in the 1960's might also be among information-providing companies, for the need for more and better data will grow and grow and grow, but opportunities might also occur among service companies that provide completely different types of needed service to their customers.

All through the 1950's, the stock of Dunn & Bradstreet proved a magnificent investment to its holders. This company established itself as the source to get routine credit information. As business grew and more and more of such data was needed, the base had been created to supply this need without a corresponding increase in cost.

Similarly, late in 1958, the stock of the A. C. Nielsen Co. was first offered to the public. As its relative newness in the financial community results in the investment characteristics of this security being somewhat less well-known than they otherwise might be and as it is an excellent example of the type of investment for which investors might well be alert during the 1960's, it might be fruitful to examine this situation in some detail. The company has other activities but the bulk of the profits come from supplying a large number of the nation's outstanding manufacturers of standard consumer product items (canned foods, cigarettes, soups, paper goods, etc.) with accurate up-to-the-minute data on how each item in both their own and their competitors' product lines are selling in each area served. Results are attained by actual audit of carefully selected sample retail outlets. Because the company can do this for many customers significantly cheaper than either one manufacturer could do it for himself or even a number could by working together, it is unlikely a newcomer would be able to cut seriously into this business unless, as also seems unlikely, the quality of this company's service to customers should markedly deteriorate. Meanwhile, year after year, the business grows at a remarkable rate. This has been due to three separate growth influences. These are (1) existing customers using the service for more and more subdivisions of their product lines, (2) the service being developed for an increasing number of different types of products—a growth factor appearing to have considerable further possibilities, and (3) extension of these services to foreign operations, the profitability of which is just beginning. Finally, the company for the past few years has received some revenue from a television-rating service and a coupon-handling service which are also just starting to become profitable. Not because the business had grown for years but because there were such strong prospects of its growing equally steadily for many more to come, it is hardly surprising that little more than six months from the time of original public offering these shares were already showing handsome profits to their owners and that large institutional investors were deciding that here was a growth stock with a degree of intrinsic safety that fitted in with their needs.

It might be asked, why give all this detail about the Nielsen company, since it is a rather unique business which by its very nature precludes another investment opportunity just like it from making an appearance. The answer, of course, is that this is exactly what I desire to show about this or any other service business that is to prove a spectacular investment. It is only the one that is unique, that provides something that many others cannot readily duplicate, that is likely to prove the bonanza investment. However, in the economy as a whole, the business of supplying services is growing even more rapidly than the business of supplying tangible products. As, just to give examples, a Dun & Bradstreet and A. C. Nielsen appeared on the investment scene, so others will, I suspect, appear in the decade just starting. They can be very much worth waiting for, provided they qualify as to the basic ingredient of all outstanding investments. This is a management with high ethical standards and unusual ability that will steer the company's activities into fields of above-average growth in demand. Usually these fields should be ones which for one reason or another are sufficiently hard for newcomers to enter so that the company will continue to get its full share of the expected growth. Occasionally, however, if the growth potential is great enough and if the management involved is unusually ingenious and able, a major investment opportunity may still arise in a specialized subdivision of this service field that, at least superficially, seems to offer much less natural protection against a multiplicity of other companies rushing in to divide up this growth.

An example of this sort was introduced to the investment community even more recently than the first public offering of A. C. Nielsen stock. I am referring to the shares of Manpower, Inc. This company, which was only founded in 1948, is the largest nationwide organization engaged in furnishing temporary help for many kinds of business requirements. By June, 1959, it and its licensees had one hundred and sixty-nine offices in forty states and ten foreign countries. It was being regularly called upon for its services by many of the largest industrial, financial, and retail companies of the nation. This type of growth would not have happened if the company had not filled a real need. It recognized that, varying all the way from individual law offices to giant corporations, illnesses, vacations, or the arrival of a temporary abnormal work load created a need for trained people who could be hired for short periods of time. Meanwhile, a huge reservoir of such skills existed among such groups as housewives, students, teachers, retired people, etc. who might desire to work certain days of the week or certain months of the year, but were not in a position to seek full-time employment. These people are paid by Manpower for actual hours worked at the various Manpower customers to whom they are sent, and the customer is freed of both the difficulty of obtaining temporary people of the required skills and the various costs of placing them on his own payroll. With "fringe benefits," insurance costs, and other hidden payroll charges what they are today, such savings are often fully comparable to the excess of Manpower's fees over basic pay scales entirely aside from the elimination of the risk of selecting undesirable temporary help. Small wonder then that the business has grown rapidly.

However, is this a business that is really suited to long-range investment? The amount of capital that it takes to set up such an organization in any one community is relatively small. Anyone with lots of friends and acquaintances in a city or its suburbs could employ ingenuity and salesmanship and might obtain a worthwhile volume of business in his area. Is not this just the sort of field where so many could so easily compete for a growing market as to make it generally unattractive for investment?

This whole service is so relatively new that only the future will provide a positive answer. However, I believe, the indications are that in spite of these apparent weaknesses the intrinsic investment worth of Manpower will have proved itself and the sharp rise that has occurred in the price of these shares will have been justified. Manpower's management has shown great ingenuity in pioneering its services in many quite unrelated fields. Its office division supplies skills ranging from stenographers, switchboard operators, and file clerks to bookkeepers, tabulators and operators of the more complex modern office equipment. Its industrial division provides perhaps an even wider range of skills such as warehouse workers, janitors, inventory takers, messengers, and even car washers. Its sales-aid division—in addition to the obvious functions of supplying sales clerks—provides demonstrators, models, and crews trained in obtaining data for market research studies. Its technical division offers trained personnel for temporary work in such skilled fields as engineers, draftsmen, and accountants. With all this experience behind it, the company has learned how to go out and get business and how to handle it at a relatively low overhead. It sets rates that might make competition difficult for newcomers who had neither its volume of business nor its experience in how to promote customers and how to locate skilled people desiring part-time work.

Investors who would look to the service field for some of the great investment opportunities of the 1960's should keep in mind that the new situations which offer themselves in this area will differ in their activities from the examples I have cited by as great a degree as Dun & Bradstreet, A. C. Nielsen, and Manpower, Inc. differ from each other. Many by their varied nature will not be of long-term investment calibre. In regard to each, the investor should ask himself three questions. These are: Does this field promise great growth? Is the management of this company genuinely outstanding? Does obtaining leadership in this field offer real assurance that many others may not be able to come in later and compete for this growth at relatively little disadvantage from the pioneering company? It is only when all three questions can be answered in the affirmative that the service field offers maximum appeal. When they can be so answered, such stocks can prove among the most rewarding in the decade we have just entered.

The False Growth Stocks of the Immediate Post-War Years

One of the great influences tending to cause many investors to obtain much poorer results than would otherwise occur, is the common investment fallacy of uncritically assuming that whatever has happened in the recent past will assuredly continue to happen in the indefinite future. For years, if not decades, after it had become clearly apparent that other investment media offered greater prospects to the conservative investor than did most railroad shares, institutional buyers all over the country who should have known better kept a significant percentage of their common-stock holdings in these shares largely because it was the accepted thing to do. Similarly, because most of the stocks of certain industries such as paper, cement, and lumber producers afforded their owners tremendous percentage appreciations, if prices of the late 1950's are compared to those of from ten to twenty years before, I believe many of these shares are enjoying an investment glamour that a critical investment investigation of just what has happened will show to be unjustified.

One of the characteristics of these industries is the large amount of capital required by them. A cement or paper plant needs a quite large dollar investment per ton of capacity. A lumber mill does not, but the spectacular lumber stocks have not been those merely having milling facilities but also having their own lumber supply. The ownership of forest lands also requires large amounts of dollars tied up in the investment.

Now let us go back to the generally depressed 1930's. These same industries—paper, cement, lumber—were among the more depressed then. In each of them, to a greater or lesser degree, excess production capacity was causing both idle plants and slim profit margins for such plants as were operating at all. The result was that, since stocks generally sell in relation to what they can earn and not in relation to the fixed assets behind them, most of these shares were selling at a quite sizable discount in relation to the original cost of the cement plants, the paper mills, and the timber lands which they represented.

In the period that shortly followed the end of World War II, a great change occurred in these industries. This change had not one but two major aspects. On the one hand, the great tide of economic growth that affected almost all industry meant that the demand for cement, for paper, and for lumber had shot up to a point where not only was all the excess pre-war capacity now needed but also where it was vital to build still more plant as well. Meanwhile, the second great influence was making itself felt. The spiralling post-war inflation had resulted in a price structure in which each additional ton of cement, plant capacity, or of paper production could only be erected at a cost tremendously higher than that which had prevailed in the 1920's when much of the newer plants had been built. Similarly, the acquiring of additional cutable timber lands could only be accomplished by paying corresponding increases for such assets.

Since all these additional facilities were genuinely needed, the market in time adjusted itself to price structures that would afford a normal profit to the new production brought on stream on a postwar cost basis. But look what this did to the earning power resulting from pre-war plant, which still represented the greatest part of the output of these industries. Since they were now operating at capacity, this in itself would cause a sizable increase in profits over the old pre-war tendency of operating at much under capacity. However, in addition to this, they were operating under a price structure calculated to give a worthwhile return on very much higher competitive cost plants. It is small wonder then that a tremendous jump in profits occurred or that the percentage gain in the price of these cement, lumber, and paper shares proved so spectacular.

My reason for believing that with rare exceptions stocks in these groups will not prove outstanding equity investments in the 1960's is not because the very large increases that took place in the value of many of these shares in the immediate post-war years was not entirely justified. It is that the two sets of circumstances which together produced this great rise will not again occur. One of them, inflation, will probably continue to make itself felt, as it has in the recent past. But with these industries generally prosperous and giving every sign of continuing to be, there is little or no likelihood of there being any repetition of these inflationary influences being tremendously reinforced by an emergence from a state of selling on a "bare bones" basis to these shares being priced at a normal, healthy level which contributed so much to the rise of most of these securities.

Compare what has happened marketwise to the cement, paper, and lumber stocks on the one hand, and the chemical, electronic, and drug shares on the other. The latter group never were selling at a few cents on the dollar in the latter years of the 1930's. Many of them were selling at rather generous prices in relation to earnings in those years and at several times their book value. The huge rises that have occurred since have nearly all been due to new products that these companies themselves have generated in the intervening years, largely due to their own research or engineering effort, a process which gives every promise of continuing all during the 1960's. This is a quite different thing from the one-time "rags to respectability," if not "rags to riches" evolution that has played such a contributing role in these other industries.

Of course, with all the variations that exist between one company and another, no sweeping general statement on industries, such as this one, should be made without qualifying it so far as certain individual companies are concerned. There are chemical and electronic companies conspicuous for their tendency to attempt to compete in these dynamic industries, and yet they gradually shrivel away because they do not seem to have the knack of developing new products. In contrast, certain outstanding paper companies such as Scott and Crown Zellerbach have, through ingenious development and marketing of important new paper products, genuinely built up their businesses through just the type of growth that decade by decade is likely to prove so rewarding to shareholders. The huge per capita consumption in the post-war years of a long series of paper products such as napkins, towels, cups, and particularly milk and frozen food cartons gives eloquent tribute to what ingenious management such as that found at Scott and Crown Zellerbach has already done. However, as plastics and synthetic textiles are steadily declining in price and becoming more varied in characteristics, the challenge of the chemical industry to certain of the heretofore paper-dominated markets such as disposable cups, certain frozen food containers, and bags for dry cleaning establishments, is becoming more clearly defined. It will be interesting to observe as the 1960's progress whether or not the leading paper-goods producers will be able to stave off this challenge to some of the lines they had previously carved out for themselves or whether in the face of ever-improving synthetic textiles they may be able to open up new sales outlets in such a field as, for example, disposable paper clothing.

Because it has been so much in the limelight in recent years, perhaps there is one more great industry which should be mentioned among those which may not offer comparable opportunities in the 1960's to the magnificent ones afforded in the earlier post-war years. I refer, of course, to the petroleum shares. No group was in great investment favor during all but the very end of the 1950's. Even as recently as 1958, various compilations of institutional holdings showed no dimunition in the almost unbridled enthusiasm for these shares. Most such lists usually showed a larger percentage of oil shares than those of any other single industry—although for reasons already explained, such figures are not too meaningful since they depend upon more or less arbitrary definitions of just what are the boundaries of any particular industrial classification.

Following this, however, there came a sudden but most pronounced chilling of the warm regard the financial community had been building up for oil shares. The reasons for this were many but were not hard to find. In the United States, the annual increase in petroleum demand was running at a slightly lower rate than had generally been anticipated. Furthermore, two factors were on the horizon threatening to further cut into anticipated growth. One was the unexpected enthusiasm the American public was showing for the small or "economy" automobile with its greater mileage per gallon of gasoline. The other was the manner in which competitive fuels offered tough price competition to oil for industrial and space heating purposes. Meanwhile, as the shallow and easy-to-find sources of domestic petroleum seemed more and more to have already been discovered, the cost of replacing oil taken from the ground was steadily rising as it became necessary to go deeper and deeper. At the same time, foreign activities were starting to lose their glamour. The more rapid annual increase in petroleum demand abroad and the prolific fields that were being discovered had made it appear as though the "International Companies" might be exempt from the ills of the purely domestic producers. But now waves of extreme nationalism, often accompanied by popular resentment at the "foreign oil exploiters," were showing themselves in the Arab world, in Venezuela, and in Indonesia. The worst to be expected might be outright confiscation. The least might be sharply increased taxation. In view of all these things, it is hardly surprising that many keen investment minds began wondering if they were not too heavily involved in the group which, against a background of steadily rising sales and earnings further buttressed by the proving up of ever-increasing amounts of underground oil, had been one of the most outstanding performers of the previous fifteen years.

For those who, like myself, believe that for most people the only common stock worth holding is one that affords major prospects of years of abnormal growth ahead, I feel there is much reason for giving great weight to the current critical appraisal of oil shares. To an even greater degree than may exist for many industries, the most important factor in the profit level of most oil producing companies is the price level of their products. Because it is getting steadily harder (and therefore more expensive) to find fresh oil and because wages and other costs of this industry are constantly rising just as they are for all others, further increases in crude prices will be required if the earnings of most of these companies are to grow significantly. Yet the huge amounts of oil being found in so many different places throughout the world make me believe that such increases are quite unlikely on a world-wide level. Domestically, when even existing price structures are largely dependent on government-imposed import quotas and state-enforced prorations, it would seem to me that much of a rise in price would be politically rather embarrassing.

However, if today's changed conditions may cause the oil stocks significantly to disappoint the many ardent boosters they still have, I believe they will prove equally disillusioning to the more extreme of their detractors. There are those who read the more extreme statements of various politicians in the Middle East, in Latin America, or Indonesia and who fear that revolution and local political action will cause confiscation of the huge holdings of our bigger oil companies. The very glut of oil, which is making the business less attractive so far as common-stock holdings are concerned, gives strong protection against most countries doing this for very long. The experience of Iran in the mid 1950's, when confiscation was tried, shows that oil at the refinery is not of much economic use. It has to be marketed in distant lands. Only the big companies have the tankers and the storage facilities close to customer outlets. Above all, only they have the organization capable of doing the selling. Meanwhile, so much oil is today available that if any one country or ethnic group attempts to keep oil off the market the deficit can easily be made up elsewhere. It is hardly likely that such diverse free world groups as Canada, Venezuela, Indonesia, the Arabic Middle East, and Iran (which is not Arabic) will always act in concert. Now equally great storehouses of oil are beginning to show up in North Africa and possibly in other parts of Latin America. Under these circumstances, the high cards in negotiations are not all in the hands of the producing nations. While street mobs or their equivalent may at any time seize control and stop production in one particular country, such moves are apt to be painful but temporary.

However, if the producing nations do not have all the high cards in their hands, they do have some quite strong ones. My guess is that the 1960's will see a continuation of the trend of the recent past. Slowly but steadily, the tax take of these countries (or their share of the total profit, which is the same thing) will be gradually increased. This means that for each barrel of oil produced, the oil companies will gradually earn less and less. On the other hand, with growing worldwide demand for oil, the total number of barrels produced will continue to grow. My further guess is that these two influences will about offset each other. This means that, in the years immediately ahead, the giant international oil shares are neither going to be the magnificent performers they have been in much of the recent past nor are they going to prove the sources of investment danger feared by certain alarmists.

If I am correct in this, it does mean that contrary to the sincere views of many prominent in the managements of some of our best run oil companies, the golden age of oil company investments is over. Perhaps, if it has ended for this once so favored group, it is soon to start for another group of energy producers, who for many years have been considered one of the least desirable of industries for investment. Perhaps steady progress in mechanization and possibly even in chemical processing of coal in the ground is soon to open new vistas for the handful of coal companies with the imagination and personnel capable of looking forward to these new horizons.

Index